DENIED F.C.

The Football League Election Struggles

By Dave Twydell

Published by:
Yore Publications
12 The Furrows, Harefield,
Middx. UB9 6AT.

© Dave Twydell 2001

....

British Library Cataloguing-in-Publication Data.
A catalogue record for this book
is available from the British Library.

ISBN 1 874427 98 4

Printed and bound by
Bookcraft, Midsomer Norton, Bath.

Introduction and Acknowledgements:

An introduction is barely necessary, since the various sections of the book provide their own headings. The aim of the book was to record a comprehensive record of the successful (and otherwise) clubs that have applied to join the League, an aspect within the realms of football history that has barely been touched upon before in print.

In many respects *'Denied F.C.'* reflects one of my particular football interests, that of the somewhat obscure and hitherto unresearched (in detail) aspects of the game - as did my earlier 'Rejected F.C.' books (histories of the ex-League clubs). Therefore my researches have stretched far and wide over several years, and consequently it would be difficult to make a complete list of references. The main sources for the voting figures have come from early reports of the Association of Football Statisticians, *'The Story of the Football League'* (1938), and *'The Official History of the Football League'* (1888-1988) by Simon Inglis. There were some omissions or contradictions within these publications, and other references were sought, especially the 'Athletic News', as was this worthy old newspaper for other subjects. Principally, for the individual clubs' section, many variable references were made, including club histories, non-League directories, local libraries and newspapers, etc. The illustrations were from my own (small) collection of such artifacts, plus those of other collectors.

These brief acknowledgements however would be incomplete without my sincere thanks to - like myself - one with a combined non-League and Football League interest, Mick Blakeman. Mick diligently ploughed through the vast majority of my manuscript, and from his own references corrected numerous errors that I had made! However, if any mistakes have still crept through, then they remain my sole responsibility!

Dave Twydell
September 2001

This book is dedicated to
Arran and Nicholas

Cover Design: Dave Twydell   Cover Cartoon: Dave Baxter

CONTENTS

The Football League: 1888 - 2001

Formation:

By 1888, following two decades or so, football had gradually become organised and clubs were arranging fixtures with each other, and playing under the same rules. Cup competitions had developed during this time which gave an edge to such encounters, but as time passed, the interminable Friendly matches needed spicing up. The game was gradually becoming more of a spectator sport, especially in the North of England and the Midlands, and the gradual introduction of professionally paid players ensured that fixtures needed to be more competitive in nature.

Cricket's County Championship had been formalised in 1872, and the Champions of the nine 'First Class' Counties were adjudged solely on the basis of the opinion of the Sporting press. In 1887, a simple points system was introduced, whereby a win was awarded one point, and a drawn match gave each side a half point each. Whereas this produced a more realistic system of judging the relative merits of each County, it was not mandatory for each side to play each other on a home and away basis. Cricket in fact had to a degree emulated the U.S.A. system of defining the Champions from the National Association of Base Ball Players who had devised a system in 1869, and awarded a pennant for the Championship winning side. In 1876, a National League of Professional Base Ball Clubs superseded the Players Association, with eight teams playing each other on a 'home' and 'away' basis.

Following the developments in Cricket, the Sporting press introduced merit tables from the early to mid-1880's, for both Football and Rugby. These tables listed the number of matches played, together with those won, drawn and lost (not unlike the modern version).

Broadly the order of merit in the table related principally to the number of games lost, the least at the top, the most at the bottom, although a 'Goal Average' column was also included to separate teams with equal numbers of defeats. This did not fully take into account the number of matches played or the distinction of 'home' and 'away' matches.

William McGregor of Aston Villa produced a draft rule for an organised system, from which the order of merit depended on an average being taken from victories, draws and defeats, rather than the goals scored factor.

The first attempt to draw suitable clubs together in order to play home and away fixtures on an organised basis originated in a letter from McGregor to five clubs viz. Blackburn Rovers, Bolton Wanderers, Preston North End, West Bromwich Albion and Aston Villa. Only two replies were received, including one from Mr. Bentley of Bolton Wanderers, who suggested the inclusion of eight more clubs, viz. Wolverhampton Wanderers, Accrington, Burnley, Halliwell, Notts County, Mitchell St.George's, Stoke and Old Carthusians.

A meeting was arranged for the 22nd March 1888, and was attended by representatives from Aston Villa, Notts County, Blackburn Rovers, Wolverhampton Wanderers, Burnley, West Bromwich Albion and Stoke (Derby County was also represented, but only to observe). The meeting decided to invite 12 teams that were to eventually form the League.

A parallel league was proposed by others, which became known as The Combination, with the following 18 clubs first proposed:

Crewe Alexandra, Blackburn Olympic, Derby Junction, Mitchell St.George's, Small Heath Alliance, Bootle, Walsall Town Swifts, Derby Midland, Notts Rangers, Burslem Port Vale, Leek, Newton Heath, Witton, Darwen, Sheffield Wednesday, Long Eaton Rangers, Nottingham Forest and Halliwell.

The Football League was formerly created on the 17th April at the Royal Hotel, Manchester, and it was agreed that at the season's end, the four bottom teams would be required to stand for re-election. The title of the competition was decided upon. Originally the 'Football Association Union' was suggested but, this it was argued could be confused with the Rugby Football Union. 'Football League' was finally decided upon, despite some misgivings with regards to its possible political connotations. It wasn't until November 1888, that it was decided to award two points for a win and one for a draw.

The 'alternative' league, the Combination, which also ran for the 1888/89 season, resulted in the full fixtures never being completed. The idea of The Combination came from J.G.Hall, the Secretary of Crewe Alexandra. Ten days after the creation of the Football League, a meeting was held in Crewe, and of the 18 invited, 11 clubs attended, with three expressions of interest by post; that day The Combination was formed.

One of the prime objectives was that fixtures should be played when arranged, and at least eight matches should be undertaken, rather than expecting every club to play each other twice - once each home and away. By the 15th May, 20 clubs - it is believed - became members of The Combination, viz. Birmingham St.George's, Blackburn Olympic, Bootle, Burslem Port Vale, Crewe Alexandra, Darwen, Derby Junction, Derby Midland, Gainsborough Trinity, Grimsby Town, Halliwell, Leek Town, Lincoln City, Long Eaton Rangers, Newton Heath, Northwich Victoria, Notts Rangers, Small Heath, South Shore, and Walsall Town Swifts.

Of these, all but Blackburn Olympic, Derby Junction, Derby Midland, Halliwell, Leek Town, Long Eaton Rangers, and Notts Rangers, were to either become later members of the Football League or at least apply for election.

But there was less discipline within The Combination, than the Football League, and consequently clubs frequently cancelled matches at short notice. However, by early April, only Blackburn Olympic had played fewer than eight matches (five), whilst at the other end, Burslem Port Vale completed 25 (these figures are based on assumptions that all matches were in fact Combination games rather than Friendlies). At a meeting held on the 5th April 1889, eleven of the Clubs withdrew (most to become founder-members of the Football Alliance), and The Combination effectively folded.

However, Mr Hall (of Crewe) was determined, and selected eleven from the original members (plus Sheffield Wednesday) to form The New Combination. Sheffield Wednesday soon withdrew, and three additional clubs applied to take their place, one of which was Nottingham Forest. But following further drop-outs due to Football League applications and the formation of the Midland League, The New Combination never took effect. A year later 'The Combination' was re-formed, which covered a wide area, but whose members could reasonably be regarded as having less of a standing in the football world than the original competition.

The Football Alliance was formed in 1889, embracing 10 of the former Combination clubs, and this became the unofficial Football League Second Division (not unlike the modern Alliance/Conference being the unofficial Fourth Division), with founder-members: Birmingham St.George's (formerly 'Mitchell St.George's), Bootle, Crewe Alexandra, Darwen, Grimsby Town, Long Eaton Rangers, Newton Heath, Nottingham Forest, Sheffield Wednesday, Small Heath, Sunderland Albion and Walsall Town Swifts (12 teams).

The Football Alliance
Milestones :

1890: Long Eaton Rangers resigned (moved to Midland League), and Stoke were elected in their place. There was no no re-election voting, and the competition continued with 12 teams.

1891: Stoke and Darwen were elected to the Football League. Sunderland Albion resigned (moved to Northern League). Ardwick, Burton Swifts and Lincoln City were elected (12 teams maintained)

1892: All Clubs, except Birmingham St.George's, were voted into the Football League. Newton Heath, Nottingham Forest and Sheffield Wednesday into the First Division, and the remaining eight into the new Second Division (with the addition of Burslem Port Vale, Darwen, Northwich Victoria and Sheffield United).

The Football League: Principal Milestones:

1889: The bottom four clubs: Stoke, Burnley, Derby County and Notts County were the first clubs to stand for re-election, and all were successful

1890: No votes were taken at the re-election meeting. Stoke were not re-elected, but Burnley and Notts County were, and 9th place Bolton Wanderers were excused from applying. However, Aston Villa and Bolton finished on 19 points, with incredibly close goal averages (Villa's was 0.84314, and that of Bolton, 0.84375 which would have placed the former in 9th place), and Villa would have been required to apply for re-election. But in what was later to become seen as an unprecedented move, it was agreed at the meeting to not require them to seek this endorsement (William McGregor the Football League Chairman also fulfilled the same role at Villa!). However, an error later found in Bolton's goal tally, when corrected, would in fact have resulted in them, and not Villa finishing 9th.

1891: League extended to 14 teams.

1892: West Bromwich Albion were not required to seek re-election by virtue of them winning the F.A.Cup (a ruling which it was intended to apply in later years - but was never necessary). Second Division formed (12 clubs) and First Division extended to 16 clubs. At the end of the season, Test Matches played between First Division bottom three and Second Division top three, to determine promotion and relegation.

1893: Second Division extended to 16 clubs, although Bootle resigned in August thereby leaving 15 in contention.

1894: Only three clubs (this season) required to seek re-election as Northwich Victoria resigned before the re-election meeting, Middlesbrough Ironopolis resigned in June, but 16 clubs maintained with Rotherham Town, who had not been earlier re-elected, taking their place. Rumours of a Second Division split into two new sections were unfounded.

1895: In future, test matches reduced to bottom two (Division) One and top two (Division Two).

1896: In future, where points are equal, final positions to be settled on goal average.

1898: After the re-election meeting it was decided to increase the membership to 36 (18 clubs in each division). Automatic promotion and relegation between divisions introduced (two up and two down).

1901: Burton Swifts (bottom) were required to seek re-election, however, they amalgamated with Burton Wanderers (also former members) before the re-election meeting, and as 'Burton United' were re-elected. New Brighton Tower resigned in September, and Doncaster Rovers took over their fixtures.

1905: League increased to 40 clubs (20 in each division).

1907: Burslem Port Vale resigned after the re-election meeting. Burton United, who were unsuccessful in their re-election bid, applied to take over their fixtures, but the position was offered and accepted by Oldham Athletic (the original non-elected club with the most votes). A proposal put forward by the Southern League to combine and form a new National League, but this was rejected by the Football League member clubs. Clubs were becoming increasingly professional with regard to their applications to join the League; Oldham produced an election brochure (probably the first to do so) that year.

1908: Stoke resigned during the Summer, then rescinded their decision, but this was not accepted by the League. A second vote was necessary, which included Stoke who also applied, but they were unsuccessful. A proposal was made to form a Third Division of 20 clubs (18 from the Southern League), but was rejected by the Football League member clubs.

1909: Only two clubs now required to seek re-election. No applications for membership from Southern clubs were received due to the continued animosity between the two leagues regarding transfer fees. There was a proposal again to form a Third Division (a 60 club amalgamation of the two leagues), and although it received 27 votes in favour and only 13 against, this did not reach the required three-quarters majority and so was therefore defeated.

1910: A degree of harmony was reached with the Southern League after 16 years of varying degrees of conflict.

1911: A third attempt was made at forming a Third Division (independent from the Southern League as in previous years), which was instigated by Darlington, Chesterfield, Hartlepools and Rochdale (the four clubs who applied for election that year), plus Lincoln City who had been voted out.

1911: (Contd.) A further 15 (20 in total) applications for this new division came from former Football League members, Port Vale, Crewe Alexandra and Walsall (plus a reformed Rotherham Town), and seven from clubs who (in some form) at later dates would become members - Macclesfield, Southport Central, South Shields Adelaide, Portsmouth, Southend United, Cardiff City and Merthyr Town. The remaining numbers were made up with Burton Town and South Liverpool (who were to apply at later dates) plus St.Helens Town and Croydon Common, which represented their only attempt of any kind to obtain League status. The proposal was comfortably defeated (11 for, 26 against, 1 abstention).

1915: Despite the normal re-election meeting, the League ceased operations due to the First World War.

1919: League extended to 44 clubs (22 in each division), which required two elections - the first for additional First Division members (the 1918/19 season did not operate, therefore there were no clubs automatically eligible for promotion), and for two extra Second Division members (no teams were required to seek re-election). Despite Arsenal only finishing 5th in the last Second Division season (1914/15), there was the unprecedented action (apparent outright favouritism), when they were promoted to the First Division, whilst third and fourth placed Wolverhampton Wanderers and Barnsley continued in the Second.

1920: 22 club Third Division South formed, with the Southern League (First Division) members being voted in en-bloc, and without voting. However, Cardiff City were 'promoted' to the Second Division, taking the place of Grimsby Town who were relegated to the new Third. Total League membership of 66 clubs. Significantly the Third Division clubs - 'Associate Members', would have no voting rights.

1921: The 20 club Third Division North was formed, with Mr. Alderman Cropper from Chesterfield being its principal instigator. Fourteen clubs were elected without being voted on. Lancashire Combination: Accrington Stanley, and Barrow. North-Eastern League: Ashington, Darlington, Durham City and Hartlepools United. Midland League: Chesterfield and Lincoln City. Central League: Crewe Alexandra, Nelson, Rochdale and Tranmere Rovers. Birmingham League: Walsall and Wrexham). The final four clubs (Grimsby Town were transferred from the Southern Section and Stockport County were relegated), were: Halifax of the Midland League, Southport and Stalybridge Celtic (Central League) and Wigan Borough from the Lancashire Combination. The decision to create the Third Division North (originally conceived in principal a year earlier) was made at a Football League meeting in London on 7th March 1921. One club to be promoted (and two relegated) between each Third Division and the Second Division. Total League membership of 86 clubs. Brentford and Gillingham, were the only two clubs required to seek re-election, and were re-elected without a poll being taken (this proposal had been carried unanimously except Birmingham who voted against). For the first time applicants had to answer questionnaires and have their Grounds ratified as being suitable.

1922: Two clubs from each Third Division required to seek re-election.

1923: Third Division North extended to 22 clubs. Total League membership of 88 clubs.

1924: For the first time, there were no applications for League membership, therefore the four clubs required to seek re-election were re-elected without voting.

1926: No clubs sought election to the Third Division South, therefore the two seeking re-election were re-elected unopposed. Coventry City were transferred from Third Division North to Third Division South, as both Second Division relegated clubs Stoke City and Stockport County - moved to the Third Division North.

1927: Walsall were transferred from Third Division North to Third Division South, as both Second Division relegated clubs - Darlington and Bradford City - moved to the Third Division North.

1931: Walsall were transferred from Third Division South to Third Division North, and both Second Division relegated clubs - Reading and Cardiff City - moved to the Third Division South. Wigan Borough resigned in October. Merthyr Town (who, uniquely, had applied for membership of both the North and South Third Divisions) had their offer to take over the fixtures turned down, as was the offer of Manchester Central. Third Division North continued with 21 clubs (Wigan's results were deleted).

1932: Only one club required to seek re-election to Third Division North (due to resignation of Wigan Borough); 22 clubs continued once again in this division. Mansfield Town were transferred from Third Division South to Third Division North.

1934: No clubs applied for membership of the Third Division North, therefore the two clubs seeking re-election, were re-elected unopposed.

1936: Walsall were transferred from Third Division North to Third Division South, as both Second Division relegated clubs - Port Vale and Hull City - moved to the Third Division North.

1937: Mansfield Town were transferred from the Third Division North to Third Division South, as both Second Division relegated clubs - Bradford City and Doncaster Rovers - moved to the Third Division North.

1938: Port Vale were transferred from the Third Division North to Third Division South, as both Second Division relegated clubs - Barnsley and Stockport County - moved to the Third Division North.

1939: Re-election meeting held as usual, but after three matches played by each club, the League did not continue for the rest of that season due to the Second World War.

1945 Third Division block votes increased from 4 to 12 (of 57 total).

1946: League fixtures recommenced, but no re-election meeting was necessary as fixtures for the 1939/40 season used for the 1946/47. However, New Brighton, having lost their Sandheys Park Ground due to enemy bombing and who remained inactive during the War were considered vulnerable. They arranged to play at the Tower Ground (the home of the former New Brighton Tower F.C.), but the League looked upon their continuing with scepticism, and announced at the A.G.M. that if necessary the Third Division North would function with only 21 clubs for the ensuing season. 14 applications had been received for election, but there was no question of the necessity of a re-election meeting. The clubs applying were: Chelmsford City, Colchester United, Gillingham, Hyde United, Merthyr Tydfil, North Shields, Scunthorpe & Lindsay United, Shrewsbury Town, South Liverpool, Wellington Town, Wigan Athletic, Worcester City, Workington and Yeovil & Petters United. (Hyde United was the only club who did not previously or subsequently apply for election).

1947: It was reasoned that in order to allow clubs to reinstate themselves properly after the War, the four clubs for re-election were re-elected without a vote being taken, despite the fact that there were 25 non-League clubs who had applied. Mansfield Town were transferred from Third Division South to Third Division North, as both Second Division relegated clubs - Swansea Town and Newport County - moved to the Third Division South. A proposal was made to form national 3rd and 4th Divisions (generally the 3rd North section was against the idea), but the proposal was turned down at the League's AGM.

1950: Both Third Divisions extended to 24 clubs. All four clubs for re-election, re-elected without voting. Total League membership of 92 clubs. The applications of Merthyr Tydfil, Llanelly and Cradley Heath were allowed, despite the fact that all three had greyhound racing at their grounds, which was frowned upon.

1951: Shrewsbury Town were transferred from Third Division North to Third Division South, as both Second Division relegated clubs - Chesterfield and Grimsby Town - moved to the Third Division North.

1952: Port Vale were transferred from Third Division South to Third Division North, as both Second Division relegated clubs - Coventry City and Queens Park Rangers - moved to the Third Division North.

1958: Fourth Division formed (from clubs who finished in lower halves of the two Third Divisions). Promotion and relegation, between Divisions One, Two and Three - two up and two down. Between Division Three and Four - four up and four down. Bottom four in Division Four to apply for re-election. There were 12 non-geographical separate applications for membership of the new division.

1959: Four clubs required to seek re-election from the (single) Fourth Division.

1960: A club was voted out of the League (Gateshead), the first time since 1951.

1962: Accrington Stanley resigned in March, and their results were deleted. Discussions were held with regard to re-formatting the Fourth Division into two new regional sections, and bringing in eight new clubs (but this never came to fruition). Record number of 26 clubs applied for membership of the League.

1964: Eight clubs from the Southern League (the overall strongest competition) were barred from making an election bid due to their signing of Football League players on free transfers. A League Management proposal to create three regional divisions from the Third and Fourth was defeated by the clubs.

1966: Three (unknown) non-League clubs had their applications to join refused due to their signing of Football League players without consent The first suggestion regarding the formation of a 'Super League' was made, and also the possibility of including extra clubs to form a new 4th Division.

1968: Peterborough United demoted to Division Four due to illegal payments to players; only bottom three clubs relegated to Fourth Division. The Chester Report reccommended that the League be increased by 6 to 10 clubs within 5 divisions (3 National), and with four up/down for promotion/relegation. A club applying for re-election for two consecutive seasons would automatically be demoted.

1970: A Club voted out of the League (Bradford Park Avenue), the first since 1960.

1972: Barrow voted out of the League after a drawn vote with Hereford United.

1973: Promotion and relegation between 1st, 2nd and 3rd, changed to three up and three down.

1976: The Football League announced an agreement with the Northern Premier and Southern Leagues, that the latter two would submit a list of clubs that had been approved to make an election bid. The League would then select from that list two clubs to join the four re-election candidates at the appropriate meeting. Goal difference (as opposed to goal average) introduced to separate teams with same number of points.

1977: New rule allows only two clubs to seek membership of the League.

1978: Last club (Southport) to be voted out of the League (replaced by Wigan Athletic).

1980: New rules allows only one club (from Alliance Premier League) to seek membership of the League.

1981: Three points for a win (formerly two) agreed for following season.

1986: Enfield become the last (unsuccess-ful) club to seek election to the League.

1987: First season of automatic promotion and relegation outside of the Football League. Lincoln City relegated, Scarborough promoted. Play-off system commenced. The club in the higher division immediately above the relegated clubs joined the three clubs in the lower division below those promoted. The four teams played off to decide who would be promoted/remain in the upper division.

1989: Play-off system modified. In each division, after the promoted clubs, the next four teams play-off to produce another promotion team.

1990: Despite Swindon winning First Division Play-off Final, they were 'demoted' (due to illegal payments), and Sunderland - the losers - promoted instead.

1991: Reorganisation - two extra clubs in First Division (to 22), two less in Fourth (to 22).

1992: Retitling of Divisions - 1st becomes Premier, 2nd - First, 3rd - Second and 4th - Third. Maidstone United fold in August.

1995: Reorganisation - two less clubs in Premier Division (to 20), two more in Fourth (to 24).

1999: Scarborough become the first auto-matically promoted Club who are subsequently relegated.

'A' -The kiss of death?

With the notable exception of Arsenal (and - more recently - A.F.C.Bournemouth), if your club heads the alphabetical listings then your time will probably be limited! Aberdare Athletic were voted out of the League in in 1927, and Ashington followed two years later, after a fairly short stay. Accrington voluntarily departed (in 1893), whilst Accrington Stanley reigned, in 1962, and likewise Aldershot thirty years later. The Argonauts had no luck with their applications in the 1930's, nor did five other 'A's'. Of that quintet, Altrincham were perhaps the unluckiest of all clubs not to be elected.

THE FOOTBALL LEAGUE
~ THE ELECTION OF THE CLUBS ~

(Column headings: 1 = no. of votes. 2 = Club re-elected. 3 = New club elected. 4 = club not elected. 5 = club not re-elected.)

1888

Club	1	2	3	4	5
Accrington			X		
Aston Villa			X		
Blackburn Rovers			X		
Bolton Wanderers			X		
Burnley			X		
Derby County			X		
Everton			X		
Notts County			X		
Preston North End			X		
Stoke			X		
West Bromwich Albion			X		
Wolverhampton Wanderers			X		

1889

Club	1	2	3	4	5
Stoke	10	X			
Burnley	9	X			
Derby County	8	X			
Notts County	7	X			
Mitchell St. George's	5			X	
Sheffield Wednesday	4			X	
Bootle	2			X	
Sunderland	2			X	
Newton Heath	1			X	
Grimsby Town	0			X	
South Shore	0			X	
Sunderland Albion	0			X	
Walsall Town Swifts	0			X	

1890 (No votes taken)

Club	1	2	3	4	5
Notts County		X			
Burnley		X			
Stoke					X
Sunderland			X		
Bootle				X	
Darwen				X	
Grimsby Town				X	
Newton Heath				X	
Sunderland Albion				X	

A. Villa (8th) and Bolton W. (9th) finished on equal points, and both were excluded from having to apply for re-election

1891 League increased to 14 clubs

Club	1	2	3	4	5
Aston Villa	8	X			
Accrington	8	X			
Darwen	7		X		
Stoke	7		X		
Derby County	6	X			
West Bromwich Albion	6	X			
Ardwick	4			X	
Nottingham Forest	1			X	
Sunderland Albion	1			X	
Newton Heath	0			X	

1892 - League increased to 16 clubs

Club	1	2	3	4	5
West Brom. Alb. (no poll)		X			
Sheffield Wednesday	10	X			
Nottingham Forest	9	X			
Accrington	7	X			
Stoke	6	X			
Newton Heath	6		X		
Sheffield United	5			X	
Darwen	4				X
Burton Swifts	1			X	
Newcastle East End *	1			X	
Middlesbrough/					
Middlesbrough Ironopolis**	1			X	
Liverpool Caledonians				X	
Liverpool (Rejected before voting)					

* Declined invitation to join 2nd Division
** Declined invitation (as combined club) to join 2nd Division

Newly formed 2nd Division
Election without voting

Club	1	2	3	4	5
Ardwick			X		
Bootle			X		
Burton Swifts			X		
Burslem Port Vale			X		
Crewe Alexandra			X		
Darwen			X		
Grimsby Town			X		
Lincoln City			X		
Northwich Victoria			X		
Sheffield United			X		
Small Heath Alliance			X		
Walsall Town Swifts			X		
Liverpool Caledonians				X	

1893   2nd Div. increased to 16 clubs

Club	1	2	3	4	5
Lincoln City		X			
Crewe Alexandra		X			
Port Vale		X			
Walsall Town Swifts		X			
Rotherham Town			X		
Newcastle United			X		
Woolwich Arsenal			X		
Liverpool			X		
Accrington *					
Middlesbrough Ironopolis					
(in place of Accrington)			X		
Bootle (Resigned)					
Loughborough (Rejected before voting)					
Doncaster Rovers (Rejected before voting)					

* Resigned after losing Test Match to retain 1st Division status (refused 2nd Division membership) No record of voting figures traced.

Left Column

Club	1	2	3	4	5
1894 (2nd Division, 16 clubs restored)					
Ardwick/ Manchester City	20	X			
Leicester Fosse	20		X		
Bury	17		X		
Burton Wanderers	17		X		
Rotherham Town *	15				X
Blackpool	8			X	
Loughborough	8			X	
Accrington	7			X	
Rossendale	0			X	

Northwich Victoria (Resigned before meeting)
Middlesborough Ironopolis (Resigned after meeting)
* (later invited to join in place of Middlesborough Ironopolis)

Club	1	2	3	4	5
1895 (Non-elected clubs votes not recorded)					
Lincoln City	22	X			
Burlsem Port Vale	22	X			
Crewe Alexandra	18	X			
Loughborough	18		X		
Blackpool				X	
Fairfield Athletic				X	
Walsall Town Swifts					X

Club	1	2	3	4	5
1896					
Blackpool	19		X		
Walsall	16		X		
Gainsborough Trinity	15		X		
Luton Town	10			X	
Burslem Port Vale	10				X
Crewe Alexandra	4				X
Fairfield Athletic	3			X	
Glossop North End	3			X	
Macclesfield	2			X	
Tottenham Hotspur	2			X	

Rotherham Town (did not seek re-election)

Club	1	2	3	4	5
1897					
Lincoln City	21	X			
Burton Swifts	15	X			
Luton Town	13		X		
Burslem Port Vale	11			X	
Burton Wanderers	9				X
Nelson	7			X	
Glossop North End	5			X	
Fairfield	3			X	
Crewe Alexandra	2			X	
Millwall Athletic	1			X	

Club	1	2	3	4	5
1898					
Lincoln City	21	X			
Burslem Port Vale	18		X		
Loughborough	16	X			
Darwen	15				X
New Brighton Tower	13			X	
Nelson	3			X	
Bristol City	1			X	

(After above voting, League increased to 36, with two Divisions of 18 each)

Right Column

Club	1	2	3	4	5
(1898 Continued - 1st Division election)					
Blackburn Rovers	27		X		
Newcastle United	18		X		
Manchester City *	10			X	
Small Heath *	4			X	
Newton Heath *	3			X	
Woolwich Arsenal *	2			X	

* Remained in 2nd Division)

Club	1	2	3	4	5
(Elected - no voting - to 2nd Division)					
Darwen			X		
New Brighton Tower			X		
Glossop North End			X		
Barnsley			X		

Club	1	2	3	4	5
1899					
Loughborough	28	X			
Chesterfield Town	17		X		
Middlesbrough	17		X		
Blackpool	15				X
Stockport County	11			X	
Chorley	7			X	
Wigan County	7			X	
Coventry City	0			X	
Ashton North End	0			X	

Darwen (Resigned)

Club	1	2	3	4	5
1900					
Barnsley	29	X			
Stockport County	28		X		
Blackpool	24		X		
Doncaster Rovers	5			X	
Loughborough	3				X
Kettering	2			X	
Stalybridge Rovers	1			X	

Luton Town (Did not seek re-election)

Club	1	2	3	4	5
1901					
Burton United *	23	X			
Bristol City	23		X		
Stockport County **	16(21)	X			
Doncaster Rovers ***	16(13)		X		
Walsall	7				X
Stalybridge Rovers	7			X	
Crewe Alexandra	5			X	
Darwen	0			X	
Southport Central	0 ?			X	

(New Brighton Tower resigned)

* Combined club, formerly Burton Swifts and Burton Wands.
** Re-elected after initial tied vote with Doncaster Rovers.
*** Elected after New Brighton Tower resigned.

Club	1	2	3	4	5

1902

Club	1	2	3	4	5
Chesterfield	33	X			
Gainsborough Trinity	31	X			
Stockport County	29	X			
Walsall	?			X	

1903

Club	1	2	3	4	5
Bradford City	30		X		
Stockport County	20	X			
Burnley	19	X			
Doncaster Rovers	14				X
Crewe Alexandra	7			X	
West Hartlepool	7			X	
Southport Central	4			X	
Willington Athletic	1			X	

1904

Club	1	2	3	4	5
Leicester Fosse	33	X			
Glossop	27	X			
Doncaster Rovers	21		X		
Stockport County	11				X
Crewe Alexandra	10			X	

1905 (1st Division increased to 20 clubs)
(Bury and Notts County not relegated from 1st Division)

Club	1	2	3	4	5
Leeds City	25		X		
Burslem Port Vale	21	X			
Chelsea	20	X			
Hull City	18			X	
Burton United	10			X	
Crewe Alexandra	10			X	
Doncaster Rovers	4				X
Stockport County	3			X	
Clapton Orient	1			X	

(After first vote, 2nd vote taken, 2nd Division increased to 20)

Club	1	2	3	4	5
Burton United	36	X			
Hull City	36		X		
Clapton Orient	26		X		
Stockport County	26		X		
Doncaster Rovers	20				X

1906

Club	1	2	3	4	5
Chesterfield Town	36	X			
Burton United	32	X			
Clapton Orient	21	X			
Oldham Athletic	20			X	
Wigan Town	5			X	

1907

Club	1	2	3	4	5
Lincoln City	28	X			
Fulham	28		X		
Chesterfield Town	23	X			
Oldham Athletic *	17			X	
Bradford Park Avenue	11			X	
Burton United **	7				X
Rotherham Town	0			X	
Salford United	0			X	
Wigan Town	0			X	

* Subsequently replaced Burslem Port Vale who resigned.
** Applied to replace Burslem Port Vale but failed.

1908

Club	1	2	3	4	5
Grimsby Town	32	X			
Chesterfield	23	X			
Bradford Park Avenue	20		X		
Lincoln City	18				X
Tottenham Hotspur	14			X	
Burton United	1			X	

Rotherham Town and Queens Park Rangers withdrew before voting. Stoke resigned in close season. A Special General Meeting was called to elect another club, but Stoke then changed their minds, but this was too late to stop a second vote taking place:-

Club	1	2	3	4	5
Tottenham Hotspur *	20(20)5	X			
Lincoln City	20(20)3			X	
Stoke	6			X	
Rotherham Town				X	
Southport Central				X	

* After 2 tied votes with Lincoln City, final voting of 5-3, made by Management Committee.

1909

Club	1	2	3	4	5
Blackpool	27	X			
Lincoln City	24		X		
Chesterfield Town	21				X
Stoke	6			X	
Rotherham Town	0			X	

1910

Club	1	2	3	4	5
Birmingham	30	X			
Huddersfield Town	26		X		
Grimsby Town	12				X
Darlington	7			X	
Chesterfield Town	6			X	
Stoke	3			X	
Hartlepools United	1			X	
Rochdale	1			X	

Club	1	2	3	4	5
1911					
Barnsley	28	X			
Grimsby Town	18		X		
Lincoln City	17				X
Darlington	7			X	
Chesterfield Town	6			X	
Hartlepools United	1			X	
Rochdale	1			X	
1912					
Leeds City	33	X			
Lincoln City	27		X		
Gainsborough Trinity	9				X
Chesterfield Town	6			X	
Cardiff City	1			X	
Darlington	1			X	
Newcastle City	1			X	
Doncaster Rovers	0			X	
1913					
Blackpool	32	X			
Stockport County	22	X			
Chesterfield Town	10			X	
Stalybridge Celtic	6			X	
Darlington	4			X	
Gainsborough Trinity	4			X	
South Shields	0			X	
Nelson (withdrew before vote)					
1914					
Nottingham Forest	34	X			
Lincoln City	24	X			
Stoke	16			X	
Darlington	2			X	
Chesterfield Town	1			X	
South Shields	1			X	
Gainsborough Trinity	0			X	
South Liverpool	0			X	
1915					
Leicester Fosse	33	X			
Stoke	21		X		
South Shields	11			X	
Chesterfield Town	8			X	
Darlington	4			X	
Glossop	1				X
Coventry City (withdrew before vote)					

League suspended 1915/16 to 1918/19
World War 1

Club	1	2	3	4	5
1919 - League extended to 44 clubs					
(Election for 1st Division):					
Chelsea (Elected without voting)		X			
Woolwich Arsenal	18	X			
Tottenham Hotspur	8			X	
Barnsley	5			X	
Wolverhampton Wanderers	4			X	
Nottingham Forest	3			X	
Birmingham	2			X	
Hull City	1			X	
(Election for 2nd Division):					
Coventry City	35	X			
West Ham United	32	X			
Rotherham County	28	X			
South Shields	28	X			
Port Vale *	27			X	
Rochdale	7			X	
Southport	7			X	
Chesterfield Town	0			X	

* Leeds City expelled October 19, Port Vale took over fixtures.

1920 - 3rd Division formed (initially Southern Section only) All members of Southern League accepted without voting: Portsmouth, Watford, Crystal Palace, Plymouth Argyle, Queens Park Rangers, Reading, Southampton, Swansea Town, Exeter City, Southend United, Norwich City, Swindon Town, Millwall, Brentford, Brighton & Hove Albion, Bristol Rovers, Newport County, Northampton Town, Luton Town, Merthyr T., Gillingham.

Club	1	2	3	4	5
Leeds United	31	X			
Cardiff City	23	X			
Grimsby Town *	20				X
Lincoln City	7				X
Walsall	3		X		

* Accepted into new 3rd Division - place available due to the election of Cardiff City - from the Southern League - direct to the 2nd Division.

1921 - 3rd Division North Section formed

Club	1	2	3	4	5
Brentford (no poll taken)		X			
Gillingham (no poll taken)		X			
Aberdare Athletic *	38	X			
Charlton Athletic *	30	X			
Bath City	12			X	
Pontypridd	5			X	
Abertillery Town	4			X	
Barry	1			X	

Aberaman and Bridgend both withdrew before voting.
* Replaced Crystal Palace (promoted) and Grimsby T. (who moved to new 3rd Div. North)
(3rd Division North) - automatic election
Accrington Stanley, Ashington, Barrow, Chesterfield, Crewe Alexandra, Darlington, Durham City, Hartlepools United, Lincoln City, Nelson, Rochdale, Tranmere Rovers, Walsall, Wrexham.

Club	1	2	3	4	5

1921 3rd Div. North Section (continued)
(Final 4 places went to the vote)

Club	1	2	3	4	5
Wigan Borough	34	X			
Halifax Town	25	X			
Southport	25	X			
Stalybridge Celtic	25	X			
Castleford Town	18		X		
Rotherham Town	13		X		
Blyth Spartans	9		X		
Gainsborough Trinity	8		X		
Doncaster Rovers	6		X		
West Stanley	6		X		
Wakefield City	4		X		
Lancaster Town	3		X		
Scunthorpe & Lindsey U.	3		X		
South Liverpool	1		X		

Division made up to 20 clubs - Grimsby T. moved from the 3rd Div. South and Stockport C. relegated from the Second Div.

1922
(South Section)

Club	1	2	3	4	5
Southend United	36	X			
Exeter City	32	X			
Pontypridd	21		X		
Bath City	1		X		
Llanelly	0		X		

(North Section)

Club	1	2	3	4	5
Halifax Town	42	X			
Rochdale	31	X			
Doncaster Rovers	9		X		
New Brighton	7		X		
York City	1		X		
Castleford	0		X		

1923

The two relegated clubs from the 2nd Division, Rotherham County and Wolverhampton W., moved to the 3rd Division Northern section. Stalybridge Celtic resigned and their place was allocated to the Southern Section.

(Southern Section)

Club	1	2	3	4	5
Aberdare Athletic	45	X			
Newport County	45	X			
Bournemouth & Bos.Ath	28		X		
Llanelly	9			X	
Pontypridd	8			X	
Torquay United	0			X	

(North Section) - increased to 22 clubs (2 extra places)

Club	1	2	3	4	5
Ashington	45	X			
Doncaster Rovers	45		X		
Durham City	45	X			
New Brighton	45		X		
Nuneaton Town	0			X	
Wallasey United	0			X	

1924 All four bottom clubs re-elected without vote, with three dissentions. No other clubs applied.
(South Section)

Club	1	2	3	4	5
Bournemouth & Bos. Ath.		X			
Queen's Park Rangers		X			

(North Section)

Club	1	2	3	4	5
Barrow		X			
Hartlepools United		X			

1925
(South Section)

Club	1	2	3	4	5
Brentford	44	X			
Merthyr Town	44	X			
Mid-Rhondda	0			X	

(North Section)

Club	1	2	3	4	5
Rotherham United	44	X			
Tranmere Rovers	32	X			
Mansfield Town	13			X	
Blyth Spartans	3			X	

1926
(South Section)

Club	1	2	3	4	5
Charlton Athletic (unopposed)		X			
Q. P. Rangers (unopposed)		X			

(North Section)

Club	1	2	3	4	5
Walsall	33	X			
Barrow	25	X			
Carlisle United	12			X	
Blyth Spartans	10			X	
Mansfield Town	10			X	

1927
(South Section)

Club	1	2	3	4	5
Watford	44	X			
Torquay United *	21(26)		X		
Aberdare	21(19)				X
Kettering Town	1			X	
Yeovil & Petters United	1			X	
Ebbw Vale	0			X	

* Elected on second vote.

(North Section)

Club	1	2	3	4	5
Accrington Stanley	36	X			
Barrow	30	X			
Mansfield Town	8			X	
York City	6			X	
Carlisle United	5			X	
Blyth Spartans	3			X	

Club	1	2	3	4	5

1928
(South Section)

Club	1	2	3	4	5
Torquay United	42	X			
Merthyr Town	27	X			
Argonauts	16			X	
Kettering Town	3			X	
Peterborough & Fletton Utd.	2			X	

Aberdare & Aberaman (single club) also applied, but withdrew before the meeting.

(North Section)

Club	1	2	3	4	5
Nelson	37	X			
Carlisle United	33		X		
Durham City	11				X
York City	7			X	
Chester	2			X	

1929
(South Section)

Club	1	2	3	4	5
Exeter City	42	X			
Gillingham	35	X			
Argonauts	6			X	
Aldershot	5			X	
Kettering Town	1			X	
Thames Association	1			X	
Llanelly	0			X	

Mansfield Town also applied to the South Section, but withdrew before the meeting.

(North Section)

Club	1	2	3	4	5
Hartlepools United	33	X			
York City	24		X		
Mansfield Town	16			X	
Ashington	14				X
Manchester Central	2			X	
Prescot Cables	1			X	
Chester	0			X	
Rhyl	0			X	
Workington	0			X	

Connahs Quay & Shotton applied but withdrew before vote

1930
(South Section)

Club	1	2	3	4	5
Gillingham	33	X			
Thames Association	20		X		
Aldershot	19			X	
Merthyr Town	14				X
Llanelly	4			X	
Argonauts	0			X	

(North Section)

Club	1	2	3	4	5
Halifax Town	40	X			
Barrow	22	X			
Mansfield Town	15			X	
Manchester Central	13			X	
Prescot Cables	0			X	

1931
(South Section)

Club	1	2	3	4	5
Norwich City	38	X			
Mansfield Town	25		X		
Newport County	19				X
Aldershot	14			X	
Merthyr Town *#	2			X	
Llanelly	0			X	

(North Section)

Club	1	2	3	4	5
Rochdale	40	X			
Chester	27(28)**		X		
Nelson	27(20)			X —	
Manchester Central	4			X	
Merthyr Town *	0			X	

\# Wigan Borough resigned on October 26th, Merthyr offer to take over fixtures refused.
* Applied for both sections.
** Elected on second vote.

1932
(South Section)

Club	1	2	3	4	5
Gillingham	41	X			
Newport County	36		X		
Aldershot *	35		X		
Llanelly	25			X	
Guildford City	8			X	
Merthyr Town	2			X	
Thames Association (Resigned)					

* Replaced Mansfield Town who were transferred to North section.

(North Section. Only 1 vacancy, as only 1 club required to apply following Wigan Borough's mid-season resignation, and Mansfield's transfer to the North Section)

Club	1	2	3	4	5
Rochdale	47	X			
Rhyl	2			X	
Wigan Athletic	0			X	

1933
(South Section)

Club	1	2	3	4	5
Swindon Town	45	X			
Newport County	26	X			
Llanelly	20			X	
Folkestone	5			X	
Merthyr Town	1			X	
Nuneaton	1			X	

(North Section)

Club	1	2	3	4	5
Darlington	47	X			
New Brighton	47	X			
Scarborough	4			X	

Club	1	2	3	4	5
1934					
(South Section)					
Bournemouth & Bos. A.	48	X			
Cardiff City	48	X			
Folkestone	0			X	
(North Section)					
Rochdale (unopposed)		X			
Rotherham Utd. (unopposed)		X			
1935					
(South Section)					
Southend United	48	X			
Newport County	43	X			
Bath City	1			X	
Folkestone	1			X	
(North Section)					
Carlisle United	46	X			
Southport	46	X			
Shrewsbury Town	6			X	
1936					
(South Section)					
Exeter City	48	X			
Newport County	40	X			
Bath City	9			X	
Dartford	1			X	
Folkestone	1			X	
(North Section)					
Southport	47	X			
New Brighton	38	X			
Shrewsbury Town	7			X	
Wigan Athletic	6			X	
1937					
(South Section)					
Exeter City	40	X			
Aldershot	34	X			
Ipswich Town	24			X	
(North Section)					
Darlington	47	X			
Gateshead	34	X			
Shrewsbury Town	12			X	
South Liverpool	4			X	
Wigan Athletic	1			X	
1938					
(South Section)					
Ipswich Town	11(36) *	X			
Walsall	11(34)	X			
Gillingham	18(28)			X	
1938 (Continued)					
(North Section)					
Accrington Stanley	41	X			
Barrow	35	X			
Shrewsbury Town	15			X	
South Liverpool	5			X	
Scunthorpe & Lindsey Utd.	1			X	
Wigan Athletic	1			X	
1939					
(South Section)					
Bristol Rovers	45	X			
Walsall	36	X			
Gillingham	15			X	
Chelmsford City	1			X	
Colchester United	1			X	
(North Section)					
Hartlepool United	38	X			
Accrington	28	X			
Shrewsbury Town	22			X	
South Liverpool	5			X	
Scunthorpe & Lindsey Utd.	4			X	
Burton Town	0			X	
Wigan Athletic	0			X	

* Elected after a first 'preliminary ballot' was taken.

1940 - 1946: No re-election meetings (World War Two)

Club	1	2	3	4	5
1947 (All four teams re-elected without vote or dissention)					
(South Section)					
Norwich City		X			
Mansfield Town		X			
(North Section)					
Southport		X			
Halifax		X			

Unsuccessful election applicants (no vote taken):

(South)	(North)
Barry Town	Annfield Plain
Bath City	Ashington
Chelmsford City	Ashton United
Colchester United	Bangor City
Gillingham	Consett
Gravesend & Northfleet	Dudley Town
Guildford City	Nelson
Llanelly	North Shields
Merthyr Tydfil	Northwich Victoria
Peterborough United	Scunthorpe & L.U.
Worcester City	Shrewsbury Town
Yeovil Town	Stockton
	South Liverpool
	Wigan Athletic
	Workington

Club	1	2	3	4	5

1948
(South Section)
Club	1	2	3	4	5
Norwich City	47	X			
Brighton & Hove Albion	47	X			
Colchester United	2			X	
Gillingham	1			X	
Worcester City	1			X	
Bath City	0			X	
Bridgend	0			X	
Chelmsford City	0			X	
Lovell's Athletic	0			X	
Merthyr Tydfil	0			X	
Peterborough United	0			X	
Yeovil Town	0			X	

(North Section)
Club	1	2	3	4	5
Halifax Town	47	X			
New Brighton	38	X			
Shrewsbury Town	8			X	
Scunthorpe & Lindsey Utd.	2			X	
South Liverpool	1			X	
Nelson	0			X	
North Shields	0			X	
Northwich Victoria	0			X	
Wigan Athletic	0			X	
Workington	0			X	

1949
(South Section)
Club	1	2	3	4	5
Aldershot	41	X			
Crystal Palace	40	X			
Gillingham	5			X	
Worcester City	5			X	
Merthyr Tydfil	3			X	
Yeovil Town	2			X	
Peterborough United	0			X	

(North Section)
Club	1	2	3	4	5
Bradford City	45	X			
Southport	42	X			
Shrewsbury Town	5			X	
Scunthorpe & Lindsey Utd.	4			X	
Nelson	0			X	
North Shields	0			X	
South Liverpool	0			X	
Wigan Athletic	0			X	

1950 - League extended to 24 clubs per 3rd Division.
(South Section)
Millwall and Newport County (re-elected without vote)

Club	1	2	3	4	5
Gillingham	44	X			
Colchester United	28	X			
Worcester City	11			X	
Chelmsford City	8			X	
Peterborough United	5			X	
Merthyr Tydfil	1			X	
Yeovil Town	1			X	
Llanelly	0			X	
Cradley Heath	0			X	
Nuneaton Borough	0			X	

Bangor City (withdrew before vote)

1950 (Continued)
(North Section)
Halifax Town and York City re-elected without vote.

Club	1	2	3	4	5
Shrewsbury Town	30 50	X			
Scunthorpe & L. U.*	17(15)(30)	X			
Wigan Athletic *	19(15)(18)	X —			
Workington *	19(14)			X	
Nelson *	11 (5)			X	
Northwich Victoria	1 (o)			X	
South Liverpool	1 (o)			X	
Ashington	0 (o)			X	
North Shields	0 (o)			X	

8

* Four clubs went to second vote. Three clubs went to third vote (Nelson dropped out). 2

1951
(South Section)
Club	1	2	3	4	5
Watford	48	X			
Crystal Palace	45	X			
Bath City	3			X	
Merthyr Tydfil	1			X	
Worcester City	1			X	
Chelmsford City	0			X	
Hereford United	0			X	
Llanelly	0			X	
Peterborough United	0			X	
Yeovil Town	0			X	

(North Section)
Club	1	2	3	4	5
Accrington Stanley	46	X			
Workington	28		X		
New Brighton	18				X
Wigan Athletic	4			X	
Nelson	1			X	
North Shields	1			X	
Northwich Victoria	0			X	
South Liverpool	0			X	

1952
(South Section)
Club	1	2	3	4	5
Exeter City	47	X			
Walsall	45	X			
Worcester City	3			X	
Bath City	1			X	
Merthyr Tydfil	1			X	
Peterborough United	1			X	
Headington United	0			X	
Yeovil Town	0			X	

(North Section)
Club	1	2	3	4	5
Darlington	49	X			
Workington	40	X			
Wigan Athletic	9			X	
Nelson	0			X	
New Brighton	0			X	
North Shields	0			X	

Club	1	2	3	4	5
1953					
(South Section)					
Shrewsbury Town	46	X			
Walsall	41	X			
Peterborough United	6			X	
Bath City	2			X	
Yeovil Town	2			X	
Hereford United	1			X	
Headington United	0			X	
Worcester City	0			X	
(North Section)					
Accrington Stanley	45	X			
Workington	36	X			
Wigan Athletic	17			X	
Nelson	0			X	
New Brighton	0			X	
North Shields	0			X	
1954					
(South Section)					
Colchester United	45	X			
Walsall	32	X			
Peterborough United	18			X	
Worcester City	2			X	
Merthyr Tydfil	1			X	
Bath City	0			X	
Yeovil Town	0			X	
(North Section)					
Chester	48	X			
Halifax Town	28	X			
Wigan Athletic	19			X	
Nelson	3			X	
North Shields	0			X	
1955					
(South Section)					
Colchester United	44	X			
Walsall	33	X			
Peterborough United	16			X	
Worcester City	3			X	
Headington United	2			X	
Bedford Town	0			X	
Yeovil Town	0			X	
(North Section)					
Grimsby Town	49	X			
Chester	47	X			
Wigan Athletic	2			X	
Burton Albion	0			X	
Nelson	0			X	
North Shields	0			X	

Club	1	2	3	4	5
1956					
(South Section)					
Crystal Palace	44	X			
Swindon Town	42	X			
Peterborough United	8			X	
Boston United	1			X	
Gloucester City	1			X	
Bedford Town	0			X	
Chelmsford City	0			X	
Hastings United	0			X	
Headington United	0			X	
Hereford United	0			X	
King's Lynn	0			X	
Worcester City	0			X	
Yeovil Town	0			X	
(North Section)					
Bradford P.A.	47	X			
Crewe Alexandra	45	X			
Wigan Athletic	2			X	
Burton Albion	1			X	
Nelson	1			X	
1957					
(South Section)					
Norwich City	48	X			
Swindon Town	42	X			
Peterborough United	7			X	
Bedford Town	1			X	
Headington United	0			X	
Kettering Town	0			X	
King's Lynn	0			X	
Worcester City	0			X	
Yeovil Town	0			X	
(North Section)					
Tranmere Rovers	48	X			
Crewe Alexandra	47	X			
Burton Albion	1			X	
Wigan Athletic	1			X	
Morecambe	0			X	
Nelson	0			X	
North Shields	0			X	
1958 - 4th Division formed					
(South Section)					
Millwall	46	X			
Exeter City	43	X			
(North Section)					
Southport	42	X			
Crewe Alexandra	35	X			
Peterborough United	15			X	
Wigan Athletic	4			X	
Hereford United	3			X	
Bedford Town	2			X	
Headington United	2			X	
King's Lynn	2			X	
Kettering Town	1			X	
South Shields	1			X	
Burton Albion	0			X	
Gloucester City	0			X	
Morecambe	0			X	
Yeovil Town	0			X	

Club	1	2	3	4	5

1959 Election of clubs was conducted in one ballot, instead of, as previously, two from each section.

Club	1	2	3	4	5
Oldham Athletic	46	X				
Southport	34	X				
Barrow	32	X				
Aldershot	31	X				
Peterborough United	26				X	
Headington United	7				X	
Worcester City	7				X	
Wigan Athletic	3				X	
Cambridge City	2				X	
Gloucester City	1				X	
Kettering Town	1				X	
Scarborough	1				X	
South Shields	1				X	
Bedford Town	0				X	
Hereford United	0				X	
King's Lynn	0				X	
Morecambe	0				X	
Yeovil Town	0				X	

1960

Club	1	2	3	4	5
Oldham Athletic	39	X				
Peterborough United	35		X			
Hartlepools United	34	X				
Southport	29	X				
Gateshead	18					X
Headington United	10				X	
Wigan Athletic	6				X	
Chelmsford City	3				X	
Bedford Town	2				X	
Cambridge City	2				X	
Guildford City	2				X	
New Brighton	2				X	
Romford	2				X	
Scarborough	2				X	
Worcester City	2				X	
Ellesmere Port Town	1				X	
Kettering Town	1				X	
Morecambe	1				X	
South Shields	1				X	
Hereford United	0				X	
King's Lynn	0				X	
Yeovil Town	0				X	

1961

Club	1	2	3	4	5
Chester	45	X				
Exeter City	44	X				
Barrow	35	X				
Hartlepools United	32	X				
Oxford United *	19				X	
Bedford Town	4				X	
Wigan Athletic	4				X	
Chelmsford City	3				X	
Gateshead	3				X	
Cambridge City	2				X	
Hereford United	1				X	
Kettering Town	1				X	

(* Formerly Headington United)

(1961 Continued)

Club	1	2	3	4	5
Romford	1				X	
Scarborough	1				X	
South Shields	1				X	
Bexleyheath and Welling	0				X	
Gravesend and North.	0				X	
Guildford City	0				X	
King's Lynn	0				X	
Morecambe	0				X	

1962 - Accrington Stanley (resigned during season)

Club	1	2	3	4	5
Chester	46	X				
Doncaster Rovers	45	X				
Hartlepools United	40	X				
Oxford United	39			X		
Wigan Athletic	5				X	
Chelmsford City	4				X	
Gateshead	4				X	
Cambridge City	2				X	
Worcester City	2				X	
Bath City	1				X	
Hereford United	1				X	
King's Lynn	1				X	
Morecambe	1				X	
New Brighton	1				X	
Bedford Town	0				X	
Bexleyheath and Welling	0				X	
Corby Town	0				X	
Folkestone	0				X	
Gravesend and North.	0				X	
Guildford City	0				X	
Kettering Town	0				X	
North Shields	0				X	
Poole Town	0				X	
Romford	0				X	
Scarborough	0				X	
Sittingbourne	0				X	
South Shields	0				X	
Wellington Town	0				X	
Yeovil Town	0				X	

1963

Club	1	2	3	4	5
Bradford City	47	X				
Lincoln City	47	X				
Chester	43	X				
Hartlepools United	34	X				
Scarborough	5				X	
Gateshead	4				X	
Guildford City	3				X	
Morecambe	2				X	
Romford	2				X	
New Brighton	1				X	
South Shields	1				X	
Wellington Town	1				X	
Weymouth	1				X	
Yeovil Town	1				X	
Bexleyheath and Welling	0				X	
Corby Town	0				X	

Club	1	2	3	4	5
1964					
York City	48	X			
Southport	45	X			
Barrow	42	X			
Hartlepools United	36	X			
Wigan Athletic	5			X	
Gateshead	4			X	
Romford	4			X	
Yeovil Town	3			X	
Guildford City	2			X	
New Brighton	2			X	
South Shields	2			X	
Gloucester City	1			X	
Morecambe	1			X	
Weymouth	1			X	
Bexley United	0			X	
Poole Town	0			X	
Scarborough	0			X	
1965					
Lincoln City	48	X			
Stockport County	45	X			
Barrow	41	X			
Halifax Town	41	X			
Bedford Town	4			X	
Gateshead	4			X	
Guildford City	3			X	
Hereford United	2			X	
Wigan Athletic	2			X	
Cambridge United	1			X	
Morecambe	1			X	
Romford	1			X	
South Shields	1			X	
Wellington Town	1			X	
Wimbledon	1			X	
Bexley United	0			X	
Corby Town	0			X	
New Brighton	0			X	
1966					
Lincoln City	43	X			
Bradford City	42	X			
Wrexham	40	X			
Rochdale	36	X			
Cambridge United	5			X	
Wigan Athletic	5			X	
Hereford United	4			X	
Bedford Town	3			X	
South Shields	3			X	
Morecambe	2			X	
Romford	2			X	
Corby Town	1			X	
Gateshead	1			X	
Wellington Town	1			X	
Folkestone	0			X	
Scarborough	0			X	
Wimbledon	0			X	
Yeovil Town	0			X	

(Three other - unknown - clubs had their applications rejected due to their signing of Football League players without consent).

Club	1	2	3	4	5
1967					
Lincoln City	46	X			
York City	45	X			
Bradford P.A.	45	X			
Rochdale	38	X			
Romford	5				
Wigan Athletic	5			X	
Hereford United	4			X	
Bedford Town	2			X	
Chelmsford City	1			X	
Wellington Town	1			X	
Wimbledon	1			X	
Yeovil Town	1			X	
Cambridge City	0			X	
Cambridge United	0			X	
Corby Town	0			X	
Guildford City	0			X	
Kettering Town	0			X	
New Brighton	0			X	
Scarborough	0			X	
1968					
York City	46	X			
Chester	44	X			
Bradford P.A.	44	X			
Workington	38	X			
Cheltenham Town	3			X	
Bedford Town	2			X	
Cambridge City	2			X	
Cambridge United	2			X	
Chelmsford City	2			X	
Runcorn	2			X	
Wigan Athletic	2			X	
Guildford City	1			X	
Hereford United	1			X	
New Brighton	1			X	
Wellington Town	1			X	
Wimbledon	1			X	
Worcester City	1			X	
Yeovil Town	0			X	
Nuneaton Borough	0			X	

Port Vale were to be expelled, due to irregularities, but voted back in again by 40 votes to 9.

Club	1	2	3	4	5
1969					
Grimsby Town	47	X			
York City	45	X			
Bradford P.A.	38	X			
Newport County	27	X			
Wigan Athletic	11			X	
Kettering Town	3			X	
Cambridge City	2			X	
Cambridge United	2			X	
Hereford United	2			X	
Romford	2			X	
Bedford Town	1			X	
Chelmsford City	1			X	
Worcester City	1			X	
Nuneaton Borough	0			X	
Wimbledon	0			X	

Club	1	2	3	4	5
1970					
Darlington	47	X			
Hartlepool United	42	X			
Cambridge United	31		X		
Newport County	31	X			
Wigan Athletic	18			X	
Bradford P.A.	17				X
Cambridge City	2			X	
Bedford Town	1			X	
Hereford United	1			X	
Morecambe	1			X	
Romford	1			X	
Yeovil Town	1			X	
Boston United	0			X	
Chelmsford City	0			X	
Hillingdon Borough	0			X	
Telford United	0			X	
Wimbledon	0			X	
1971					
Lincoln City	47	X			
Barrow	38	X			
Hartlepool United	33	X			
Newport County	33	X			
Hereford United	22			X	
Wigan Athletic	14			X	
Cambridge City	2			X	
Telford United	2			X	
Yeovil Town	2			X	
Boston United	1			X	
Bradford P.A.	1			X	
Romford	1			X	
Bedford Town	0			X	
Chelmsford City	0			X	
Gateshead	0			X	
Hillingdon Borough	0			X	
Kettering Town	0			X	
1972					
Northampton Town	49	X			
Stockport County	46	X			
Crewe Alexandra	46	X			
Hereford United *	26(29)		X		
Barrow	26(20)				X
Bradford P.A.	1			X	
Cambridge City	1			X	
Wimbledon	1			X	
Bangor City	0			X	
Bedford Town	0			X	
Boston United	0			X	
Hillingdon Borough	0			X	
Romford	0			X	
Telford United	0			X	
Wigan Athletic	0			X	
Yeovil Town	0			X	

* Voted in on second vote (with Barrow).

Club	1	2	3	4	5
1973					
Colchester United	48	X			
Northampton Town	43	X			
Crewe Alexandra	36	X			
Darlington	26	X			
Yeovil Town	14			X	
Kettering Town	12			X	
Wigan Athletic	10			X	
Chelmsford City	4			X	
Cambridge City	1			X	
Nuneaton Borough	1			X	
Telford United	1			X	
Barrow	0			X	
Bedford Town	0			X	
Boston United	0			X	
Bradford P.A.	0			X	
Wimbledon	0			X	
1974					
Doncaster Rovers	46	X			
Stockport County	38	X			
Crewe Alexandra	37	X			
Workington	21	X			
Kettering Town	16			X	
Yeovil Town	14			X	
Wigan Athletic	10			X	
Chelmsford City	8			X	
Nuneaton Borough	1			X	
Telford United	1			X	
Cambridge City	0			X	
1975					
Swansea City	43	X			
Scunthorpe United	41	X			
Darlington	32	X			
Workington	28	X			
Kettering Town	20			X	
Wigan Athletic	8			X	
Yeovil Town	8			X	
Wimbledon	4			X	
Bedford Town	2			X	
Goole Town	2			X	
Northwich Victoria	2			X	
Scarborough	2			X	
Gainsborough Trinity	1			X	
Nuneaton Borough	1			X	
Telford United	1			X	
Weymouth	1			X	
Boston United	0			X	
Chelmsford City	0			X	
1976					
Stockport County	42	X			
Newport County	41	X			
Southport	38	X			
Workington	21	X			
Yeovil Town	18			X	
Kettering Town	14			X	
Wigan Athletic	6			X	
Chelmsford City	3			X	
Wimbledon	3			X	
Nuneaton Borough	2			X	
Telford United	2			X	
Gainsborough Trinity	1			X	
Scarborough	1			X	

Club	1	2	3	4	5

1977 (New ruling restricting maximum two new applications)

Club	1	2	3	4	5
Halifax Town	44	X			
Hartlepool United	43	X			
Southport	37	X			
Wimbledon	27		X		
Workington	21				X
Altrincham	12			X	

1978

Club	1	2	3	4	5
York	49	X			
Rochdale	39	X			
Hartlepool United	33	X			
Wigan Athletic *	26(29)		X		
Southport	26(20)				X
Bath City	23			X	

* Voted in on second vote (with Southport)

1979

Club	1	2	3	4	5
Doncaster Rovers	50	X			
Crewe Alexandra	49	X			
Darlington	42	X			
Halifax Town	37	X			
Altrincham	13			X	
Kettering Town	12			X	

1980 (New ruling restricting application from one Alliance Premier League club only)

Club	1	2	3	4	5
Darlington	49	X			
Crewe Alexandra	48	X			
Hereford United	48	X			
Rochdale	26	X			
Altrincham	25			X	

1981

Club	1	2	3	4	5
Tranmere Rovers	48	X			
Hereford United	46	X			
York City	46	X			
Halifax Town	41	X			
Altrincham	15			X	

(Wycombe Wanderers withdrew their application before the meeting)

1982

Club	1	2	3	4	5
Northampton Town	53	X			
Crewe Alexandra	50	X			
Scunthorpe United	48	X			
Rochdale	48	X			
Telford United	13			X	

1983

Club	1	2	3	4	5
Blackpool	52	X			
Crewe Alexandra	49	X			
Hereford United	49	X			
Hartlepool United	36	X			
Maidstone United	26			X	

1984

Club	1	2	3	4	5
Chester City	52	X			
Halifax Town	52	X			
Rochdale	50	X			
Hartlepool United	32	X			
Maidstone United	22			X	

1985

Club	1	2	3	4	5
Halifax Town		X			
Stockport		X			
Northampton Town		X			
Torquay United		X			

1986

Club	1	2	3	4	5
Preston North End	62½	X			
Exeter City	64	X			
Cambridge United	61	X			
Torquay United	61	X			
Enfield	7½			X	

1987   Automatic promotion and relegation commenced - subject to Ground, etc. approvals - with Alliance Premier (GM Vauxhall Conference).
Lincoln City - relegated
Scarborough - promoted.

1988
Lincoln City replaced Newport County

1989
Maidstone United replaced Darlington

1990
Darlington replaced Colchester United

1991
Barnet promoted (League re-organistaion, no team relegated)

1992
Colchester United promoted
(Aldershot folded and no Club was relegated, in addition, Maidstone United later also folded, prior to the start of the season)

1993
Wycombe Wanderers replaced Halifax Town

1994
No movement.
(Kidderminster Harriers not promoted - Ground not suitable. Northampton Town avoided relegation)

1995
No movement.
(Macclesfield Town not promoted - Ground not suitable. Exeter City avoided relegation)

1996
No movement.
(Stevenage Town not promoted - Ground not suitable. Torquay United avoided relegation)

1997
Macclesfield Town replaced Hereford United.

1998
Halifax Town replaced Doncaster Rovers.

1999
Cheltenham Town replaced Scarborough.

2000
Kidderminster Harriers replaced Chester City.

2001
Rushden and Diamonds replaced Barnet.

ABERTILLERY TOWN

(1921)

The development of the coalmining industry in the 19th century resulted in an influx of workers to South Wales, including those from the rugby loving areas of the English West country, and there is no doubt that around 1900, Rugby was the principal ball sport in South Wales.

Abertillery Town, were just another Welsh club that - relatively - flourished around the First World War period. Football (soccer), following its popularity in the North of the principality, fairly rapidly spread to the Rugby strongholds in the South which led, around the turn of the 20th century, to a prolific number of football clubs in the area. An influx, which continued to rise, also arrived from the Midlands and South-east of England, together with those from North Wales, all from areas which were football strongholds. The legalisation of professionalism in 1900 in South Wales, coupled with the founding of a South Wales League a decade earlier, laid the foundations for the sport.

In 1909, three Welsh clubs (Aberdare, Ton Pentre and Merthyr) were elected to the pinnacle of non-League football, the Southern League, albeit the Second Division (Section 'A'). Treharris joined their compatriots one year later, and four further clubs were added in 1911. The 1912/13 season saw the Second Division of the Southern League totally dominated by Welsh clubs - ten of the thirteen members - and one year later, when Cardiff City became the first Welsh team in the First Division.

From 1909, Welsh clubs continued to join the Southern League Second Division, and within three years the teams from the Principality dominated the competition.

One of the best Grounds in Wales, but the team never stood a chance.

In 1913 Abertillery Town became the latest recruit. The Club made a steady start in the Southern League Second Division, finishing 11th of 16 teams, but made a quick exit from the competition, for along with fellow South Wales teams Mardy and Caerphilly they resigned during the following season, due to drastically reduced gate receipts.

But in any event, with War clouds looming, the Southern League closed down for the duration. When the League started up again in 1919, the three absentees returned to the eleven strong Second Division, which at this time consisted solely of Welsh Clubs. It is believed that the post-War Abertillery Town was not the same club as their predecessors; doubtless the earlier club had folded during the hostilities. Once again a team from Abertillery made no great impression, finishing 8th in the final table.

In 1920 a major change occurred in the Football League, when the Southern League en masse became the new national Third Division. The remaining Southern League clubs formed two divisions, the 'English Section' with 10 of the 13 being all Reserve elevens of former first team members, and a 'Welsh Section' which was little changed from the previous Second Division.

Abertillery was still a Rugby stronghold, but the 'Town' club made an encouraging start to the season, now under the guidance of player/manager James Blessington (who was one of the instigators of the Abertillery Schools League) - the ex-Scottish international - when a crowd of 1,000 was present to see their Practise match on the 16th August.

"A most successful season" was forecast by the local Press, especially since two notable signings had been made in Fred Fox from Preston North End, and E.McGuire a prominent Irish player who was signed from the Distillery club.

A short 'honeymoon' period was experienced in the town when both the local Rugby team and the football club enjoyed good support. The Town's final league record showed a slight improvement, for the team finished in 6th place of the 11 competitors. But in December the club were in trouble with the F.A. of Wales, when they were suspended as a result of their conduct and disrespect shown after several requests for information on a player were ignored.

The 1920/21 season saw the club, now running on professional lines, and also entered in the Western League First Division (to augment the lack of regular Southern League fixtures), where they finished a very respectable 3rd. There was an - albeit brief - boom in football popularity in South Wales, coupled with the success of those teams who were now members of the Football League, which contained four from the principality (the most successful being Cardiff City who had moved straight into the Second Division where they finished runners-up).

The lesser Welsh teams were encouraged to also attempt a move upwards, despite limited resources which were matched by small crowds spectating at very basic grounds, and at the Football League election meeting, no less than five teams from Wales applied for membership. Aberaman Athletic, in view of their close proximity to Aberdare, sensibly withdrew before the voting took place, and Abertillery Town were amongst the group, but they hardly had a pedigree worthy of serious consideration.

There were in effect two places vacant, in addition to the places of the two teams for re-election, but this pair was welcomed back without a vote being taken, and the rest were allowed to personally state their case. Aberdare Athletic - who were runners-up in the Southern League Welsh section - although only a recently reformed team had the Ground and support and were overwhelmingly approved, and for the three remaining clubs there were few votes left.

Pontypridd were a reasonably established club but only managed five votes, Welsh Section Champions Barry surprisingly fared the worst of all, gaining just a solitary vote. Abertillery, who it was considered had one of the best Grounds in the Country, had pledged to increase their capital by £10,000 if they were accepted, but with only four votes they were well short of the required number.

The rejected clubs never came even near to acceptance (Charlton Athletic were the other successful team with 30 votes), and reason prevailed one year later when only Pontypridd (together with new aspirants Llanelly) tried their luck again and came fairly close to gaining recognition.

Meanwhile Abertillery Town, who shared their ground, The Park, with the local rugby club (Abertillery - 'The Tilleryites'), proved that they would have been totally unsuitable for Football League membership, for in 1922 they finished one off the bottom of the Southern League Welsh Section, and the following season, together with three other clubs, they failed to complete their fixtures in a decimated Division. Yet they had been optimistic, although acknowledging that unemployment in the area was always going to be a problem, and but for the local industrial unrest were confident of financial success; at this time the club had an active supporters club. Finance was without doubt the main factor for the club's demise, and on some occasions the club were unable to pay the players their wages.

The devastating effects of the troubles in the local coal industry soon took their toll on such football clubs, and Abertillery Town withdrew their team (the reserves) from the Welsh League, and by the end of the 1922/23 season the Club had disappeared.

Abertillery was never to have a Senior football team again, and the town continued as a Rugby Union stronghold. Located in the South Wales Valleys, and within twenty miles or so of Cardiff, Newport, Aberdare and Merthyr (all Football League members at the time), notwithstanding several other semi-professional clubs, the Abertillery club had clearly fought a battle for support they could never win.

ALTRINCHAM

(1977, 1979, 1980, 1981)

Altrincham F.C. was founded back in 1903, yet it was nearly three-quarters of a century before the club found itself in a suitable position to apply for membership of the Football League. The club's formative years were low-key, but success was almost immediate with three Manchester League Championships in four years. In 1908 they moved onwards and upwards, becoming members of the Lancashire Combination, one of the most Senior of semi-professional leagues in the North. After the First World War they moved across to their own County League, The Cheshire, a competition which despite its apparently insular outlook, was deceptively strong, with many later leading Northern non-League clubs who at one time had been members.

Altrincham rarely challenged for honours, although they generally finished in the top half of the table, before a slump in the late 1920's saw a final wooden-spoon position in 1930. On the back of this the club rapidly became a force in the Cheshire League, once again generally finishing in the top half of the table, with a runners-up place on one occasion, but the Championship itself always eluded them.

Returning to the Cheshire League after the Second World War, the team did not impress, and although support was at a high (gates of 3,000 were not uncommon at Moss Lane despite the team's mediocrity), "Alty" finally slumped to a low in 1953, when they finished bottom. The Club's fortunes turned slightly for the better over the next few years until another slump saw the team finish second from bottom in 1961. However, Alty gradually became a force to be reckoned with, which culminated in the Championship, at last, in the 1965/66 season. This Championship season was repeated the following year, and the runners-up spot was claimed in 1968. In the slump years the attendances at home matches dipped to around the 1,000 mark, but the club's new found success led to hitherto unheard of support, with gates of 5,000 not being uncommon.

The unluckiest club never to get elected?

With fellow Cheshire Leaguers Wigan Athletic making their perennial applications for Football League recognition, it is perhaps somewhat strange in the circumstances that Altrincham's first bid for higher status was not made for another decade. Perhaps, however, the club's reluctance to better themselves was well-founded, for they were unable to repeat their Cheshire League successes in the Northern Premier League, of which they became founder-members in the 1968/69 season. The first few years saw the team generally languishing around mid-table, until another surge saw them finishing in third spot for two seasons running.

The following year they finished 7th, and in 1977, 10th, but by now attendances at Moss Lane had slumped to little above four figures. Yet 1977 was the year chosen for the team to make their first bid for a coveted Football League place. By now the usual plethora of aspirant clubs had been reduced to an agreed two, and along with Wimbledon (of the Southern League), they made their bid.

It was a good year to try for recognition, for constant strugglers Workington were rejected in their re-election bid, but it was Wimbledon who made it with 27 votes, compared to the Cumbrians 21, whilst "Alty" became also-rans with just 12 in support. It was the first year, after many previous attempts, that Wigan Athletic were unable to make a bid, which was unfortunate for them, but their 14th place in the Northern Premier table on this occasion hardly warranted inclusion.

Wimbledon were not particularly strong candidates, and must have considered themselves somewhat fortunate to get the seal of approval. From the Northern Premier League, both Boston United (Champions) and even Bangor City (4th) had better credentials than Altrincham, and would appear to have been the more suitable names to put forward.

One year later, the ever-persistent Wigan Athletic were the Northern League candidates, finishing as runners-up, whilst Altrincham improved on a year earlier to fifth, yet, ironically this season it was not good enough. Wigan at last got their just rewards (at the expense of Southport), whilst "Alty" had the opportunity to try again twelve months later. In 1979, the Champions of the Northern Premier (Mossley) had no aspirations or were ill-equipped to move up to the Football League, and the by now rapidly emerging Altrincham - as runners-up - were given their second try. However, their 13 points were well short of the 37 that kept Halifax Town in the Football League.

The 1980/81 season saw the introduction of the Alliance Premier League (later named GM Vauxhall Conference), when the elite of the non-Leaguers (from the Southern and the Northern Premier Leagues), combined. Altrincham had by now reached their peak, and they became worthy Champions of the new competition in its inaugural season. Aided by an incredible home record, when the team remained undefeated and shared the points on only three occasions, Alty managed to edge ahead of runners-up Weymouth by just two points. The Club had a Ground that was already up to Football League standard (albeit in the 'pre-Taylor Report' era when such requirements were not so stringent), with seating for 1,200, covered standing to embrace 5,000 and a Ground capacity of 10,000.

At the start of the season the club were determined that everything would be in place for their hoped for-election and over £50,000 was spent on additional concrete terracing. Financially as well as on the administration side they could prove their stability, and their support had reached an average of around 2,000 at home matches. In the F.A.Cup that season the team had a fine run, winning through to the third round after beating both Crewe and Rotherham, and thereby adding two more Football League scalps to their list of past successes in the competition.

Meanwhile, in the Football League, it was looking grim for the often struggling Rochdale, who were making their second re-election application in three years, to add to their embarrassing list of previous poor seasons.

This season they finished hopelessly outclassed at the bottom, and eight points adrift of the next club, Crewe Alexandra. Alty had good reason for their optimism, for they had spent over £10,000 on a campaign to convince the other members of the League that they were worthy of inclusion.

At the Football League's election meeting, Altrincham were devastated to lose out by just one vote (25 votes to Rochdale's 26), but the story did not end there. Two clubs who had promised their support for the non-Leaguers bid were Grimsby Town and Luton Town. It transpired that neither club had voted at the meeting, for the Grimsby representative was in the wrong part of the meeting room (which prevented him from voting), and the Luton man, who mixed up the time of the meeting, arrived late! Two more votes and the verdict would have swung over to Altrincham. Surely the closest, and the cruellest, denial of Football League 'promotion' ever experienced by a club.

It must have been difficult for Altrincham to pick up the pieces during the 1980/81 season, but this they managed to do, for they were again Alliance Premier League Champions and achieved another good F.A.Cup run. Yet once again bad luck came to the fore at the election meeting. This year the four re-election candidates - Tranmere Rovers, Hereford United, York City and Halifax Town - were not perennial strugglers.

The most likely candidates for the drop were Halifax, who were making their second application in three years (after a long period of security), but who only finished second from bottom. In the circumstances it would have been hard on any one of the four to be denied another chance, and this was reflected in the voting, when Altrincham could only muster 15 votes, whilst Halifax managed 41.

That year was to be the last that Altrincham featured in a re-election bid, and in the meantime their fortunes have slumped, which saw them relegated from the Alliance (Vauxhall Conference), and playing in the Northern Premier League by the late 1990's. The club, through no fault of their own, have probably missed their best chance of reaching the Football League.

ANNFIELD PLAIN

(1947)

Annfield Plain made just one election attempt - in 1947 - and they probably could not have chosen a worse time!

It is a strange fact that the North-East of England is a veritable goldmine for producing famous players, and can attract fanatical support at the big three centres of Newcastle (United), Sunderland and Middlesbrough, yet is almost completely neglected by the fans elsewhere; just ask Hartlepool and Darlington! This indifference extends to the non-League scene, where there is a plethora of teams, with grounds - although in many cases by now very much run-down - deserving of better support, and well run leagues of varying standards.

The area has had its chances, for apart from the five current members mentioned above, South Shields/Gateshead, Ashington and Durham have all been members of the Football League in the past, and all three have failed, principally through lack of support. And even at a lesser level, particularly in the former Amateur days, there were the 'Giants' in Bishop Auckland, Crook Town, and West Auckland.

Into this scenario appear Annfield Plain. Founded in 1890, as 'Annfield Plain Celtic', the club was admitted to the Northern Alliance in 1902, where they stayed until 1926, when the First Division of the Alliance amalgamated with the North-Eastern League (the Second Division retaining the old name).

The club had become a force to be reckoned with, claiming the Alliance Championship in 1920 and 1923.

Annfield were now playing alongside the reserves of Sunderland and Middlesbrough in this semi-professional competition, plus Carlisle United, who gained admission to the Football League in 1929 (they in fact changed places with Durham City).

League Cup Winners, and 6/6d as their share of the gate!

In their debut season in the North-Eastern League, the Annfield team fought their way through to the first round of the F.A.Cup for the first time, but only to lose 4-2 at home to fellow leaguers Chilton Colliery.

In 1928, Annfield again reached that stage of the competition, this time (in stormy weather) losing out at home to Southport of the Football League Division Three North, 4-1; the game produced Annfield's all-time record attendance of 7,200. The club managed to hold their own in the league that was dominated by Football League reserve elevens, but without winning any major honours.

The immediate years after the Second World War was a boom time for football throughout the country. Now freed from the dark days of hostility, the returning Servicemen helped to swell the crowds at football matches to unprecedented levels, and as with the majority of clubs they had never experienced greater prosperity.

The North-East of the Country saw high levels of employment with a booming shipbuilding industry - notably on the Tyne - and a demand for coal from the many mines in the area.

During the 1946/47 season, Annfield Plain achieved their most notable success in the North-Eastern League when they won the League Cup.

This success came on the back of a fifth from top placing in the final table a year earlier. It was these moderate achievements which no doubt prompted the club to apply for Football League status, despite that season only finishing 10th (of 20) in the league itself. But crowds were reaching high levels, a factor which no doubt encouraged the club to make this bold move.

In the best match at Derwent Park that season, the homesters beat Stockton 2-1 in the League Cup Semi-final before an attendance of 4,000, and earlier even a league game with nothing at stake against Eppleton (an entertaining 8-2 victory) produced a gate of around 2,000. In the League Cup Final itself, 7,500 were present at Murray Park, West Stanley, to see the Plain win the League Cup, although this was hardly a financial bonanza, for the club received only travelling expenses as their share, a paltry 6/6d. (32p) from a gate which realised £320!

Annfield Plain's Football League ambition was shared with an unprecedented, and record total, of 27 non-League hopefuls that year. Amongst these contenders were Ashington, Consett, South Shields and Stockton, all from the North-Eastern League.

South Shields (who finished third), former Football League members Ashington (fourth), plus Stockton and Consett who finished 7th and 8th respectively, all had more realistic claims than Annfield Plain.

In addition, from their own locality, there were also other aspirants elsewhere that would have surely received more credibility, such as the up and coming Merthyr Tydfil from Wales, former members Gillingham (and Southern League Champions) plus Scunthorpe and Lindsey United of the Midland League.

Apart from their reasonable performances in the two post-War seasons, the Derwent Park club hardly had a football record that was worthy of serious consideration.

But in the final event all these applications were academic, for the Football League took the, not unrealistic, view that it would be unreasonable to cast aside one of their own, whilst their clubs were still regrouping so soon after the War. And so the four teams up for re-election were welcomed back without even the necessity of a vote.

At least Annfield Plain have gone down in history as a club which once applied for Football League status, although in reality if voting had taken place, their bid would almost certainly have attracted no support! The Club was to prove that they really did not have the ability to rise above their status, for the ensuing years in the North-Eastern League were to produce no further honours, and they eventually dropped down to the lesser Wearside League, where they have hardly excelled!

ARGONAUTS

(1928, 1929, 1930)

In the dim and distant past history of the Football League, there have been a number of clubs seeking Football League status who failed woefully, and have now faded into oblivion. Indeed there have even been a few somewhat strange applicants who made it to this level but soon departed. Yet, in relatively modern times, there can surely have been no stranger case than that of the Argonauts. In fact this outfit, for they can scarcely be called a 'club', never played a game (before or after their election attempts), and never even had a named squad of players, yet had made arrangements to play home games at the most famous Stadium in the world!

Home Ground - Wembley Stadium!

The Argonauts were to be England's answer to the famous Amateur Queen's Park team of Scotland, who at this time were still a powerful First Division force north of the border. One has to delve back to around the turn of the century to appreciate the scenario that brought about the creation of the Argonauts. Although the game of football originated in the South of England amongst the Public Schools of the like of Eton and Winchester, 'ambassadors' from these learned academies spread the word to the industrial Midlands and North, from whence emerged the clubs who were to create the first Football League in 1888. However, by this time, professional (paid) players had become the norm, a situation which was generally frowned upon - with a few exceptions - in the South. Such was the feelings against these 'mercenaries', that their very presence was to lead to the formation of the Amateur Football Alliance in 1907.

Although by this time several professional Southern-based clubs had entered the Football League fray, there was still much support for quality Amateur clubs, not least the renowned Corinthians. For many years they refused to lower their own ideals and compete with others in either Cup or League competition.

Eventually they succumbed and for a number of years competed well against their professional counterparts in the F.A.Cup.

Against this background, the Argonauts came upon the scene in 1928. The formation of the club was the brainchild of R.W. (Dick) Stoley, the former Cambridge University and England Amateur International player, who at that time was associated with Ealing AFC. In the post of secretary he rapidly recruited others to form a committee, and the news broke in late March 1928, of the club's intentions. They let it be known that they were to be a National - Amateur - team, and that they had already secured the venue for their home matches, at no lesser venue than the White City Stadium in West London.

Stoley announced that the Stadium, with a 100,000 capacity, would provide the ideal setting for his team of top class amateur players, with quality dressing-room accommodation and top facilities for spectators.

Despite the rapid formation of the Club, at this time Stoley assured the public that it was already properly constituted, had the necessary financial backing, and the promises of many top class amateur players, all of whom had won representative honours in some form. However, at this stage names were not divulged, no doubt confidentiality was necessary since these players had been committed to other top Amateur clubs. *"This is not an affair of the Parish pump"*, Stoley stated, emphasising that although formed in a short time it was no wild, ill-conceived idea.

Stoley wrote to every League club, and there were few who objected, except for two Third Division South clubs who were very much opposed to the idea. Both Queens Park Rangers - whose Loftus Road Ground was but a short walk from the White City Stadium - and

Brentford, just a few miles distant, already had enough problems attracting support, and hardly wanted further competition. The Argonauts committee emphasized that they were not a 'local' club as such, and that they would only appeal to the large numbers of untapped amateur followers in London.

In reality, support for Amateur and Professional clubs at this time was, to a large degree, independent of each other, but there was always the possibility of a shift of Bees and Rangers fans, in favour of the Amateurs. But the club took the objections seriously, and they soon made plans for an alternative venue, *"We have the pleasure to inform you that we have definitely concluded arrangements to play our home matches at the Ground of the Final tie* [the F.A.Cup Final] *at Wembley Stadium"*, it was announced!

The influential 'Athletic News' took up the cause. An outspoken - for the time - sporting newspaper, they severely criticised the F.A. for not openly supporting the Argonauts, were they against the Amateurs? They considered that for the good of the Amateur game, the F.A. (who of course were the controlling body for all clubs) should have encouraged the top Amateur clubs to offer some of their players to the newcomers!

This somewhat audacious statement did have a certain logic, for the Athletic News felt that the club would benefit the game in general, since their prominence would tend to stop the schools - particularly Public ones - move away towards Rugby. Help or no help, just prior to the election meeting in June, the club claimed to have promises from 33 top class players. They reasoned that a large squad would be necessary in view of the long travelling distances to matches, which would mean the unavailability of some, in view of their paid employment commitments.

After much publicity, and the open encourage-ment from the influential Athletic News, the day of the election meeting came. The Argonauts were unsuccessful in their bid, but they received an exceptional degree of support. Whilst Torquay United were warmly welcomed back - with 42 votes - Merthyr Town could only manage 27. The Amateur team however received the lion's share of the remaining votes, with 16 (the next placed hopefuls - Kettering Town - could only muster three).

The Argonauts committee had been really confident of acceptance, and they must have been severely shaken by this rebuff. In essence, the team did not exist, for the players were not publicly known, and a match had never been played by the club. Crestfallen, it was announced that after this snub there was no alternative but to disband. But one year later the Argonauts were back! The same arguments in their favour were used, Wembley Stadium as a home venue was again secured, and once again promises from many top players had been received. *"We are in a stronger position than a year ago"*, the club announced.

1929 was a bad year for those in the South who applied for advancement, for both re-election candidates Exeter City and Gillingham had strong cases, each having only been required to go cap in hand once before. As expected, the pair were comfortably voted back in, and the Argonauts, despite once again claiming the most votes of the others, this time they could only muster six in support. The Argonauts announced after the meeting that this was their last attempt, and they would now definitely *"shut down"*. Yet one year later they were there again!

But their third attempt did not prove to be lucky, just the reverse in fact. Their bid this time around did not produce the publicity of before, and although Merthyr Town were voted out, Gillingham, despite this their third re-election application, received good support. The Argonauts failed dismally, for they did not receive a single vote, whilst even fellow no-hopers Llanelly managed four. This somewhat romantic interlude in the history of the Football League at last came to an end, and the Argonauts were never heard of again.

Meanwhile, Merthyr's place in 1930 was taken by Thames Association, whose short member-ship of the League was to prove to be as bizarre as those of the Argonauts three attempts to join the elite.

However, the 'Wembley Stadium Saga' was not yet fully completed, for Stoley - the aspirant Argonauts secretary - still made use of the venue; quite possibly his commitment had entailed some payment in advance. For his 'other' club, Ealing AFC, appeared on the hallowed turf on no fewer than eight occasions, when it was used as a 'home' ground during the following season.

ASHTON NORTH END

(1899)

Look in an atlas and it is obvious that 'Ashton' is a very popular place name. However, this particular little known club provides clues to its geographical placing.

The 'North End' suffix no doubt was adopted from that of the famous Preston club of the period - that was also used by Glossop (in Derbyshire) prior to their election to the Football League one year earlier. The period also gives a clue, for the Southern based clubs had barely come upon the scene at this time, and therefore this Ashton would almost inevitably have come from the North of the country. This still gives a number of possibilities, but in fact this 'North End' was from Ashton-under-Lyne, in Lancashire.

Their bid was turned down .....

and they never played another game!

There was at this time many clubs in the area, of varying standards, but a few years earlier Ashton North End shot to relative prominence. Virtually unheard of prior to their entry into The Combination in 1894, their one season in this company was to be highly successful.

The Combination was formed in 1890, just two years after the Football League itself, and was soon to attract a number of worthy clubs. It was initially centred around the Manchester environs, but soon the net spread further, notably to Cheshire and Derbyshire. From the 10 Founder-members, Chester, Burton Swifts, Northwich Victoria and Wrexham were all at one time destined to be elected to the Football League.

After the first season, The Combination was dominated by Everton Reserves, who had a hat-trick of Championships, before moving on elsewhere for one season.

Amongst other newcomers in 1894, was Ashton North End. 'The Onions', as the team was nicknamed - for no obvious reason - took the Combination by storm, and in this, their debut and only season, they claimed the Championship.

It was a fairly close-fought competition, for Ashton just edged ahead of the 'other' North End, from Glossop, by one point at the finish. Support was at a high for the Onions, and when they entertained challengers Chester, at their Manchester Road Ground on the 24th November, there was a large crowd of around 4,000 present.

The spectators were not disappointed for Ashton ran out as 6-4 winners, after a three goal lead at half-time. In the return, at Faulkner Street, on the 13th April, the Ashton supporters, who numbered around 1,000, saw their team play out a goalless draw.

In those far off days, over one hundred years ago, the value of playing in the League was not necessarily perceived to be as important as in the modern game, and the Onions - despite their Championship win in 1895 in a competition second only to the Football League itself - decided to join the Lancashire League for the 1895/96 season.

Yet that year they may well have stood a chance of being elected, should they have so wished, for with the resignation of Northwich Victoria from the Second Division, Loughborough (Midland League Champions) were elected in their place. No doubt they would have struggled financially in the higher league, a factor which led to them swopping over to the more localised, but lower status, County league.

In the Lancashire League, Ashton North End were in good company, for other teams included Fairfield Athletic and Blackpool (1894/95 Champions and runners-up respectively, who also made unsuccessful bids for Football League status in 1895); other member clubs were Nelson, who folded during the 1898/99 season - but resurrected years later became members of the League - Southport Central, Stockport County, and Stalybridge Rovers.

But the Onions were never able to emulate their success of 1895, although they held their own for several years. The 1898/99 season proved to be the best, and at one time the team made a serious challenge for the top, but by early April the chance had gone, and they had slipped to 5th (of 13 teams).

The last match of the season, and it transpired, the Club's last ever game, was played at the Manchester Road enclosure on the 24th April. Haydock provided the opposition (this club having earlier taken over the fixtures of Rock Ferry who had retired from the league), and the homesters triumphed by virtue of a single goal scored by Wilson. The team finished in a very creditable 3rd place (with a league record which read: P.24 W.12 D.5 L.7 F.35 A.31); their 29 points were ten short of Champions Chorley.

On the 6th May 1899, a few weeks before the Football League election decision, a meeting was held to decide which way the Club should move.

The situation in respect of a financially critical period was acknowledged, and those present were told that: *"If the public rally round them at this juncture, the future of the club, they are confident, would be assured. They are anxious to climb into the Second Division - it is now or never."* Obviously a change of heart from four years earlier.

The Club's application was duly made at the League's meeting, and it surely must have come as no big surprise - in view of the credentials of the other applicants - when their bid was turned down; Ashton North End (together with Coventry City) were the only bidders who received no votes.

Soon after the Football League meeting, a Public meeting was held at the Feathers Inn, in Old Square, when the future of the Club was discussed. Few followers turned up, which illustrated the apathy shown towards the Football Club, and it was decided that Ashton North End should fold.

This became the only occasion when an established Club was never to play another game, after an unsuccessful bid to gain Football League status. With the absence of North End, it was left to Hurst Ramblers to take up the mantle of the most Senior club in the town, and many years later, plus a name change, once again saw the town of Ashton-under-Lyne making a bid for the Football League.

ASHTON UNITED

(1947)

Conveniently following on (alphabetically) from the previous non-League hopefuls (Ashton North End), Ashton United were, it is often claimed, formerly known as Hurst Ramblers, who supposedly were formed in 1878 or 1879. However, early references relate to plain 'Hurst', and the Ramblers suffix doesn't appear until around 1892. Hence it is most likely that these were two different clubs, and Ashton United a more likely follow-on club, from the Ramblers, but from c.1892.

Hurst, were probably around at about the same time as their neighbours North End, and in these earlier days were most likely the more Senior of the two clubs, for they first entered the F.A. Cup in 1883. At this time they initially beat the renowned Turton team, before scratching in the second round to Irwell Springs, after their opponents lodged a protest following Hurst's earlier victory. They were to only reach the second round, in 1885, before fading from the Cup scene in 1887, never reaching the first round (proper) stage again. But their successors - Ashton United - have repeated this feat, the first time in 1952/53.

Hurst were also the first winners of the Manchester County Cup, in the 1884/85 season, when they beat Newton Heath (later Manchester United) 3-0 in the Final that was played at Whalley Range. Hurst Ramblers were runners-up in the Federation in 1892-93 and champions in 1893-94, before moving up to the Combination for one season in 1894-95, when they finished 8th.

Second from bottom in the league... hardly the right credentials for a bid!

Football prominence in the town was taken over by Ashton North End, until they folded in 1899, when Hurst Ramblers took control again, which coincided with their first season in the Lancashire Combination (1898/99).

However, this prominence was shortlived for they too disbanded during the following season, having played their home games on Grounds in Darnton Road, and at Rose Hill. On their reformation (without the Ramblers suffix), they made their new home in Surrey Street, Hurst Cross, in 1909, when they joined the Manchester League.

In their first season they were runners-up, having the same points but a slightly inferior goal average to Salford United, who beat them 2-1 in the championship decider. Hurst were also the last champions of the original Manchester League, in 1911/12. An upward move to the Lancashire Combination was made in 1912, as members of the Second Division. In view of the time gap (1900 to 1909), it is debateable if the two were one and the same club, but the current Ashton United assume this as fact.

Hurst made little impact on the Lancashire Combination, apart from their initial season when they were promoted to the First Division (after finishing in only fifth place), and a runners-up spot, in the higher division, at the end of the 1914/15 season (although they were Champions in the 1916/17 first competition War league). In 1923, they transferred to the Cheshire League, where they remained until the Second World War.

During this period they were neither Championship contenders nor strugglers - except for the 1936/37 and the following season when they finished as wooden-spoonists.

They rejoined their Cheshire colleagues in 1945, and in 1947 the Club made its one and only bid for Football League status.

The first post-War season was a shot in the arm for football, for never had the sport been so popular. At Hurst Cross crowds of two to three thousand were common, and with expectations at such a high, it is little wonder that the Club felt confident that they could compete in the Football League. However, this thought crossed the minds of 27 other clubs who also applied; but Ashton United (they formally changed their name on the 1st of February 1947), by finishing second from bottom of the Cheshire League could hardly have been optimistic about the outcome of their bid. Wigan Athletic also made a bid, but as they finished as wooden-spoonists in the same league, their chances were even slimmer!

Financially the Club at this time was stable, they had demonstrated that they could attract reasonable crowds, and they had expressed their intention of becoming a Limited Company. In addition a proposal was made that the top clubs in the two regional Football League Third Divisions would combine (this was to happen some ten years later), whilst additional members would form two new (regional) Fourth Divisions. Therefore the plethora of applications, even some unsuitable ones, was perhaps hardly a surprise.

The expansion proposal was defeated, the retiring clubs were re-elected without a vote, and this was to become the 'new' Ashton United's sole bid for Football League status.

The following season was no better for Ashton United in the Cheshire League for they finished in the same position, but this time conceding 143 golas in their 42 matches, and it is little wonder that their decision to apply for Football League status was not repeated!

They moved back into the Lancashire Combination First Division until 1961, when they were relegated to the Second Division (it is not clear why, for they finished 12th of 22). They immediately became the Second Division Champions, but moved to the Midland League in 1964. Two years later they returned to the Lancashire Combination Second Division before completeing the circle and moving back to the Cheshire League in 1968. The rest of the Club's days in the Cheshire were poor, and they transferred to the North-West Counties League in 1982. Relegated from Division One in 1984, Champions of Division Two and promoted in 1987-88, then champions of Division One four years later with promotion to the Northern Premier League Division One have been the Club's lot over the last 20 years or so.

To date they have remained in Division One, and obviously although possible, the likelihood of ever being promoted the the League is most unlikely.

BANGOR CITY

(1947, 1972)

From the early days, football was far more popular in North Wales, compared to the Southern area of the Country, before an awakening to the sport finally arrived after the turn of the century. Bangor City were one of the pioneers in the North, having been founded in 1876, although it was of course to be some years before the team came to prominence outside their own locality. The Club's first major honour was their winning of the Welsh Cup in 1889, a feat which was repeated seven years later, and again in 1962; in addition the club were finalists on six occasions, under its old format when the more powerful Football League clubs were also entrants.

Whilst football was popular in the North, there were few clubs of sufficient standard to warrant a major league competition in the early days. But after five seasons in the localised North Wales Coast League (which included such teams as Flint, Rhyl, Colwyn Bay and Holywell), from 1893 as founder-members, the ambitious Club moved upwards to The Combination for 13 years. A brief return to the Welsh Coast was then made, before another period, once again based in the English football structure, within the Cheshire League and the Lancashire Combination.

Between the First World War and 1930, the Club possibly faded away from Senior football, but the situation is made confusing due to 'different' Bangor clubs around this time, which may have been one or more separate organisations. But 'Bangor' were still able to acquit themselves well in the various Welsh cup competitions.

Good crowds, European Cup entrants, but no place in the League for these Welshmen

In the early post-Second World War years, Bangor City was playing in the Lancashire Combination, and in 1947, they made their first bid for Football League status. It was rather ironic that after popularising the game in the North, it was the South which had the lion's share of League Clubs, with three then current members (and two former members), whilst Wrexham was the sole representative at the other end of the Country.

The Post-war football boom produced a host of clubs who felt they could make the grade at the highest level in 1947. But their efforts were to no avail, for the clubs seeking re-election were welcomed back without a vote, thus ensuring equal disappointments for the hopefuls. In any event Bangor City hardly had a good case, having finished in only 15th place of 22 clubs in the Lancashire Combination, despite having achieved the runners-up position in the last, post-War, full playing season.

Despite their lowly position, there was little doubt that support would be forthcoming at the gate, for that season a record attendance (10,212) was present for the North Wales versus Queens Park match, and the standards at the Ground in Farrar Road were acceptable, for many representative matches and Amateur Internationals were staged there; a far cry from the Club's earlier Ground at Maes-y-Dref in lower Bangor, which had little more than fairly narrow flat standing enclosures around the pitch, plus a squat and compact Stand down one side.

Bangor City was hardly a force to be reckoned with for the next three years in the Lancashire Combination, and after a rebuff from the Cheshire League in 1949, following an application to join their ranks, it was hardly an opportune time for the Club to try their luck with the Football League once again, just one year later. The only real advantage in Bangor's favour was their continued support, for home League attendances in excess of 2,000 and up to 3,000 were the norm, whilst an excellent run in the Welsh Cup saw a crowd of 7,582 (receipts of £919) for the 7th round tie with Merthyr Tydfil.

The Club's decision to apply for Football League membership was probably a late one, for early in March they re-applied to join the Cheshire League, and it wasn't until the 6th of April, that the Club formerly announced their intentions. The local newspaper brought up the subject of the team's chances of gaining entry into the Northern section of the Third Division, and stated that: *"City officials are observing the 'silence is golden rule.'"* The reporter went on to admit that, *"Northern football circles are already weighing up the chances as - not so good."*

The Club must also have realised that they had only a slim chance of success, despite the fact that at least two newcomers would join both the North and the South Third Divisions due to a proposed increase of four clubs. In the final event, rather than apply to join the North, they decided to stake their claim in the South! Geographically this made little sense, and at the last moment the Club saw the futility of the situation, and withdrew their application completely.

At least the team's final placing of 7th in the Combination was sufficient for the Cheshire League to finally accept them into their competition for the following season.

Eighteen generally unremarkable seasons (apart from a memorable entry into the European Cup-Winners Cup in 1962), ended with the Club becoming founder-members of the Northern Premier League. It was whilst in this competition, in 1972, they made their third and final bid for Football League status. Yet again there was no particular merit in their attempt that year, for they only finished 9th in the League, whilst third place Wigan Athletic must surely have felt more confident. Perhaps the Club's financial stability, with home crowds far in excess of most of their contemporaries (normally around 1,500), led them to believe that their application may be viewed favourably.

At the re-election meeting, Bangor City failed dismally, recording no votes (as did most of the 12 aspirants, including Wigan). This was to sensibly be the Club's final attempt, for in their two attempts they had received no votes.

The Club did later reach the Alliance Premier League on two occasions, where they remained for only two seasons each time, and in 1992, they were virtually obliged to leave the English football pyramid, and try their luck in their own national league. Whilst publicity and a chance of glory may be possible in the European competitions once again, Bangor City have now relinquished any possible chance of promotion to the Football League.

BARRY/BARRY TOWN

(1921, 1947)

Football arrived in the Barry area in the late 1880's, and was therefore one of the earlier centres in South Wales that recognised the sport. However, Barry A.F.C. in name was not formed until 1912, at the start of the upsurge in interest in this area at a higher level. In 1908, a Club by the name of 'Barry District' played in the Western League until 1913, at which time 'Barry Town' (probably the same club with a new title) was accepted into the Southern League, the name change coming into being a year earlier.

The team played in the Southern League Second Division, together with Croydon Common, Luton Town, Brentford and Stoke, plus a predominance of (South) Wales Clubs - twelve in total - who therefore made up the bulk of the 16 club membership. Barry opened their new Ground at Jenner Park with a visit from fellow-leaguers Mid-Rhondda, and a final placing of 10th was reasonable, if not spectacular, and one year later they ended just one place higher. The First World War put paid to any chance of progress, and on the re-grouping of the Southern League Division Two, the competition became totally Welsh. After a moderate 1919/20 season, Barry became Champions of the renamed 'Welsh Section'.

Barry were enjoying a very successful season in the league, whilst support was good with Jenner Park crowds of 4,000 being not uncommon; an F.A.Cup match with Mid-Rhondda attracted a massive attendance of around 10,000, who somehow managed to pack into the tight little enclosure. By the end of April, the local Barry Herald newspaper announced that the team were... *"shaping up to become Champions of the Southern League, a position which will have great influence in support of their application for admission into the Third Division of the Football League."*

The first attempt was a failure.... why Aberdare and not Barry?

The Championship was confirmed following the Club's victory over Mardy, yet they lost their last League match 3-1 at home to Pontypridd; no doubt fatigue was a contributing factor for the team was required to play 15 games in the last three weeks of the season!

By now the upsurge of interest in football had reached a high in South Wales, and already the country had four representatives in the Football League, viz. Cardiff City, Swansea Town, Newport County and Merthyr Town, therefore there was good cause for optimism in Barry that their application would be accepted. Cardiff in fact had gone straight into the Second Division a year earlier, and followed this with immediate promotion to the First. *"Cardiff's promotion to the First Division should help Barry's bid, one of the pioneers of the code in South Wales,"* the Newspaper announced.

Yet there were two big problems that were to hamper the Club's ambitions. Despite their successes over the season, they were not a wealthy club and had experienced financial problems which would not be looked on favourably by others, *"It is hoped that the finances will be repaired in the Summer,"* it was reported. In addition Jenner Park had a small, cramped playing area, and little to offer the spectators in the way of facilities or comfort when large crowds were present. The hill on the West side had to be cut into.... *"volunteers shaped the hill in a thorough manner"...* as soon as the season ended, whilst the spare soil was used to enlarge the playing area. It was confidently predicted that the Ground, when finished, would be one of the best in the Country. The Football League meeting when the Club's immediate future would be decided was on the 23rd May, and Councillor C.B.Griffiths O.B.E. represented them.

The bottom two League clubs were re-elected, with no poll being carried out, but with Crystal Palace being promoted from the Third Division (and no club replacing them), plus the transfer of Grimsby Town to the new Third Division North, there were two places vacant in the newly designated Third Division South. Barry were devastated when they not were not voted in, and even worse they were virtually snubbed with just a single vote. Runners-up to Barry in the Southern League, Aberdare Athletic, were almost unanimously welcomed in (plus Charlton Athletic), and from Wales both Pontypridd (4th) and even Abertillery (6th) polled more votes - 5 and 4 respectively - than the Champions.

A disconsolate Councillor Griffiths later reported to the Barry Supporters Club, when he confirmed the, *"keen disappointment felt."* He acknowledged that Barry's failure was due to the *"lack of preparation"*, particularly in respect of the Ground, which was still being improved. Conversely Aberdare was backed with considerable funds and they had completed the improvements at Pennydarren Park. Additionally the Aberdare club had produced and distributed an impressive brochure to 'sell' the Club, whilst Barry had naively ignored such an approach. The Councillor assured the supporters that, *"the club will eventually attain election"*, and would present *"a stronger case next year."* He also acknowledged that considerable funds would be necessary for their next bid.

Barry got off to an indifferent start to the 1921/22 season in the Welsh Section of the Southern League, and the club spirit waned as they rapidly lost support; even an attractive F.A.Cup match versus Cardiff Corries only attracted 2,000 through the gate. Worse was to come, for the economic situation in the country rapidly worsened, to such an extent that the following year, four clubs failed to complete their fixtures, leaving just seven teams left at the season's end. Barry had a wretched time, slumping to fifth, and reporting a massive loss of £ 896 on the season.

There was no question of the Club applying for election to the Football League that season, nor indeed for many years to come. A near perpetual struggle in the Southern League, both on the pitch and financially, was the outcome in the years leading up to the Second World War. Somehow the Club pulled through, and were present for the first post-War season of 1945/46. This interim competition (the first 'proper' season started one year later) was moderately successful, and one year later they finished in a very encouraging seventh final place.

In April the team had high hopes of finishing even higher with two home thrashings of Bedford Town (6-0) and Hereford United (7-0), but then disappointed their followers with defeats in the last two matches.

Little was said of the Club's second attempt at election in 1947, but they - together with 11 other Southern-based teams - applied for the regional Third Division of the Football League. But both Mansfield Town and Norwich City were re-elected without dissention, and the abandonment of the plan to extend the membership of the League that season resulted in no vote even being taken for the hopefuls.

That year was the second, and last, attempt by the now renamed Barry Town, yet with Championship successes in the 1950's these years would appear to have been the more opportune ones. Until 1982, the Club maintained their Southern League status, never threatening the leaders, but occasionally in danger of being voted out, until finally - ironically after a few years when they were well placed in the top division - they resigned, and opted for the Welsh League.

Later, after a few brief seasons back in the Southern, they eventually rejoined the revamped Welsh National League in 1994, where they have become a force to be reckoned with. There is now the promise of frequent appearances in the UEFA competitions, but with no chance of ever gracing the Football League.

BATH CITY

(1921, 1922, 1935, 1936, 1947, 1948, 1951 - 1954, 1962, 1978)

Of all the clubs that have applied to join the Football League, there are few to match Bath City's tenacity over such a long period, when strangely they tended to make separate two year bursts over a period of nearly sixty years.

Bath have arguably one of the best credentials for Football League membership.... they play in a City with a large catchment (a population of over 80,000 which would probably be doubled with surrounding towns and areas included), they have little competition at a high level (whilst Bristol is only 13 miles away, with this City's own population of around ½ million there should be plenty of support to share), their Ground at Twerton Park is perfectly capable of staging League football (as it already did over several years for Bristol Rovers), and their non-League crowds whilst not spectacular are quite capable of rising to the big occasion. The only minus against them, ironically the most important one, is the Club's general lack of real success on the field!

Formed in 1889, the Club's initial progress was very slow - especially when compared to their two neighbours in nearby Bristol - for it took 19 years for the team to adopt professionalism, with their entry into the Western League in 1908. Yet despite the vast area for support, success at Western League level was only marginal, and a further thirteen years ensued before the Club rose further up the football ladder, to the level of the Southern League.

Despite still only holding membership of the moderate rated Western League, Bath City made a bold, and some might say, foolish first bid for the Football League in 1921. Yet, no doubt aided by their potential and the fact that the Third Division South was to increase by two, they surprisingly managed to capture 12 votes, by far the best of the four 'also-rans'. Quite probably the Club had already been promised a Southern League place for the 1921/22 season, and therefore this would have aided their credibility.

But only a moderate, albeit steady, first showing at this higher level, with a final mid-table finish was the outcome, before the Club made their second bid for Football League status. With only themselves plus Guildford and Boscombe fielding first teams in the still highly rated Southern League (English Section), Bath City had a clear field, for the other pair did not apply. Yet Pontypridd, only a moderate performer in the nine club Welsh Section of the Southern League, also made a bid for membership (as did fellow countrymen, Welsh Leaguers Llanelly), and amazingly they captured 21 of the 22 available votes; Southend and Exeter were comfortably re-elected, and Bath received the one remaining vote. The Somerset club must have been somewhat disconcerted after this lack of faith in them, and it was to be another thirteen years before they tried again.

A Deserving Case?

Perhaps the time gap was not altogether surprising, for the Club hardly provided good credentials for an upward move, since for several years they finished well down the Southern League table (and were actually bottom of the Western Section in 1926). Then a remarkable transformation came about, when from a poor contender, they became a powerhouse. The (Western) Championship in 1930 (repeated three years later), gave them respect amongst their competitors.

Following a further period of indifferent performances, Bath made another election bid in 1935, when their first team played in both the Western and Central sections of the league, yet hardly the ideal time after finishing bottom in the latter competition! The team received just one vote for their trouble, yet a year later - when their performances on the field had barely improved - they captured nine votes of approval, by far the best of the three contenders from the South. It can only be assumed that prospective candidates at this time were sought who displayed potential rather then performance!

In a sense Bath City achieved Football League status during the War years! For the team participated in the Wartime League South for three seasons, when they regularly met the first teams of Cardiff City, Swansea Town and Bristol City; remarkably they usually finished above their illustrious opponents. In fact they made such a good impression that a local reporter stated that: *"Their performances should earn Bath City League membership one day."* But history shows that it wasn't to be.

Bath City seemed to have a penchant for applying for League status at all the wrong times! The first season after the Second World War, saw them make another bid, in 1947, following a campaign that left them second from bottom in the Southern League. But since all re-election candidates were allowed back in, no voting was taken for the ludicrous number of 29 applications from non-League clubs. A year later, after a slightly better season, it was another forlorn hope, for the Club were rebuked, receiving no votes (along with six others amongst the ten Southern hopefuls).

From 1951, Bath City applied for four consecutive seasons, and although their perform-ances gradually improved in the Southern League (they finished fourth in 1954), their support at the re-election meetings ironically dwindled - but only from a few votes to none! Sensibly, the Club decided to suspend any further bids for some years.

At last the Championship came to Twerton Park, in 1960, and another third round appearance in the F.A.Cup (the first, in 1931, helped provide the funds to buy Twerton Park, which they had moved into in 1932) was enjoyed. With an all-time record attendance in Bath of 18,020 for the visit of Brighton, all seemed set for a realistic Football League election bid. But Bath City declined! Perhaps sensibly they waited for two further years, during which time they established themselves, finished runners-up in the Southern League and therefore may well have considered that by then they were in a stronger position. Unfortunately the Club could not have chosen a worse season, once again, for no fewer than 18 clubs from the the Southern League Premier Division (plus Corby from the First) decided to apply.

With the sudden resignation of Accrington Stanley this left the way clear for one definite addition to the League, to a competition which was continually criticised for its 'old boys' network, and prevented the introduction of new blood to the competition. Champions Oxford United overwhelmingly received the votes of confidence, and the remaining 22 were sparsely shared amongst no fewer than 25 applicants. Bath City received just one.

The 1962/63 season was a poor one for Bath City and so they declined to make a 'promotion' bid, but one year later, with a finish of third in the table, plus another third round F.A.Cup appearance the signs were once again good. However they, and seven other Southern League members were barred from applying as punishment for their acquiring players from Football League clubs without paying a transfer fee.

A definite prolonged lean period followed, but after a vastly improved 1976/77 season, when they finished fourth, they followed this with the Championship one year later. With this record behind them, and a sensible policy by now adopted whereby just one club from the North and one from the South would apply for Football League membership, the chances looked good for the City. But the Club were destined to be unlucky once again, for their challengers from Lancashire, Wigan Athletic, had an even stronger claim for a move upwards. Three of the re-election candidates were comfortably wel-comed back, which left just one place for three bidders. Tantalisingly Bath City failed by just three votes, Wigan and Southport obtaining 26 each, and the former being elected on a second vote.

1978 presented, without doubt, the Club's best chance for election to the Football League, and although they have had their 'ups and downs' (with membership of the Conference for most of the period from 1979), the team have not come close to the later introduced automatic promotion position. However, the opportunity is there, and with a stronger challenge on the pitch, it would not be that surprising to see Bath City promoted to the Football League Division 3 sometime in the future.

BEDFORD TOWN

(1955 - 62, 1965 - 73, 1975)

Bedford have a unique record with regard to election bids, which they share with just two other clubs - Chelmsford City and Kettering Town - and ironically the trio are geographically quite close. All three have made the joint second most number of Football League applications, without being elected - 18.

Although by the early post-War years Bedford Town had become a force to be reckoned with, it was to be many years after their formation (they were reformed in 1908), before they graduated to the Southern League, until that time playing in the United Counties League. For the 1945/46 season, Bedford Town were accepted into the Southern League, but for some years they made a hard job of it, and indeed came close to losing their membership after twice becoming wooden-spoonists.

They were one of the most persistant triers!

Only a third from bottom final table position in 1950 ensured their continued membership. There is no doubt that the appointment of Ronnie Rook (ex-Arsenal) as player/manager in February 1951 had a profound effect, for immediately the attendances soared from around 3,600 in the pre-Rook period to 5,600 in the latter part of the season. From bottom at the beginning of the year the team rose to finish 17th of 23. A good F.A.Cup run and a best ever final league position the following season, ensured that interest remained at a high, and the average home crowd that season was a very healthy 5,190.

Despite a final third place one year later, the attendance figures inexplicably dropped, and though carrying a large playing staff, a financial loss on the season was reported. The next two seasons saw drops in the final tables, but then the 1955/56 campaign was memorable for the F.A.Cup exploits by the team.

By now Ronnie Rook's contract had expired, but under new leadership, Bedford Town proved they were a force to be reckoned with, and in the Cup they not only reached the third round, but even held Arsenal to a draw at Highbury. But for the financial rewards from the Cup, the coffers would have been empty, and spurred on by this success (despite only finishing fourth in the league), the Club made a concerted effort to obtain membership of the Football League.

Surprisingly they had already made a bid a year earlier, an ill-conceived move for they only obtained a final place of 18th in the Southern League, and surely - as was the case - must have expected not one vote in support. Their Cup run and good league performances would have been expected to gain some votes, yet in 1956, a nil response was again recorded.

In 1957, they managed one vote, and this was doubled a year later, yet with two runners-up places to their credit, more could surely have been expected. The real snub came in 1959, when despite winning the (now regionalised) Championship, and with average home crowds approaching 4,000 (a big drop over the years, but still better than virtually all others), not one vote of support was obtained. Whilst the lionshare went to the redoubtable Peterborough United, the likes of Headington (later Oxford) United and Worcester City - both teams finishing well down the pecking order in their division - each claimed seven votes.

One year later the Club did receive two votes, but with non-League Peterborough United deservedly at last 'moving upstairs' (with more votes than re-elected Hartlepool and Southport), there were few spoils left for the rest.

This season, Headington United received eight more votes than the Eagles, but since they were runners-up of the new Premier Division, and Bedford finished only seventh, this result was hardly surprising. Bedford finished two places lower in the 1961 table, yet managed four votes, equal with Wigan Athletic as the top 'also-rans'. No doubt their case was helped by continued good attendances - relative to others - and their well appointed Eyrie Ground.

The following year, the Club made their eighth consecutive election bid, but it must have been a forlorn hope, for they were well out of the running with a dismal season in the Southern League, and with no less than 26 aspirants, there were many far more worthy of consideration. The Club's nil vote led them, sensibly, to wait for better times before trying again.

In 1964, Bedford would surely have had a reasonable claim for a higher status, following a top half of the table finish, and an amazing F.A.Cup run which saw them beat Second Division Newcastle United at St. James' Park, and only depart at the hands of Carlisle United in the 4th round. But they, along with several other Southern League teams, were barred from making an application that year, due to these clubs obtaining Football league players without paying transfer fees. Bedford therefore had to wait another year (which saw a positional drop in the League table and no Cup run). Even so their four votes was very creditable, and although well below the required number, they topped the hopefuls chart. The inconsistencies came to the fore once again one year later, when a fourth final place in the League, and another excellent F.A.Cup run - through to the fourth round - produced only three votes. Yet the Club obviously continued to have some support at the re-election meeting, and whilst they only received two votes in 1967, the Club's relegation to the First Division of the Southern League hardly merited an attempt or any support!

But a run through to the third round of the F.A.Cup (six matches were necessary to navigate the 1st and 2nd rounds), must have helped their case.

The team immediately bounced back to the top Division, receiving just two election votes in 1968, but relegation, and one less vote was their lot a year later. The Championship of the lower division in 1970 did little to impress the voters (just one vote), yet a year later, with a consolidatary 7th final position in the Premier Division, no votes were credited to the Club. By 1972, the Club was running out of steam, and with yet another disappointing finish, no votes was hardly a surprising outcome. In 1973, Bedford Town tried yet again, in a consecutive run of nine, election attempts. But there was no support for their bid, and they waited for two years for their next, and final, assault.

Another relegation (in 1974), followed by an immediate Championship of the First Division North, whilst very encouraging, was hardly a good enough cause for Football League recognition. But even so, there were two votes in their favour in 1975, although several Premier Division clubs also made a bid. This was to be The Eagles last attempt at the Football League.

Around the mid to late 1950's, the Club had a good case to argue; a well equipped Ground, a consistent team and large attendances, however, so did Peterborough United (who finally managed the move upwards) as did several others. By the 1970's, the Club had faded from the limelight, and although they briefly came to the fore once again, they folded in 1982, following the loss of their Eyrie Ground. Realistically, the chance of League football in Bedford has gone, although a 'new' Bedford Town eventually arose from the ashes, and after plying their trade in the lower divisions of the Ryman (Isthmian) League, they made it to the Premier in 2001 - so who knows!

BEXLEYHEATH & WELLING/
BEXLEY UNITED

(1961 - 1965)

Although in reality two separate clubs, the two - Bexleyheath & Welling and Bexley United - were one and the same in all but name.

The senior football team in the town of Bexleyheath, in Kent, underwent a number of major changes over the years, with the presence of several different clubs with varying names. It all started in 1917 with Bexleyheath Labour who gained admittance to the Kent League in 1919. But they soon found that their ambitions were too high, for within a few months the club folded mid-season, and the remainder of the their fixtures were played out by the newly formed Bexleyheath Town club. The new outfit reached their pinnacle of success by becoming Champions in the 1928/29 season, and two years later they became known as Bexleyheath & Welling.

In line with most non-League Clubs, Bexleyheath & Welling closed down for the duration of the War, although they were somewhat slow in making a re-appearance, for they did not reform until 1951. The team were once again admitted to the Kent League, and although they did not achieve anything of note, they soon became renowned for their youth policy which was recognised as one of the best in the country. As in the pre-War days, the Club had links with Charlton Athletic, but in 1953, they turned professional and steadily made upward progress. Much of their success, albeit they were never Kent League Champions, was credited to player-manager Charlie Vaughan who had spent most of his Football League career with Charlton Athletic.

The Southern League underwent major changes in the late 1950's, when they extended their membership greatly in order to form two divisions. Many of the newcomers were recruited from the Kent League, including Bexleyheath & Welling in 1959, which had the knock-on effect of decimating the latter competition, and led to the disbanding of the competition. Under Vaughan's leadership the Club were very successful, and earned themselves a rather surprise promotion to the Premier Division of the Southern League at the end of the 1960/61 season after finishing in third place.

Despite making five consecutive attempts, the Club never stood a realistic chance!

Somewhat ludicrously over ambitious, Bexleyheath & Welling made an application to join the Football League in 1961, when they were one of fifteen making a bid. The four re-election candidates comfortably retained their places, and with Oxford (recently changed from Headington) United grabbing 19 of those left, the few votes left were sparsely scattered amongst nine of the hopefuls. With ten other applicants from the Southern League, all of whom (except First Division Champions Kettering Town) were from the Premier section, it must surely have been a forlorn hope by the Bexleyheath contingent to expect any support.

One year later the situation regarding applicants was somewhat farcical, for virtually the whole of the Southern League Premier Division tried their luck (18 of the 22 members), plus Corby from the First, to give a grand total of 26 bidding clubs. With only three Football league clubs needing to seek re-election - Oxford United received the lionshare for the fourth place.

The former 'Headington United' were duly taken on board in place of Accrington Stanley who had already resigned - there were 22 votes left for the rest. With Bexleyheath finishing around mid-table in their league, it was once again no little surprise when they received not a single vote of support.

In 1963 the number seeking re-election was a little more rational, albeit there were still 12 trying their luck. Bexleyheath were one of the aspirants again, and for the third time they received no votes, only one of two to receive 'nil points'. The other club to receive no vote of confidence was Corby Town who were also the supreme optimists since they could only finish seventh in the First ('Second') Division!

Prior to the start of the 1963/64 season, the Club's name was changed to the more convenient 'Bexley United', and they expended a great deal of money in levelling and relaying the playing area at their Park View ground, which had been used in the pre-War days. Determined to climb up into the Football League, further expenditure was made on enlarging the Seated Stand, and covering the terrace opposite. These improvements were proved to be carried out in haste rather than with proper planning, for during the Winter a few months later, the pitch became a morass, so much so that some 'home' matches had to be played at Woolwich Army Stadium.

For a while it appeared that all the Club's ambitions would be thwarted, as they lay dangerously around the relegation zone, but a 2-2 draw at home to Cambridge United, before a poor attendance of 1,330 (when on a good day 3,000 was not uncommon) in April ensured Premiership football for the following season. Bexley finished the season around mid-table, acceptable, but hardly cause for yet another bid to join the Football League!

By now the former Manager, Charlie Vaughan was Chairman, and together with the then current Manager, Harold Tanner, and Secretary Bernard Lee, the Club confirmed that they felt it important to make the attempt every year as part of their long term policy.

" *Like their previous three* (applications), *it is unlikely to gain any votes.*" Bexley compared their efforts with those of Peterborough United who only 'made it' after many attempts; but in view of the Midland club's playing record fair comparisons could hardly be drawn. There was, on this occasion, perhaps some justification, for there had been talk of splitting the Fourth Division into a 'Football Alliance' with two sections the following year. This would mean the addition of 14 new teams, most of whom would come from the Southern League. In addition eight Southern league clubs were prevented from making an election bid as punishment for their signing of Football League players on free transfers. With Chelmsford City and Bath City (who finished second and third respectively), this gave greater hope for the other contenders. But even with only thirteen bids (and only seven from the Southern League), Bexley United were yet again snubbed, and were one of three clubs who received no votes.

One year later, the Club made its fifth and final application to join the League, and as before they received no votes. Five attempts and a total of no votes, must have been a record, and at last the Club must have got the message. Geographically they were well placed with a good catchment area, they were reasonably supported at the gate, and with improvements the Ground could probably have been brought up to an acceptable standard. But the Club was not particularly successful, in fact they were relegated at the end of this season, 1964/65, and never regained their Premier Division status. Presumably Bexley United at last saw the futility of their efforts, and in any event ever mounting financial problems eventually led to the Club folding in June 1976, with debts of 30,000.

Welling United were later to install themselves at the Park View Ground, a 'fairytale' story of a club who came, in just a few years, from park football to the highest competition in non-League football. But United were never to make an election bid, and therefore, as they say, "that is another story"!

BLYTH SPARTANS

(1921, 1925, 1926, 1927)

Blyth Spartans, hailing from the North-east of England, were founded in 1899 although an earlier club in the town, named simply 'Blyth', had played in the Northern Alliance from 1892. In their first season they were runners-up, a feat which was repeated two years later. The original club last appeared in the Alliance in 1899, therefore it is very likely that they folded, and from their ashes the Spartans were created. However, it was eight years before the new club regained this status, playing Friendly matches for the first two seasons, before joining the Northumberland League in 1901, of which they were Champions three years later.

Spartans have had a colourful history over the past century, having alternated between Professional and Amateur, aspired to Football League status, had a record-breaking F.A. Cup run, yet have also struggled at times.

The team spent six seasons in the Northern Alliance, from 1907, and captured the Championship twice. Around 1910, they moved to Croft Park, and there they have remained. Shortly after their ground move, the ambitious club adopted semi-professional status and accordingly were accepted into the North-Eastern League, a competition occupied at that time by the likes of the reserve teams of Newcastle United, Sunderland and Middlesbrough, plus Hartlepools United, Darlington and Carlisle United first teams.

It was not long before the First World War intervened, but when the league reconvened in 1919, the Football League was on the verge of some radical changes which were to see its membership considerably enlarged with the addition of two Third Divisions.

The first change came in time for the 1920/21 season, when the clubs in membership of the Southern League became, en masse, the new 'Third Division South'. One year later, the process of forming a 'Third Division North' - which had been conceived a year earlier - proceeded. The selection of teams for this new division was not so simple as it was for the southern part of the country, where the Southern League had no equals in terms of non-League seniority.

In the North there was more than one league which included in their memberships clubs who were worthy of Football League status, therefore although 14 clubs were selected, the remaining four (Grimsby Town from the Southern section transferred to the North, and relegated Stockport County made up the final 20) had to go through the more familiar voting system.

Of the automatically selected clubs, four came from the North-Eastern League, namely Ashington, Darlington, Durham City and Hartlepools United. The final four places went to the vote, and 14 teams from various leagues vied for coveted Football League status. With eight clubs already representing the North-east corner of the country (the 'big three', South Shields, and the quartet of new clubs), there were just two more applications, those of Blyth Spartans and West Stanley.

The state of football in this area during the early 1920's was somewhat different from that in the 1990's, for although the numbers of clubs have not diminished over the period, the economic situation has led to very much reduced support.

No more room for anymore North-Easterners!

The industrial North-east, principally with its shipbuilding and coalmining Industries was sufficient to support a number of fully professional clubs, although in view of developments just a few years later, it became obvious than even eight were not viable, even in those early post-War football boom days.

The four North-Eastern League clubs who were automatically elected were, in three cases, apparently somewhat strange choices. Darlington, a club who always finished high in the table and were 1920/21 League champions were an obvious choice, however Hartlepools United who finished 8th (and normally ended up around mid-table), plus Ashington, with a similar record, hardly had strong pedigrees. Durham City (11th), in only their second season in the North-Eastern League were hardly well-established. Yet Blyth Spartans, who finished in 5th place (and West Stanley two places below them) were virtually overlooked.

Blyth received only 9 votes (compared to Wigan Borough who were elected with 34), and it can only be assumed that perhaps the geographical situations must have been a factor. Blyth, North of Newcastle, close to Ashington, and somewhat remote, had around double the population of Durham, and the latter with its Cathedral and City status perhaps was considered to project a better image for the Football League.

Sensibly, Spartans did not make another bid for four years, for clearly the North-east had a virtual surfeit of Football League clubs, and with both Ashington and Durham having to apply for re-election after just two seasons of membership (when Blyth were runners-up in their league), and Hartlepools in 1924, there was just not the support available; in addition the grim days of Industrial unrest were on the horizon.

Blyth made another attempt in 1925, having finished only 8th in the North-Eastern League (although only first team clubs Shildon and Workington were above them), and once again there was little support with just three votes. One year later a third application was made, yet despite finishing in a poor 14th place, they received the boost of 10 votes. It had been decided at the North-Eastern League A.G.M. on the 7th of June that just two clubs names would be put forward, the other club being Carlisle United who managed 12 votes.

In 1927, the Club made their last bid for elevated status, but yet again with only a mediocre league record over the previous season. The team finished 9th (with only Carlisle and Jarrow's first teams above them), and it probably came as no real surprise when they received just three votes (the lowest number of the four bidding clubs in the northern section).

By now the economic situation had worsened in the North-East part of the country, and one year later financially decimated Durham City (for the past four seasons, with under 2,000, they had the lowest average attendance of all the League clubs) were voted out, followed by Ashington one year later.

In 1936, Blyth Spartans were North-Eastern League champions, but by now all hope of Football League status, or for any other clubs in the area, had vanished. The Club reformed after the Second World War, rejoining their old league in 1947. In 1958, the North-Eastern League was dissolved, and Blyth - now an Amateur club - finally gained election to the Northern League in 1964. The Club later returned to semi-professional football, and their amazing run through to the fifth round (an all-time non-League record) of the F.A.Cup in 1978 is the best remembered exploits of Blyth Spartans, rather than their long forgotten attempts to gain promotion to the Football League.

BOSTON UNITED

(1956, 1970, 1971, 1972, 1973, 1975)

The name of Boston United only goes back to 1934, but the Club in its original form can be traced back to the late 19th century. The current Club was first known as Boston Town, and their home Ground, then known as the Main Ridge Ground was one and the same as the current York Street venue, albeit now changed in every respect. Initially the Town's main competitor was Boston Swifts (an entirely different team, and not to be confused with this suffix that often related to the reserve eleven of a 'parent' club). But the Swifts whose 'Ground', only a pitch in reality, abutted that of Town's, failed to re-appear after the great War (1914 - 1918), and so their fellow Lincolnshire League neighbours were left to carry the torch for the town.

In 1921, Boston Town made the big step up when they joined the Midland League, and although their first season was mediocre (17th of 22 teams), for three years they became a force to be reckoned with finishing second, third and second again in the end of season league tables. But from the mid-1920's they slipped back to mediocrity and only rarely finished above mid-table. By now the Club were struggling financially, and it was mainly due to the intervention of Ernest Malkinson in 1933 that ensured their survival; the Club's saviour was to remain with the club for 50 years, mainly in the role of Chairman. In the Summer of 1933, the Club reformed and adopted their current name of Boston United.

The new United never seriously challenged for the Championship in the years leading up to the War, but their performances gradually improved and they could generally be found around, or above, mid-table. It was some years before the Club came to the fore after the hostilities, but following a decade of generally disappointing performances, they shook the football world with one feat in the 1955/56 season F.A.Cup competition. Boston United had on a number of occasions fought their way through to the final rounds of the Cup (as Boston Town even beating Bradford P.A. at home in the 2nd round 1925/26 competition, before a record crowd of 5,041), before their achievement in 1955.

In the 4th qualifying round, Sutton Town were thrashed 8-2 on their own Ground, and in the 1st round proper United edged through with the odd goal in five over Northwich Victoria. High-flying Third Division North Derby County (who finally lost only one home League match all season) were visited for the second round, and only the most optimistic gave them any chance; *"No, I shall not go to Derby because I can't stand the strain of seeing the United humiliated",* one supporter supposedly said. But with six former County players on the field, the Lincolnshire team mercilessly tore their opponents apart, and came through as 6-1 winners; arguably the greatest result for a non-League club (and a not particularly high-flying one) against a Football League team. United lost 4-0 in the next round to 'Spurs.

This stupendous victory appeared to have spurred the Club on, for aided by excellent support, and a final second place finish in the Midland League, they made their first application for the Football League in 1956. Burton Town, who are geographically South of Boston, made their application to the Northern section, whilst somewhat ludicrously Boston United tried their lot with the Southern division! There were two strong contenders for each division - Wigan Athletic and Peterborough United - and in the circumstances a single vote, one more than eight other Southern hopefuls, was a moderately hopeful sign of the future for Boston.

After finishing in third place the following two seasons, Boston United opted for the Southern League, a year which saw a number of moves in and out of the Midland League. Third in the North-West zone followed by 9th of 22 in the new Premier Division one year later was a reasonable start in this new company. A rule of the Southern League was a commitment by new clubs to remain within it for at least three years (which would have thwarted any attempts at the Football League should Boston have wished to try their luck again), but after a disastrous 1960/61 season, when the team finished bottom (conceding 123 goals in 42 games) they were relegated.

Non-League sleeping giants?

48

Almost bankrupt dropped down to the Central Alliance, having been refused a re-admission to the Midland League.

For a club who had only a few years before applied for election to the Football League, and held their own in the Southern League, this was an embarrassing fall, but they soon bounced back, capturing the Central Alliance title at the first attempt. 'Promoted' to the Midland League, two moderate seasons followed, but still in financial disarray the Club eventually came close to folding and for the 1964/65 season dropped right down to the local Boston League, with the hope of regrouping and coming back a stronger club. The next stop in this roller coaster ride was initially one season in the United Counties League (capturing the League and Cup double), followed by entry to the somewhat inappropriate West Midlands League (Boston lies on the far East coast!)

Now fully 'recovered', the team triumphed with two title winning seasons, before yet another move, this time as founder-members of the Northern Premier League (the Club's record now showed that at one time they had been members of the most senior, Southern, Midlands and Northern competitions!). After an indifferent first season, the team climbed to 3rd place (just two points behind leaders Macclesfield Town) in 1970, and - perhaps somewhat prematurely - considered they were now good enough to be considered for the Football League again. Boston United were just one of 13 hopefuls - including Cambridge United (who replaced Bradford P.A.), Hereford United and Wigan Athletic - but the Lincolnshire club received no votes.

Fourth place a year later, followed by the runners-up spot and the Championship two years running really put the Club back amongst the giants of the non-League world. During this period three more attempts in succession were made for the Football League, but still each ended in total failure, with just one vote to show for their efforts. United were somewhat unfortunate for their bids were made at a time when there were several much stronger overall contenders each season.

This was despite Boston's excellent playing record at the time, their financial stability, and the good attendances they were attracting at York Street.

One final attempt for recognition was made, in 1975, but this was as unsuccessful as the previous five attempts. If there was one major flaw it was the Ground, which although reasonable, it was realised that it was not really up to Football League standards, even with the less demanding requirements at this time. This point was cruelly rammed home in 1977, when, following the team's third title success in five seasons, they were denied permission to apply for the Football League (now limited to the two most suitable clubs, one North and one South), due entirely to their inadequate Ground. If not for this factor, they in all reality would have received their 'promotion' for their replacement applicants in 1978, also from the Northern Premier League, runners-up Wigan Athletic, were voted in, replacing Southport.

In the past, due to financial disasters, the team bounced back strongly, and they were determined to do the same, this time in respect of a total rebuilding programme, and thus ensure that should the opportunity arise again they would not lose out. The vast and costly redevelopment work took around ten years to complete, but at the end the Club had a Ground almost totally roofed, which could hold nearly 7,000 standing under cover, and around 2,000 seated. The York Street Ground is now undoubtedly one of the finest in non-League football.

Unfortunately having got everything into place, the Club has not since had the opportunity to make another bid for the Football League. The financial burden of rebuilding had a long term effect on the playing staff, and although founder-members of the Alliance Premier League, the Club was never able to capture the Championship Trophy. Relegation came in 1993, and a move back to the Southern League again five years later, where the Club continue to flatter to deceive. Undoubtedly the support is there, if somewhat dormant, there are no problems with the Ground, and Boston United, it is felt - now back in the Conference - are something of a sleeping giant that one day may realise their ambition of a Football League place.

BRIDGEND TOWN

(1948)

The single attempt by Bridgend Town to gain Football League status, 'over the border' is one that is on the fringe of farce - for at the time no suitable team existed! However, well before 1948, and again shortly after, such club names did exist, and had their moments of relative prowess.

There was an onslaught of football (soccer type) in South Wales soon after the turn of the century, and for a few years the very sanctity of the all conquering Rugby (Union) style of football was in jeopardy in this area of the principality. Bridgend Town F.C. was formed in 1920, in a town which had been totally dominated by Rugby Union, but in keeping with other towns in South Wales a serious challenge was made by new football clubs that sprang up both before and after the First World War (1914 -1918). This change in sporting attitude can be seen with the initial entry into the Southern League of Ton Pentre, Merthyr and Aberdare (the latter two had representation a few years later in the Football League itself) in 1909.

No Senior team, no decent Ground, no chance!

Within ten years the whole Second Division of the Southern League was composed of Welsh Clubs (11 in total), plus four in the top section. That same year, enthusiasm was such that a club was formed in Bridgend following a public meeting in the town. The main stumbling block in the successful creation of a team was that of aquiring a Ground, but the enthusiasm was such that the newly elected Directors, described as *"well known business and professional men of the town"*, committed themselves wholeheartedly.

The Directors, shielded by the protection of the new club's limited liability status, paid the not inconsiderable sum of £1,450 for a 6.5 acre site, in June 1920, which was to become the club's home Ground (probably that known as Newbridge Fields). For a few years, the local Rugby club had cause to fear the challenge of football, for Bridgend Town entered the Welsh League within a few weeks, and just two years later were accepted into the Southern League (Welsh Section). Despite there only being a final seven teams in this division - the economic situation countrywide, and particularly in South Wales was beginning to take effect as four other clubs had started but not finished the season - Bridgend could only finish second from bottom, although three of their players were soon destined to step up into the Football League.

The re-organised Southern League (into Western and Eastern Divisions) the following season saw Bridgend rise to 13th of 18 teams, and to the heady heights of fourth (of 20) one year later. Ironically after this best season, albeit a brief flirtation with the professional Southern League, the club were forced to resign - due to financial considerations - and they dropped back into the Welsh League where they remained until 1928. By now Rugby had regained full control of the Bridgend sporting public, and it was to be over 20 years before a football team, of anything like Senior status was to appear again in the town.

The post-War euphoria which saw unprecendented interest in leisure activities, and in particular football, spread far and wide.

Whilst there was no active football club present in Bridgend in 1948 (at least not at any Senior level), it would appear that there were the dormant remains of the former Town club, for in April, the local Press reported that the Football Club was ambitious (even if they were not prominent at that time), and that a better Ground was required, presumably this was with reference to Newbridge Fields. After discussions with the local Council to find a suitable site had come to nothing, the football officials made contact with the nearby Porthcawl Authority, with a view to transferring their operations to that town. Bridgend, *"already had an established league side and had ambitions to play in higher circles"*, it was announced, yet this would appear to have been something of an over-statement, for at this time there is no record of any team from the town playing at even an intermediate level, nor any reports of any matches in the local Press.

The Porthcawl Council were agreeable to this idea, for they were keen to build a multi-sports centre, at a suggested site to the West of Rhech Avenue. The proposed name of the club would be 'Bridgend and Porthcawl United'; *"Porthcawl would have an extremely good chance of attracting soccer international matches"*, it was somewhat over confidently stated. The existing football club, Porthcawl United were, to say the least, upset at these proposals: *"We appear to have had a polite brush-off"*, their Chairman announced.

Amid this scenario, with the suggestion of a Senior team - but where certainly no more than a minor one existed - that would play at a still to be decided location, and with not even a decision as to which town the Ground would be located in, at the Football League's 1948 re-election meeting, 'Bridgend' applied for membership! Ten non-League clubs applied for the two positions in the South section, but Norwich City and Brighton & Hove Albion were comfortably re-elected, whilst Colchester United - with excellent credentials received just two votes.

Bridgend, with six other hopefuls did not receive one vote between them. Despite this snub, which surely the Bridgend applicants must have anticipated, the local Council then decided to help the proposed Senior club in its quest, and some fields between the by-pass and Dripping Bridge were suggested. But in reality it was another six years (1954) before the 'new' Bridgend Town was formed, and a further nine before they had achieved (Senior) Welsh League status, following their Championship of the Welsh League Division 2 East at the end of the 1962/63 season.

The Club then went from strength to strength, winning the League title in 1969 and 1973, before entering the Southern League in 1977, where they immediately gained promotion to the Premier Division. Although relegated one year later, they bounced back with the Midland Division, plus the overall, Championship in 1980.

Although the Alliance Premier League was now in operation, Bridgend's ambitions did not extend that far, and their membership of the Southern League only lasted until 1983. Dropping down back to the national Welsh League, even this standard could not be sustained, and by the late 1990's, a lower level was the Club's lot.

Around the time of Bridgend's application to the Football League, the undisputed sporting king in the area, the Rugby Union club, must have had their crown dented, for in 1949, the Bridgend Rugby League team took over the Brewery Field headquarters of the Union club, where they remained until 1957, when the original occupants regained control.

And so, in Bridgend, the situation has returned to its original format; Rugby League is dead, Football is the minority sport, and Rugby Union is back on top!

BURTON ALBION

(1955 - 1958)

After the demise of Burton Town early in the Second World War, the town was left without Senior football representation until 1950. The formation that year of Burton Albion (a different name suffix from the previous clubs of Swifts, Wanderers, United and Town) kept alive the desire to bring back League football to a town which, surprisingly, had two representatives in the 1800's. The new team adopted the nickname of the 'Brewers' which very much reflected one of the main industries of this Staffordshire town.

Four more attempts from yet another club in the town... but all to no avail!

There had been rumours that the old Burton Town would reform after the War, but as nothing came to pass in this direction, it was left to a brand new club to fly the flag in the town, following an enthusiastic meeting attended by some 700 football fans.

When Kettering Town moved to the Southern League at the end of the 1949/50 season, it conveniently left a place open in the Birmingham and District League for the newly formed Club. It was quite an undertaking to be plunged straight into the highly rated Birmingham competition without past experience or even support.

Yet the public took to this new team immediately, and although on the field the team did little more than hold their own, finishing 16th of 19 teams (just two points above tailenders Lye Town), the attendances at their Lloyds Foundry Ground in Wellington Street normally numbered between four and five thousand; this left the Club to ponder on what numbers they would have attracted had they been successful! The first practise match had attracted 1,200 to Wellington Street.

And on the 17th August, 5,000 had crammed into the enclosure for the team's initial competitive match, when Gloucester City reserves were entertained in the Birmingham and District League.

A year later, the situation had improved considerably for the team slotted in at fifth from top. The Club cont-inued to improve finishing one place higher a year later, and in 1954, they claimed the runners-up spot, just three points adrift of Champions Wolverhampton Wanderers third team.

By now the Birmingham and District League had enlarged its numbers, containing an almost unwieldly 24 clubs, and therefore for the 1954/55 season the competition was split into North and South sections. With a final place of third in the Northern division, the Club considered they had reached a standard that warranted an application to join the Football League.

Whilst they may well have been well supported at this time, they could hardly be considered a power in non-League football, and they, with two other applicants, were unable to get even one vote of support, whilst the far more eleigble Wigan Athletic only received two.

Another factor against the Club was their Ground, a former basic Sports ground with only spartan amenities. Clearly the only way forward was to find a better home; but this was still three years in the future.

The 1955/56 season saw another new innovation in the Birmingham League, with a First and Second division split, with The Brewers naturally competing in the higher section. Although only finishing fifth from top, the Club felt they again had a case for 'promotion' to the Football League, yet once again they were rebuffed, albeit they did receive one vote of the four that were split amongst three hopeful clubs. One more year was spent in the Birmingham and District League, but again the team were hardly an impregnable force, for at the season's end they could only manage fourth place.

The Club's apparent hopeless attempts to better themselves have to be viewed in conjunction with Chairman Grantham and his fellow directors ambitions for their club. For some years they were at the forefront in the desire to create a 'Premier Midland League' which would be on a par with the undisputed top non-League competition, the Southern League. Even more radical were the alternative attempts to form a Football League Midland section of Division 3, alongside the North and South divisions.

Overall, at this stage of the Club's development, the repeated attempts at Football League recognition was an expensive and ill-conceived idea. The Club failed dismally with their third attempt, in 1957, albeit this time, they and one other received a single vote each, whilst the other three hopefuls in the Northern ballot obtained none.

The 1957/58 season was to be the Brewers last in the Birmingham and District League, for it was obvious that in order to better themselves the Club had to seek a higher rated league. There were only two realistic choices, the more local Midland League, which was first considered, or the higher profile Southern League. The Club set their sights on the latter, albeit the running costs would increase, but the Directors felt that the more attractive opposition would increase the crowds. However, another move also had to be considered, a physical one, for clearly the Lloyds Foundry Ground was unsuitable for higher level football.

A suitable site was identified in the Autumn of 1957, when 3.5 acres of Eatoughs Ltd Sports Ground became available. With another 2.5 acres adjacent Council land the Club would be able to build a spacious stadium. In the following January the purchase of the land was made, and then began a race against time to have the new venue ready for the start of the following season. Work started in April and the Club launched a £5,000 appeal fund to add to the £2,000 contributed by the Supporters Club for the land purchase. But by now the boom of the early post-war years had passed, for gone were the near capacity crowds; in February the attendance was just 1,275 for the visit of Bilston, and the Club knew that crowds would have to average 3,000 to make ends meet. The new Ground scheme plus the hopeful move to the Southern League was an expensive gamble, when allied to the cost of Eton Park (as it was to be known) - an enormous £15,000, which included a new 324 seater Stand costing £6,000.

The team finished the 1957/58 season disappointingly in mid-table, they were financially committed to the hilt, and they had not performed well during the season; but they still applied for Football League membership! With the applications now coming from a mixed front (following the formation of the Fourth Division), there were twelve aspirants, and Burton Albion - not surprisingly - received no votes, as did three other teams.

That was to be the last effort by Burton Albion. Their new Ground was finished, albeit after the season had started, and they gained their Southern League place (and incurred a 100 fine from the Birmingham and District League due to their late withdrawal from that competition). The last game at Wellington Street saw Cheltenham Town as visitors on the 23 August 1958, and the first game at Eton Park was watched by 5,527 (the second largest crowd to date), when Nuneaton were entertained in the F.A.Cup on the 20th of September. Currently the club are a prominent member of the Southern League, and on the verge of Conference membership.

BURTON TOWN

(1939)

With due respects to the current Burton Albion F.C., it is quite amazing that the relatively insignificant football town of Burton-upon-Trent (in Staffordshire) should feature frequently in the re-election 'game'. With four separate clubs applying for Football League membership, the town holds the most clubs record, a record jointly heid with Rotherham.

By the turn of the century, Burton-upon-Trent had remarkably seen no fewer than three clubs from the town in membership of the Football League, albeit the latter - Burton United - was a 1901 amalgamation of the previous two. Burton Swifts had earlier become founder-members of the Second Division in 1892, and were followed two years later by Wanderers. It is difficult to explain exactly why the town should have been blessed with even one, nether alone two, representatives in the Football League, and at the same time. With a population at the time of around 40,000, it was hardly a large thriving city, and there were surely many other towns in the North and Midlands (the professional game had hardly taken off in the South at this time) that could reasonably have claimed a better case for inclusion.

The League record of the three clubs was not highly successful, and it was not surprising that the final survivor, United, were voted out in 1907, and this club finally disappeared in 1910. Waiting on the touchlines was Burton Town, who were formed as 'Burton All Saints' around the time of the 1901 amalgamation of the town's two Senior clubs.

Another club in the Brewery town stakes a claim for League membership.

Initially the 'Saints' played in Junior football, but on the demise of 'United' they became the most prominent of the local teams. The club eventually developed their own enclosed Ground at 'The Crescent', which was located just off Victoria Crescent, but was built over by factories many years ago. The main facilities at The Crescent, consisted of a small seated Stand and two larger standing enclosures.

Although still a relatively minor club in 1911 they were one of 20 clubs who proposed (but this was subsequently defeated), the form-ation of a Third Division of the Football League. In 1919, the Club made an upward move when they were elected to the Birmingham Combination, and two years later the Birmingham & District League (a Senior competition of far greater status than its 'town' designation would suggest), where they stayed until 1935, attaining the runners-up position in 1927, and the Championship the next year. The team started the 1926/27 season with 14 opening victories, but extended F.A. and Birmingham Senior Cup runs, led to a fixture backlog, and they lost five of their last matches. The Club changed its name from 'All Saints' to 'Town' in 1924, and their rise to prominence was something of a surprise, for previously they rarely finished much above mid-table. They did achieve a unique record during the 1930/31 season, when in the course of three consecutive league matches (all won) they scored 32 goals; beating Stafford Rangers 12-0, Wellington St.Georges (away) 11-3, and finally Walsall Reserves 9-0 at the Crescent.

The Town was unable to obtain such lofty positions again, but after finishing 7th at the end of the 1934/35 season, they were accepted into the Midland League, where they remained, without major honours, finishing around mid-table each year, until their demise in 1940. However, in their fairly short history at Senior level, they had some memorable F.A.Cup runs, and some notable Football League 'scalps'. The 3rd round was reached in the 1931/32 season, after an excellent 4-1 home victory over Gateshead; in the 1935/36 season Third Division North York City were humiliated 5-1 at their own Ground, before the Town lost (5-0) at Southend United; they were narrowly defeated by Darlington (2-1 at home) in the 1936/37 season, and a year later lost to Rotherham United, in the 1st round, but only after a replay. The Gateshead match attracted a crowd of 5,960, whilst the visit of Blackburn Rovers produced an all-time record attendance of 9,674.

Whilst Burton Town could not claim a sustained record at the top, they had shown they could equal their betters in the F.A.Cup, and proved that good attendances could be attracted to The Crescent Ground, where even Midland League matches could often pull in crowds of around 3,000. But the Club's decision to apply for Football League membership at the meeting of the 11th May 1939, was somewhat ambitious to say the least, especially alongside the more successful Shrewsbury and Scunthorpe sides. With 22 votes, Shrewsbury came close to ousting Hartlepool or Accrington from their secure positions, but there was no faith shown in the abilities of Burton Town, who, along with Wigan Athletic, received no votes.

In order to stand for election, Burton Town had to 'technically' resign from the Midland League, but they were automatically reinstated following their failure to convince. Despite their ambitions, things were far from healthy on the financial front at The Crescent, for the Club announced a loss of £759 on the season, bringing their overall deficit to a massive £2,443. For the 1939/40 season, the Club had previously announced that several new playing professionals would be arriving, but they did not materialise, and the warning bells were beginning to toll.

On the 30th August 1939, the Club Vice-Chairman, Mr. M.Mercer gave this grim message: *"Football in Burton is on its last trial..... If we do not get a better response from the Public the Club will have to go."* The 1939/40 season fixture list had Burton Town Reserves due to play at home to Shrewsbury Town's second team, whilst the first team would travel to Barnsley for a Midland League game on the 2nd September. The match at Barnsley ended farcically, abandoned after 10 minutes due to torrential rain, with the score at 0-0. The Town had previously lost 2-1 to the same team at home on August 26, and two days later went down 4-0 at Frickley Athletic. The War brought the curtain down abruptly on normal football, although a Midland Wartime competition was run, which embraced eight teams including Burton Town. Two Burton matches remained unplayed (home and away versus Kidderminster), and the team finished 6th of 8 in the table. But the conditions proved too much for Burton Town, particularly with little income and the Club folded in 1940. As Mr. Mercer had warned a year earlier, albeit under somewhat different circumstances, the Club had played its last trial..... and failed it!

CAMBRIDGE CITY

(1959, 1960, 1961, 1967 to 1974 inclusive)

To any self-respecting Cambridge City fan (and sadly around the turn of the 21st century there are not many now), it was the greatest injustice when Cambridge United upstaged City and were admitted to the Football League. For many years City were the Senior of the two clubs, albeit for most of their history an Amateur club, whereas the modern United did not even progress to a Senior level until the 1940's, initially in the United Counties League as Abbey United; that however, as they say, is another story!

Formed in September 1908 as Cambridge Town (out of an earlier club, Cambridge St. Mary), they were the most prominent club in the University town, although an Amateur outfit, but for many years had no ambitions greater than to perform well at this level. They first competed in the Bury and District League, followed by the Southern Olympian (1911-1914). Town remained at an Intermediate level, in the Southern Amateur League (five times Champions) from 1919 until 1935, when their move upwards even then was quite modest, to the Spartan League. They were Spartan League Champions on several occasions, including the first post-War season (1945/46), and in 1950 gained admittance to the Athenian League, a competition that was generally recognised as the second most senior amateur league in the South.

When Cambridge obtained its City status in 1951, the Town club celebrated this honour, and soon after changed their name to include this suffix. Cambridge City failed to claim any honours during their eight seasons stay in the Athenian League, indeed their record was very poor - their best finish was seventh, and their positions in the last four years included three second from bottom finishes. Although a number of clubs did change from Amateur to Professional in this period, it is doubtful if any had such a poor playing record preceding the changeover.

It was surely not just a coincidence that City turned professional and gained immediate admittance to the Southern League at the same time that Cambridge United (already by now semi-professional) joined the same competition! City edged ahead of their neighbours after reaching halfway up the South-Eastern Zone table, and hence were promoted to the new Premier Division for the 1959/60 season. But it was surely somewhat optimistic when the Club applied for Football League membership in the Spring of 1959. Nonetheless the City received two votes, more than the majority of the aspirants, although with no track record, confidence in the Club could only have related to potential.

The Club were better equipped for their second application a year later, for not only did they finish in fifth place, but a brochure was produced which amongst other things showed that their Milton Road Ground, first opened in 1922, was adequate. The enclosure could boast a 1,000 seater Stand (opened in 1926), a half-pitch length covered terrace opposite, and a 12 step open terrace behind one goal. described in the brochure as: *Covering approximately 9 acres...... and has ample room for expansion and a capacity of 50,000."* Not perfect at this time before the enormous potential expansion (!), but better than some, although only two votes were obtained again at the election meeting. Then another reasonable season saw the Club obtain two votes once more, at their third attempt. By now the competition was beginning to hot up, for City were joined by United in the Southern League Premier Division, and within a few years the pair of clubs would be battling out for League recognition. Strangely, neither club seemed interested as early as the end of the 1962/63 season, when the two finished as Champions and Runners-up in the league, for this would surely have been the optimum time to attempt a rise.

No hopes of a Cambridge 'double'!

The clubs fought out the Championship neck and neck, and with City achieving the double over their near neighbours (the Milton Road match attracting a record crowd of 11,574) this was enough to edge them above United. It was left to seven other Southern League clubs, most with lesser credentials - at least on the playing front - than the Cambridge pair to try their luck in the election battle. For the next few years the two clubs finished around, or just above, the halfway mark in the Premier Division, and so closely matched that rarely were there more than a few points separating the two at each season's end. It wasn't until 1967 that City, along with United, made their next bid, but why that season is difficult to judge for it was a mediocre one for both teams. This mediocrity was reflected in the voting, for both teams received no votes!

In 1968, there were very few 'spare' votes, for most were cast for the four re-election teams, and both City and United received two each, one less than Cheltenham Town who obtained the most of the 'also-rans', with three. However with the introduction of Greyhound Racing at Milton Road, the City Club ran the risk of not being allowed membership of the Football League on this fact alone. The 1967/68 season was a significant one in Cambridge, for United began to pull away from their neighbours, finishing third in the table, whilst City after finishing one off the bottom, were relegated, which makes it all the more surprising that both clubs should have received equal votes.

After such a poor season, City had hopes of bouncing straight back into the Premier Division, but had no such luck and had to settle for around middle of the table in the First. Yet despite United building upon their success and claiming the Premier Championship, both clubs applied for Football League election. Amazingly they both received two votes each, although clearly at this time a gulf in ability had built up between the two clubs. But Cambridge City had a long history behind them, a factor which may have given them some support, and one year later they were promoted back to the Premier Division after finishing runners-up to Bedford Town in the lower section. Both clubs made their annual bid to better themselves, and another Championship success was rewarded when United gained Football League recognition at the expense of Bradford Park Avenue. Yet there was still some sympathy for City for they received their customary two votes; was it the same two Football League clubs that continued to have faith in them?

In view of the normal 'closed shop' attitude of the Football League members, City must surely have realised that they had no hopes of making it a Cambridge double in the Football League in 1971. They did have an excellent season, and finished runners-up to Yeovil Town, but in view of the rarity of even one non-League team gaining admittance to the Football League, the chances of two from the same city were remote to say the least. At the election meeting, the Club received their customary two votes, whilst Hereford United were the surprise bidders receiving 22, despite several unremarkable Southern League seasons behind them.

A year later, Cambridge City found themselves well down in the bottom half of the final table, yet they appeared to be dogmatic in their attempts for Football League recognition, and despite clearly no-hopers, their ninth bid ended with just one vote, one more than perhaps was merited! A mid-table finish in 1973 was in the eyes of the City Directors good enough for a tenth bid, and another single vote of encouragement, although with fewer applications, there were four non-Leaguers who received the lionshare of support.

1974 was to be the last desperate attempt by Cambridge City. Another mid-table placing, and this time no votes, whilst the other hopefuls received between one and 16. The Club's fortunes slumped again from this point on, and the realisation that the cherished hope of Football League football had died. Cambridge United had demonstrated that their elevation was fully deserved, and it must have been a bitter pill to swallow for the diminishing band of City supporters. Cambridge City have never played in the Conference, although they have maintained a fairly steady presence in the Premier Division of the Southern League. But support is always a problem, as the low hundreds cannot be exceeded even when the team is doing well.

The Club effectively moved to a new Ground in August 1985, albeit just a few yards, to the site of their former training pitch, and it is difficult to imagine that this much smaller enclosure could ever be enlarged sufficiently to allow for modern Football League criteria.

It was right that a town the size and standing of Cambridge should have a Football League representative, it was just unfortunate for City that those upstarts from the Abbey Stadium should have found their form when City started to struggle!

CASTLEFORD TOWN

(1921, 1922)

The mention of Castleford hardly identifies with the game of football, yet for a brief period there was a real chance of League status for this Yorkshire town - with a population in the 1920's of around 20,000 plus a reasonable catchment area, to give a total of around double that number. With little competition in the area, the Club could well have achieved this goal. Yet now there is not even a Senior non-League club in the town.

The history of the team really goes back to 1896 (although two years earlier both Castleford F.C. and Castleford Albion were founder-members of the West Yorkshire League), when the fledgeling football club, declined to amalgamate with the stronger Northern Union Rugby (League) team, who in turn had broken away from the original Rugby club, which had been founded in 1877. Although the oval ball sport dominated in Castleford, even the Rugby League team floundered, and folded in 1907, only to be revived five years later. Even at this time the Rugby club only enjoyed Junior status, and the period around the First World War provided the best opportunity for a football team such as Castleford Town to progress upward. Not only was the way open, with the formation of the Third Division North in 1921, for a large influx of clubs, but no doubt - and judging by the votes that the team received that year - they would have been welcomed with open arms by the Football League, who were ever anxious to encourage football to current or rising rugby strongholds; nearby Huddersfield Town received the greatest of assistance when they were elected to the Second Division in 1910, just two years after their formation, at a time when they could scarcely have claimed to have a been a dominant force in the football world!

A second application was made, but with little hope of success.

Such help probably enabled Castleford Town to gain entry to the Midland League in 1909, for they too had no track record (having arrived from the relative obscurity of the West Yorkshire League), yet were readily accepted to this competition, when Newark (from Nottinghamshire) resigned before fixtures that season had commenced. It was, however, a difficult baptism for the Yorkshire team and at the season's end they could only show a second from bottom placing for their efforts. The seasons leading up to the War were somewhat better, for the team finished 15th, 10th, 16th, 8th and 18th respectively.

The overall playing performances continued to improve in the aftermath of the War, since the Town finished eighth in the table at the end of the 1919/20 season. With the formation of the Third Division, which consisted of all Southern clubs and became the 'Southern Section' a year later, the path opened for many clubs to join the Football League elite in 1921 with the addition of the Northern section of the Third.

The Club's geographical area (within a rugby stronghold) was guaranteed to be favourable to the Football League, and at this time the team was certainly well supported with attendances normally in the low to middle thousands. In addition, an excellent F.A.Cup run in the 1919/20 season, which took the team from the preliminary round to the second round proper - via eight victories - undoubtedly aided their bid. At this stage they only narrowly lost (3-2) at First Division Bradford P.A. It was therefore with a certain degree of confidence that three of the Club's Directors, plus Mr.A.E.Masser, a Leeds solicitor, travelled down to London on the 5th March to state their case.

With 20 lucky clubs able to join the Football League, there had never been a better chance. However, 14 places were in effect spoken for, and with relegated Stockport County plus the addition of Grimsby Town (from the inaugural Third Division) this left just four opportunities.

Wigan Borough comfortably gained entry, whilst Halifax Town (no doubt two more popular choices in view of their rugby orientated situations!), Southport and Stalybridge Celtic all received 25 votes, nine less than Wigan. In fifth place, and hence missing out, was Castleford Town, who polled just one vote less than three of those successful clubs. The fact that Castleford were promised election should one of those elected subsequently drop out, was scant consolation, and it was a very depressed quartet that journeyed back up North.

The Supporters also had high hopes of the Club's election, and there was *"still a feeling that eventually the Town will be seen in first class company."* Such expressions of confidence are of course so common amongst fans, who normally view their team through rose tinted glasses. However in Castleford at this time there was genuinely good support, and just one week after the rejection, a crowd of around 7,000 (a season's best) was present at the Wheldon Lane Ground for the visit of Huddersfield in the 1st round of the West Riding Senior Cup. Despite their opponents fielding several players with First Division experience, the home team won the match.

The 6.3 acre Wheldon Lane (later 'Road') enclosure was located on the Northern boundary of the town, and although rather spartan by modern standards, it did have a 30 yard long wooden Stand, plus the more recent addition of dressing rooms on the Ground; a luxury at this time not enjoyed by many senior clubs. During the Summer of 1921, a Shareholders and Supporters club was formed, and the pre-season (1921/22) trial game attracted a healthy attendance of about 2,000.

The first Midland League match, which resulted in a 2-1 victory over newcomers Mansfield, attracted 3,000. Such numbers were very encouraging and augered well for the future, yet depressingly within a few months, not helped by an early F.A.Cup exit at the hands of Frickley Colliery, the support drastically fell away.

Although considered a sport-loving town, it appears that rugby was 'king', despite at this time there being no Senior club present. In addition there was now the threat of football competition from another local team, that of Castleford and Allerton, who had just been elevated to the Yorkshire League.

On Wednesday 3 May 1922, a meeting was held at the Empress Hall to discuss the prospect of applying for Football League status again. It was reported that a shilling fund had raised only £80, a poor return for a reasonably large town, and it was pointed out that should the Club be elected then gates would have to rise considerably, since a fully professional team would be required. Conversely those present were reminded that just a few years earlier Huddersfield Town had been a financially struggling club, yet they had just become the new holders of the F.A.Cup. The Chesterfield F.C. Chairman had been invited to the meeting to advise the Club on their approach, and it was decided that a second application should be made, although the general feeling was that there was little hope of acceptance. At the League's election meeting the two re-election candidates (Halifax Town and Rochdale) were comfortably voted back in, and this year, with no additions to the Third Division North, the four hopefuls failed dismally, Doncaster Rovers getting nine votes, and Castleford Town received none.

From this time on, the Club's fortunes went from bad to worse, whilst the local Rugby League club prospered. The Town remained in the Midland League, with poor final table positions until the struggle was finally given up at the end of the 1925/26 season. The team finished bottom, the goal difference produced figures of 62-130, and the Club did not even apply for re-election. Castleford voluntarily dropped down to the Yorkshire League, and although they finished runners-up at the end of their first season, no other honours came their way. Two years later they even slipped out of this competition, although they returned in 1934, but after three further seasons (they failed to complete the 1936/37 campaign), they disappeared from the football scene altogether.

The Town football club's loss was the Rugby League club's gain, for the latter - now playing at a Senior level, had already moved in to the, now renamed, Wheldon Road (former Lane) Ground, and they went from strength to strength, as the threat of football competition had been removed.

CHELMSFORD CITY

(1939, 1947, 1948, 1950, 1951, 1956, 1960 - 62 incl., 1967-71 incl., 1973-76 incl.)

There is only one other club (Yeovil Town) who can better Chelmsford - along with two other teams - for the number of attempts at Football League admission; no fewer than 18 efforts, including one run of 10 when only one year was missed. There is no doubt that for many of those years their claims for recognition were very worthy ones, yet they never had the charisma, or perhaps more realistically the consistency at the top, to seriously challenge the establishment.

Although the Club was first founded way back in 1878, as a reformed professional outfit, their history at a high level only goes back to 1938. Chelmsford City (they adopted the suffix on their reformation) were an immediate success and fully justified the faith shown in them when they gained admittance to the Southern League.

So many repeated applications, yet so little to show for their efforts. What chance now?

Although their final League placing was only moderate, the City hit the headlines with their stunning displays in the F.A.Cup, when, aided by several former League players including two ex-Internationals, they reached the fourth round. Three emphatic home victories saw them beat Kidderminster Harriers (4-0), Darlington (3-1) and Southampton (4-1) - in front of enormous gates of between 10,000 and 10,741 - before finally succumbing to First Division Birmingham.

A competent team, a good ground, and a generous catchment area for support, were all excellent ingredients for status at a higher level, yet at the 1939 election meeting the Club could only muster one point!

Perhaps City were considered too new on the scene; a club that had yet to prove itself, and of course they were in competition with old campaigners (and previous League members) Gillingham - who received 15 votes, and Southern League Champions Colchester who, surprisingly, also received just one.

Perhaps the City bid was premature, but unfortunately capable of greater things or not, the next attempt could not be made for eight years due to the intervention of War.

Chelmsford were one of many that made a bid in 1947, but the Football League quite reasonably considered it would hardly be fair to consider the banishment of any existing member who had to re-establish itself after the hostilities. The City made their third bid a year later, despite a mediocre Southern League season, and their reward was no votes, as was the lot for six other clubs. Although Gillingham were still the most dominant force in southern non-League football, it was perhaps a surprise to see that Chelmsford made no Football League bid in 1949, despite an excellent season which left them runners-up to the Kent side, although even the Gills received only five votes at the re-election meeting.

1950 brought the bidders out in their droves, for with the promise of two extra places in each Third Division, there would never be a better chance. Gillingham, despite a slight falter that season, and Colchester United, comfortably moved upward, although another good campaign ensured City eight votes, the second best of the also-rans.

But in 1951, and despite another good campaign, the Club were dismayed when they received no votes, whilst conversely mediocre Bath City managed three. Watford and Crystal Palace were almost unanimously reinstated, which was not unexpected on this occasion, but voting figures in many years proved that there was a lot of sympathy for struggling members within their own Football League numbers, than that for aspiring and no doubt capable non-Leaguers!

The latest rejection, coupled with several poor playing seasons sensibly prevented City from making any unnecessary bids. Then, in 1956, although only managing a final ninth place in the League, they renewed their efforts, but this was wasted for once again they were rebuked. Two largely unremarkable seasons followed (the team though did finish third in 1958), and with a large intake of new teams, and the geographical zoning of the two new divisions, the City disappointed within this weaker competition.

Yet they persisted in their election bids, but received just two votes in both 1960 and 1961 (when they finished runners-up in the Southern League). The 1962 re-election meeting was reduced to near farce, with the guarantee of one replacement due to the resignation of Accrington Stanley, and no fewer than 18 hopefuls made their bid. In the circumstances 3 votes for Chelmsford, the fourth best, was quite good but even so was still hopelessly insufficient.

After then missing out for four years (somewhat surprising since the team finished as runners-up in their own league on two occasions), they then went on a run of eleven years when they only failed to make a bid once, in 1972. For most of this period City were a model of consistency, including capturing the Southern League title on two occasions, and it was only in the mid-70's that their grip at a higher level faltered.

Unlike Wimbledon, Hereford United and Cambridge United, Chelmsford City tended to be only dominant intermittently, and therefore were not able to command the attention, and hence votes, for admission to the Football League. Yet their efforts surely deserved more than they usually received in this respect.

Initially the 'powers that be' had little confidence in Chelmsford, with few, if any votes cast in their favour. After coming so close in 1971 to gain admission to the Football League, Hereford United were successful one year later, when Champions Chelmsford City did not even apply. In 1973 and 1974, the Club gained their most votes (four and eight respectively) against strong competition, but even these numbers were far below that required. A mid-table finish in 1975, and even lower one year later marked the end of the Club's bids for recognition.

For some years this once powerful club lost its way, and it wasn't until the early 1980's that they came close to reclaiming their former glories, although not sufficiently to earn a place in the Alliance Premier League.

Up to the early 1990's, the Club could always depend on reasonable to good crowds at a well equipped venue (the Ground at New Writtle Street was used briefly by Southend United for their Wartime matches), but following devastating redevelopment and finally the sale of the Stadium site in 1994, the Club have only just managed to survive.

The tenacity of the Club and its band of dedicated supporters will no doubt ensure the name of 'Chelmsford City' will continue, but probably only on the smaller non-League 'stage'.

CHORLEY

(1899)

It is difficult to imagine that at one time Chorley had their sights set on the Football League. Currently languishing in the First Division of the Northern Premier League, they have tended to be one of the better supported clubs in this competition, but even crowds of around 300 (sometimes approaching 500), are dwarfed within the Club's Duke Street ground. Duke Street is one of the best of the old fashioned Football Grounds still remaining in non-League football, and once comfortably held nearly 10,000 in the 1931/32 season. However, this is far removed from the reality of the situation in 1899, when the Club made its first and only application to join the Football League.

One attempt many years ago.... and it would seem unlikely that they could make another serious challenge

The Club was founded in 1883 (although some references relate to 1875 when the Club first played under the rugby code), and after serving their 'apprenticeship' in the Lancashire Alliance from 1890 to 1894, they were admitted to the Lancashire League. From the start in 1875, the Club had played at the Dole Lane Ground (later Coronation Recreation Ground) which was located near the centre of the town. Initially it was quite small, but was later enlarged when two extra fields were integrated into the venue, and for spectators a Grandstand was eventually built. In their former Rugby days, the Club were scheduled to play the first ever match in Lancashire under floodlights on the 24th October 1878 against Swinton. A crowd of around 8,000 had assembled from far and wide to see this new spectacle.

But the Siemens Lights refused to work, and after two hours, with rain which had continued throughout the evening, the crowd were - to say the least - becoming impatient! As a security measure, two club members secreted away the takings and hid them under a bed at the Rose and Crown Hotel, which was at that time Chorley's headquarters.

The last rugby rules game was finally played against Preston on the 24th March 1883, and a few months later, a new era started on the 27th October, when the Club entertained and beat Wigan 6-2 in the first football match.

After moving up to the Lancashire League, success was soon to come Chorley's way for they won the Championship in 1897, and that same season had a good run in the F.A.Cup which took them through several early rounds (including victory over a fledgeling Accrington Stanley side), before finally losing to Blackpool.

The Club were unable to repeat their success in the league, but on entering the F.A.Cup at a later round they notably twice held Second Division Darwen to a draw before losing in the replay. The end of that season saw some dramatic changes at the Football League election meeting, where, after the customary voting, a further ballot was held to allow extra members to join, due to an extension of the Football League which would henceforth include 36 clubs (18 in each division).

The 1898/99 season was shaping up well for Chorley in the Lancashire League, and a 3-0 home win in April over Wigan County, before a crowd of over 4,000 (albeit this included around 1,400 visiting supporters) assured the team of the Championship. At that time they had a clear lead of six points, and at the end finished eight points clear of third place, and fellow Football League aspirants, Ashton United, and seven more than runners-up Southport Central. After Chorley made the decision to apply for Football League membership, their bid was duly submitted at the re-election meeting. With less of a sustained record behind them than other bidders Blackpool and Stockport County, neither of whom in any event gained sufficient support, it came as no real surprise that Chorley's votes, which totalled seven, were insufficient.

Of more notice that day was the motion forwarded by West Bromwich Albion, to radically modify the officiating at matches. However, the proposal to appoint two referees at games with four linesmen who would be nominated by the opposing clubs, was defeated.

Chorley had to return to the Lancashire League and seriously consider their future, for they, like Ashton United, were in a financially precarious position. Until their successful run-in at the end of the Championship season, crowds of 1,500 were the norm. Unlike their counterparts, Chorley managed to carry on, and after a few more years in the Lancashire League, during which time they changed their home Ground, they joined the Lancashire Combination in 1903.

The team was promoted four years later, then spent two years flitting between divisions. But they held their First Division membership from 1909 to the late 1960's when they were frequently in the honours.

They were especially successful during the inter-War years, claiming the Championship on six occasions (four times between 1928 and 1934) and were twice runners-up. It was during this halcyon period that the record attendance was achieved at Victory Park (their current Ground which they moved into in 1920), when a massive crowd of 9,679 attended a match versus Darwen during the 1931/32 season.

Immediately after the Second World War they were Champions again, in 1946, but then followed something of a slump, before they came to the fore once more, topping the table in 1960, the following year, and again in 1964. In 1969, they opted for the new Northern Premier League, but a poor season was suffered, and they moved back down into the Lancashire Combination.

After another single season, they moved back into the Northern Premier and this was the start of a period when they moved between that competition and the Cheshire County League (where they were Champions on three occasions). Finally they made it to the GM Vauxhall Conference in 1988, but it was a short stay, for only two seasons. In recent years successes have been infrequent and it would seem unlikely that they could challenge again seriously for a place in the Football League.

CONSETT

(1947)

Consett belongs to that select band of non-League clubs whose success, or perhaps more accurately - financial viability - depended so much on their economic environment. The North-East of England in immediate post-War Britain was awash with industry and jobs, and the local football teams could depend on its officials and players together with support in numbers from commerce, and in particular coal-mining which abounded in the area, as it had in the pre-War days.

Consett in County Durham was one such town, thriving with its steel industry in particular. From their formation in 1899 (as Consett Celtic), the Steelmen, as they inevitably became known, had a varied life in Senior football, which they joined in 1919 with their admittance to the Northern Alliance (the earlier Consett Town Swifts had been members around the turn of the century). Their journey took them to the North-Eastern League in 1926, with immediate promotion to the First Division one year later, a return to the Alliance in the mid-30's, and back to the North-Eastern in 1937 until the competition's demise in 1958.

Up to the Second World War the Steelmen won few major honours, and with a sparse Vicarage Field Ground perched close to, and above the Steelworks. Such was the elevation that flooding of the pitch was unknown, but soaking of spectators was common, in all truth the Club's ambitions had been probably, and realistically, quite humble.

Another moderate non-League club. With only plans for an acceptable new Ground.... there was the inevitable rejection!

With an old and patched-up army hut serving as dressing-rooms, and just a small Stand offering shelter for a few, the Ground was typical of many minor colliery sides, but certainly not for an aspiring Football League team.

In the immediate post-War years, the Consett Iron Company Ltd., the major employer in the area, announced that within the planned £7 million extensions to their site, the Vicarage Field was to be included in the development. The protests of Consett F.C. counted for little, and whilst the procurement and upkeep of the Ground no doubt was helped by the benevolence of the company in the past, it appears that in the name of progress this was now to count for nothing. The whole fate of the Club was, for a while, in the balance.

In the immediate post-War season of 1945/46, the Club had a poor return to peacetime football, at times occupying the bottom place in the North-Eastern League. Then, well into the following season the Club were faced with the bleak prospect of the loss of their Ground. Although not performing particularly well, at least the team benefitted from the post-War football boom, enjoying good support both at matches and financially, with several hundred of the Consett Iron Company workmen voluntary contributing 2d (1p) per week to the Club funds; not suprisingly the team were known as 'The Ironworkers'.

In the Spring of 1947, the Club officials and supporters decided that rather than just lie down and accept defeat, they would set about creating their own new Ground. The area was buzzing with enthusiasm, albeit their plans could not be achieved overnight, and there was a determination that a town of Consett's size should now have a Football Ground that befitted it when other centres of *"less importance"* could boast of better venues.

The 1946/47 season came to an end, with Consett finishing in a moderate eighth place, despite losing their last match 5-0 at home to Workington. On the 31st May (the season was extended due to the appalling Winter), Middlesbrough Reserves were entertained, and fought out a 2-2 draw, in front of.... *"the best gate ever"* - the attendance no doubt enhanced by the appearances of England internationals Hardwick and Mannion in the visitors side. Perhaps it was the new enthusiasm for the team that encouraged the Club's officials and supporters to aspire to greater heights, even as high as the Football League itself. On hindsight it can be seen that such hopes were merely pipedreams.

A moderate non-League club with no decent ground and only the promise of one, despite much enthusiasm would never have recruited the necessary support from the League members. Consett F.C. consequently made their application, amongst many that year, including four others from the North-East, but it will never be known what support those teams would have attracted. At the election meeting the four bottom teams in the Football League were all re-elected without any votes being taken.

Consett eventually got their ground, crafted and built by the Club and its fans themselves, with support from the local Urban Council.

After the Club's notice to quit their old Ground, they moved in with Eden Colliery, whilst work on the new Belle Vue venue proceeded. Built almost entirely by volunteer labour, working on shift systems to match their own paid work periods, an arena shaped stadium was constructed, with sloping cinder embankments all round, plus a Seated Stand along part of one side, and a covered enclosure opposite.

Finally the work was completed, and the first match in 1950 attracted 7,000 spectators, still the record, when Sunderland reserves were the visitors.

For the 1970/71 season, Consett moved to the Northern League, after short periods in the Midland, Northern Counties and Wearside leagues. They started their new career in fine form beating Ashington (who were also newcomers) 6-2 at Belle Vue Park, with four goals in the last half-hour, before a gate of 800. But this form was not maintained, and the team finished well down the final league table.

For many years they maintained reasonable form, but rarely challenged for league honours, their best performance coming in 1977, when they were runners-up (on goal average only) to Spennymoor United. A dreadful 1987/88 season saw them slump to bottom of the table, and relegation, but they walked away with the second Division title a year later.

Sadly, as at every non-League Ground in the North-East, the number of paying spectators are too few, and the acts of vandalism too many. Still playing in the Northern League, Consett struggle to make ends meet, and one thing is for sure, their single attempt for Football League status will never be repeated.

CORBY TOWN

(1962, 1963, 1965, 1966, 1967)

The town of Corby surprisingly never had a Senior football club until the early post-War years. But perhaps this was not so surprising, for like a number of other areas, especially North of London and South of Birmingham, the town virtually did not exist before 1940, and 'Corby' was destined to become one of the breed of 'new towns.' However, Corby was very different from the others, for its elevation was very much tied up with the local steelworks industry, (the works team of Stewart and Lloyds carried the football banner in the area), and the rapid growth of population came almost exclusively from North of the border.

The mass 'importation' of Scots was reflected in the new club of 'Corby Town' that was founded in 1948, with the appointment of Reg Smith the former Dundee F.C. Captain as full-time Manager.

No place in the Football League for this 'Scottish club'!

With a mixture of former Stewart and Lloyds players and fresh blood, the new club played its first match on 21st August 1948, and the team produced a sparkling 5-1 United Counties League victory over Wellingborough Town before a crowd of 2,300. The Club only made a moderate start in their first season, finishing 11th of 20 clubs, but soon rose up the table, with third place a year later, and finally captured the Championship in 1951. When this achievement was repeated a year later (five points ahead of Spalding United), the well supported professional team naturally looked for an upward move.

The Club was accepted into the Midland League, and no fewer than 16 new players were signed.

Most of the players had previous Football League experience, with several, notably, having Scottish connections.

Corby Town delighted their supporters with an excellent season which culminated in a Championship deciding match at Corby's Occupation Road Ground. The visitors on Friday 1st May 1953, were Nottingham Forest Reserves, equal on points at the top with the Steelmen. A crowd of 6,294 was unable to lift the homesters to victory, and a final runners-up place in the league had to suffice. This type of success was not repeated and after a few seasons of only moderate finishing positions in the table, the Club left in 1958 for the expanded Southern League, where they took their place in the newly formed North-Western Zone.

Although far from highly successful (a lowly final league position placed the team in the second tier 'First Division' for the 1959/60 season), in 1962 the Club made the somewhat surprising decision to apply for membership of the Football League.

Corby Town's credentials were far from impressive. A year earlier the Club had come close to folding through diminishing crowds, which was relieved only by a supportive local Council who launched an appeal to ensure the survival of the Steelmen. On the playing front, despite a best-ever start to a season - an unbeaten 13 match opening run - a final disappointing finish of 6th in the table was the conclusion.

However, latent support was still undoubtedly available, and for the right occasion and the right opposition, around 3,000 could be expected. But this did not impress the voters at the League's election meeting, which saw an unprecedented 26 clubs applying for membership. The numbers were doubtless swelled by the guarantee of at least one new club following the resignation of Accrington Stanley, but Oxford United were outright favourites, and Corby Town, along with 14 other clubs could not gain one supporter.

Despite no improvement on the pitch, and a final placing in the Southern League (First Division) of only 7th), the Club made their second application for Football League status, and this time became one of only two teams to receive no votes! With little improvement on the playing front, the Club declined from making an application in 1964, but with a fourth place finish a year later - and promotion as the reward - they tried their luck for the third time. Once again this was a forlorn bid, for there were many other more worthy bidders (including most of the Southern League Premier Division), and another 'nil' vote was the, not surprising, outcome.

Despite their promotion, the home attendances showed little improvement, with only 676 present for the opening Occupation Road 1965/66 season fixture. But an excellent F.A.Cup run which took the team through to the third round at least promoted the name of the Club to a wider audience. On the 4th December a crowd of over 6,000 packed into Occupation Road for the second round match versus Luton Town

A creditable draw was followed by a surprise replay victory, although defeat in the next round came at the hands of Plymouth Argyle, with an emphatic 6-0 result.

A final mid-table placing in the Southern League Premier Division was once again hardly the recipe for success in the Club's bid for the Football League, but the Cup run at least encouraged one solitary vote at the re-election meeting.

The 1966/67 season was another mediocre one, indeed until February the team looked a good bet for relegation. But a late season boost saw the team finally lift themselves to 16th of 22 and safety. 1967 was to become the Club's last in their Football League ambitions, and a poor season inevitably produced a poor response from the voters. Corby Town received no votes once again, as did several of the 15 hopefuls.

With relegation a year later, this signalled the end of the Club's quest for higher status. Although they have on occasions played in the Premier Division of the Southern League, the latter years of the 20th century have produced lamentably low crowds, the continual threat of the Club's very existence, and a Ground move in 1985 to the soulless Rockingham Triangle (Athletics) Stadium. Therefore the prospects of a team with Scottish support (there are local Rangers and Celtic supporters branches in the town) so far South are all but non-existent.

CRADLEY HEATH

(1950)

Cradley Heath. from the Birmingham area (not particularly prolific in terms of Football League applications despite such a large, well populated, centre), was another club where one can now look back and say..... *"Why on earth did they bother"*!

The Club first appeared in 1896 as Cradley Heath St. Luke's, and after several undeveloped grounds they finally based themselves at an enclosure in Peartree Lane, where they stayed until the end of their lease in April 1917. The Club was not heard of again until 1919, around which time they dropped the 'St Luke's' part of their name, although they retained the nickname of The Lukes for the rest of their days. The 'new' club obtained a ground at Dudley Wood Stadium, a fairly basic venue, initially with just one modest Stand, and another that was built in 1927. In 1922, the Club rose higher in Senior football, after membership of the Birmingham Combination since 1908 (or 1905 when under its former name of the Birmingham Junior League), when they were elected into the Birmingham (currently named 'West Midlands') League, its regional - or even City - title understating this competition's importance. Although the standard was inferior to the Southern and Midland Leagues, the better member clubs were not far below those of the higher competitions; Hereford United and Shrewsbury Town used it as a stepping stone, and until their election to the Football League in 1921, the Walsall first team had also been a member.

A hopeless case, with no chance of election... even the Ground would not have been acceptable!

The Lukes made rapid strides in the Birmingham League after their initial season when they finished mid-table, for two years later they were Champions with a clear ten points above runners-up Stourbridge. This winning margin was not bettered in the league for 58 years. The next few seasons the team unsuccessfully challenged the top spots, until 1931, when again they took the Championship, a feat repeated one year later. But once again leaner years followed, and at the end of the 1933/34 season they finished second from bottom. Worse was to follow, for in 1938 the team became clear wooden-spoonists, gaining only two victories and four draws in their 26 matches. The War was soon to intervene, a period when the Club may have been expected to either rise up the table or continue in the depths. In 1939, a 15 year-old schoolboy scored a hat-trick in his one appearance for Cradley Heath, the youngster was William ('Billy') Wright, who was destined to become a football legend in the post-War years.

The immediate post-War years saw major changes to the Dudley Wood Stadium, following its sale in 1939 by the Club (who had purchased the Ground in 1924), to a consortium who particularly wanted to promote Speedway in the area. The War delayed any redevelopment programme, but when this was finally undertaken in 1947 it completely changed the aspects of the venue. The traditional rectangular shaped football ground became a typical long oval shape, making football viewing uncomfortable from afar, due to the inevitable addition of the perimeter speedway track.

The only later improvement of note was a cover on the North terrace in the early 1950's.

Against a background of an uncertain successful future on the playing front, the Club regained their place in the Birmingham League for the 1947/48 season, yet amazingly in just another three years they would be staking a claim for the Football League itself. Those three intervening years were hardly dramatically lucrative on the playing front, for the team could only claim finishes of 7th, 9th and 5th respectively.

It is difficult to visualise what the thinking was behind this radical and over-ambitious move. The Club had admittedly enjoyed some good pre-War successes, but they were hardly a dominant force in a League which was in itself not one of the most Senior of non-League competitions. However, a £1,000 fund-raising scheme was launched (surely a far too modest sum!) to support their application.

Whilst 1950 was undoubtedly the best year for an attempt (since the formations of the two Third Divisions thirty years earlier) due to an expansion of the League and the introduction of four new clubs, the quality of other applicants was far higher than Cradley's. Geographically the Club was placed awkwardly, but their application was made to the Southern section of the Third Division, which included Gillingham and Colchester United (both with near impeccable credentials and both were in fact elected), plus notable other Southern Leaguers such as Worcester City, Merthyr Tydfil and Yeovil Town, with the up and coming Peterborough United from the Midland League making another attempt.

What chance did little Cradley Heath have? None, and this was reflected in the voting when the Club, with two others, received not one vote. To add further to this ill-conceived application, the Club officials clearly had not consulted the requirements for membership of the Football League, where they would have found that no new club would be accepted that groundshared with Greyhounds and the like! This factor had been a bone of contention for some years, for the introduction of Speedway to football had caused problems elsewhere, notably in the 1930's when Clapton Orient made Wembley Stadium their temporary home due to the reduced size of the football pitch at Millfields. (Gateshead and Bristol Rovers, were already groundsharing in this way and were excluded from this requirement).

If 1950 had not been a particularly good year, then the following seasons were no better. By 1955, the Club were playing in the newly formed Second Division of the Birmingham and District League, and even promotion from this undemanding level rarely looked likely.

There was never the remotest chance of Cradley Heath ever applying for the Football League again, in fact the Club moved to Ash Tree Mound in August 1959, a Ground which was completely lacking in facilities, and two years later they disbanded. With debts of £720, the Club became defunct on the 17 July 1961, and so the end came to a club that never really promised much, and never had any realistic chance of the giant leap up to the Football League.

DARTFORD

(1936)

It will probably come as a surprise to many people that Dartford F.C. made just one Football League application, and that was way back in 1936; a surprise since the club could be considered a major force in non-League football for many years, with a Ground and catchment area that was well suited for staging the game in the Football League.

Football commenced seriously in the area with the Dartford Working Mens Club and Institute, and by 1899 the club were known as simply Dartford F.C. But this club suffered serious financial problems and became defunct in 1900, to be followed in quick succession by 'Dartford United' and 'Dartford Rangers'. The Rangers, initially an Amateur club, had groundshared with United at Summer's Meadow, but they also soon dropped this suffix to their name, and they continued on until 1914. After the Great War, the Club was reformed, and they were soon to purchase land off Watling Street at a cost of £1,000. With an enclosure fence, turnstile entrances, and a large seated Stand (which cost nearly £3,000), the Club were well equipped for Senior status football. But tragedy struck in 1926 when the Stand plus the dressing rooms and offices were raised to the ground in a fire. But within a year or so these were replaced all within one structure.

The early years of the various Dartford incarnations saw the first club become founder-members of the Kent League in 1894, and two years later they were elected to the Southern League, but dropped back to their County competition in 1898, before a return to the Southern a year on. After the Great War a few seasons were spent in the Kent League, before an elevation once again to the Southern League in 1926, a competition in which they competed until their demise in 1992, save for two brief spells in the Alliance (Conference).

Only one attempt from this (former) high profile club.

Dartford made a steady, if not spectacular, return to the highest competition outside the Football League in 1926, which only a few years earlier had seen its decimation with the whole contingent forming the new Third Division. However, this league was still highly regarded, now having the reserve teams of many Football League clubs in its ranks, plus the likes of Kettering Town, Northfleet United, Aldershot Town and Folkestone.

The 1930/31 season saw the league's Eastern Division almost halved in member clubs due principally to the depression that was affecting the whole country. The Championship was fought about between Dartford and Aldershot Town, the former finally claiming the title on goal average. Two more good seasons followed (Champions again and second), and therefore with both a good team and ground, it would not have been unreasonable to have made a bid for Football League status at this time. This became apparent when the only serious challenger for a coveted place in 1933 was Llanelly, who surprisingly only narrowly missed out on replacing fellow South Wales club Newport County - despite their moderate mid-table placing in the Western section of the Southern League. The Club would rue their decision not to apply at this juncture, a move that was advised, it was revealed some years later.

Then disaster for Dartford followed, when inexplicably they finished bottom of the Eastern section table in 1934, and only a mediocre placing in the Central Division in which they, and several other clubs, also played. Despite this poor showing, the team reached the second round of the F.A.Cup, when they narrowly lost at Swindon Town. But this season was only a temporary slip, for they were back to their winning ways in the next campaign, finishing second and mid-table in the two sections, and again reached the second round of the Cup.

This time they lost by just 1-0 at home to Bristol Rovers before a 6,700 crowd. But in the F.A.Cup, the 1935/36 season was to prove the real headline maker. Drawn away to Cardiff City, winners just nine years earlier, they thrashed the Welshmen 3-0, and then produced a 4-0 trouncing of Gainsborough Trinity, at home (attendance 6,500). Then the third round draw decreed that the mighty Derby County - at the time second placed in the First Division - be visited.

The Darts took a two goal lead, but the star-studded League team fought back and eventually won 3-2. These Cup exploits coupled with another good League season, third in the Eastern Section, was enough to encourage the Directors to apply for entry to the Football League. In the Southern section of the Third Division they were up against Exeter City and perennial strugglers Newport County. Newport had only rejoined the League in 1932 and were making their 3rd re-election bid in four years. Vieing for the non-League votes were Bath City who had a less than impressive recent record in the Southern League Western section, and fellow Kentish men Folkestone who finished above the Darts in the East.

On Friday 3rd April, the local Press announced that, *"At their meeting on Monday last, the Directors* (of Dartford F.C.) *decided that application be made for admission to the Third Division and the London Combination next season. In taking this step the Directors are naturally relying on the public of Dartford and District for their support."* The latter statement was necessary for crowd numbers at home matches had been very disappointing, and apart from the extra expenses of fielding a Football League team, money would have to be found to cover Summer wages and probably transfer fees. Therefore the Directors pointed out that it was essential the attendances for the rest of the games that season increased; *"It is the duty of all supporters to do their bit if advancement is to be made",* was the stern warning! On the 18th April barely 1,000 turned up for the Cheltenham match, although the last match, a 5-0 thrashing of Folkestone was encouraging on the results front.

The voting at the re-election meeting produced somewhat strange returns. Exeter's successful re-election was reasonable, but Newport County who also comfortably retained membership was, perhaps, a surprise. Although the First and Second Division clubs, who had the lionshare of the votes, it was understood, were recommending the pair be re-elected. By now the Directors accepted that their bid was almost certain to fail - and they were not wrong. Bath City could only gain nine votes of confidence, whilst Dartford - who arguably had a better case - managed just one - as did Folkestone.

"The Club's failure to gain League status is a serious blow," it was gloomily announced; *"Charlton in the First Division will take more support away from Dartford than before."* The next season started with an encouragingly good crowd numbering 2,500, but by the year end even the better attendances had dropped to below 2,000.

In the few remaining seasons before the Second World War no further attempts were made for elevation; with indifferent performances, which culminated in the wooden spoon in the (single division) Southern League in 1939, their chances of 'promotion' would in any event have been very remote.

The Club's post-War performances were steady (with some poor seasons in the early 1950's), but generally unspectacular (one surprise Premier Southern League Championship in 1974), and they chose not to join the 'army' of clubs who made their annual appointments at the re-election meetings. Surprising perhaps, but inevitably such efforts would have been futile!

However, the Watling Street Ground did of course host Football League matches for a short period. Maidstone United during their brief career in the League groundshared with Dartford, until their shock and untimely demise, which also saw the end of Dartford (although subsequently reformed), and the Ground itself. But that, as they say, is another story!

DUDLEY TOWN

(1947)

Although it is claimed in some quarters that the 'Robins' were formed way back in the 1890's (the exact date is open to debate), it was to be many years before they would rise to a status where there was some justification, although with very little prospect of success, for an application to the Football League.

The team 'graduated' up the Senior ladder by way of the Worcestershire (later named Midland) Combination in the early 1930's to the Birmingham Combination, and then the Birmingham League, before folding in December 1938. The early post-War period saw many clubs try their luck at Football League status, and for most there was not even the remotest chance of success - Dudley Town were in this category!

Only a moderate mid-table team that played alongside Football League Clubs' third teams, clearly they had no chance!

The 1946/47 season saw the team (having reformed in 1945) making a reasonable bid for the Birmingham Combination Championship, for they were placed 3rd in mid-April, around the time to decide whether to apply for election to the League.

But the Birmingham Combination was hardly a sufficiently Senior competition when compared with the Southern and Midland Leagues, for amongst the Black Country team's opponents that season were the **Third** team of Second Division Coventry City (who beat Dudley in April), Nuneaton Borough - who thrashed them 6-0 a couple of weeks later - plus West Brom's. 'A' team and Banbury Spencer, who were both winners (4-1 and 3-1 respectively) in the last two home matches.

By finishing 8th in the Combination, it was hardly promotion-to-the-League form.

Dudley Town did decide to apply for Football League status, but even to the most optimistic this surely must have seemed a forlorn bid. Geographically speaking it was not out of the question that sufficient support would be forthcoming - especially in these post-War boom years - being placed West of Birmingham and in a densely populated area. But with West Bromwich Albion literally on their doorstep, and Walsall not far away, good crowds at the Robins' matches were not guaranteed.

They had no 'pedigree' to speak of, and were little more than a reasonably good team in a moderately high status competition. Perhaps the one factor in their favour was their home at The Sports Centre.

The Club, or at least its forerunners, first played at Shavers End, too far out of town to support good crowds and with a pitch too small to stage F.A.Cup matches. A move was therefore made, in 1911, across town - and conveniently located adjacent to Dudley railway station - to the County Cricket Ground, a venue that had been in operation since the 1840's. Although sharing with the Cricket Club, development work, to a large degree, was in favour of the footballers, including a later seated Stand on one side, by which time the Western side of the whole enclosure in effect became the Football Ground.

In 1931, the local Dudley Corporation evolved a scheme to help the unemployed, when the purpose built Sports Centre was constructed, located immediately South of the Cricket Ground on what was little more than a rubbish dump! A 6,000 crowd was present for the first match in September 1932, by which time three sides of the ground had been terraced (subsequently grassed over), and a year later a 1,800 capacity seated Stand was built.

Therefore, at least on the requirements of the period, The Sports Centre was suitable for Football League football. But a ground alone is not sufficient, and Dudley Town, along with 14 other hopefuls for the Third Division North section were not even considered, for it was decided that the two clubs for re-election (Southport and Halifax Town) should be re-elected automatically; a not unreasonable decision since the previous season was the first since 1938/39, and every club was still 'finding its feet' again.

Despite its size, it was recognised that the Sports Centre was lacking in certain aspects and for the 1947/48 season an amplifier system was purchased and catering facilities for spectators introduced. Hopes were still high of eventual election to the League, thoughts that were reinforced by new Manager Bill Morris (ex-Wolves and Birmingham), who made an announcement at the Ground in August.

He believed, he said, that a new Fourth Division would soon be formed, possibly for the 1948/49 season, and he was determined that Dudley Town would be one of the newcomers.

The team had a good season, but the Club's hopes and expectations did not materialise, for the expected influx of new clubs via a new division did not come to pass.

Dudley Town never applied for election again, and over the decades that followed the chances of eventual membership of the Football League decreased even further. The main factor that prevented this ambition was, paradoxically, the Ground itself.

There had been forewarnings that The Sports Centre could become a problem site, for built over limestone pits, subsidence problems emerged in 1932 and 1947, and then in 1957 a very deep hole 'appeared' close to the pitch. Worse was to follow, for in 1985 - ironically just after the Club had been promoted to the Southern League Premier Division - yet another crater appeared (on the cricket pitch), at which point the local council closed down the whole complex.

Dudley's fortunes since that time have plunged, for apart from the problems of finding a new Ground (many venues were used, and currently they are ground-sharing with Tividale), the team now find themselves in the relative humble surroundings of the West Midlands League.

EBBW VALE

(1927)

The whole subject of football in South Wales, in particular up to the Second World War, is deserving of detailed research in itself. Football development in Wales is more than just a sporting story, for it is a tale of industrial growth, of strikes - both local and National - of fierce competition with the oval ball version of the game... football examples of over ambition, of limited success at a high level, and often of failure. Football in the area over the first 50 years or so of the 20th century was inextricably linked with the social situation and economic pressures that were prevalent at various times.

The original Ebbw Vale football club was probably founded around 1900, and first entered the South Wales League in 1903. Embedded in the South Wales coal valleys, their rise coincided with the decline of Rugby around this time. As Rugby was relegated, Soccer was promoted, and the club rapidly became accepted in this oval ball dominated area, especially after they won, at their first attempt, the league title in 1904, a feat that was repeated five years later.

Despite a good season and reasonable support, there was really little chance, where two neighbours had already failed before them.

In 1914 they gained entry to the Southern League Second Division, a section dominated by clubs from South Wales. Of the 13 clubs who finished the season, only four came from outside the Principality, although the previous season there had been 12 Welsh teams among the 16. There were several casualties before, and early on in, the season, despite the popularity of football which was on an upward move in South Wales.

Clearly there just wasn't the numbers to support so many semi-professional teams from towns which in some cases were little more than villages. Ebbw Vale had a disastrous season, finishing the campaign with just seven points and accordingly received the 'wooden spoon'.

Despite the long lay-off due to the Great War, Ebbw Vale reappeared for the 1919/20 season and finished 5th in the table of 11 - all Welsh - teams. With coal in great demand in post-War Britain, the Welsh valleys prospered, and having weeded out the weak teams, the 1920/21 season saw the Southern League Second Division now renamed the Welsh Section. Ebbw Vale finished 3rd of the 11 teams, and then won the Championship the following two seasons, despite the loss of their Manager and the leading players to other more Senior clubs in 1922.

Whilst Ebbw Vale enjoyed their success on the pitch - and in fact became the first Welsh team to claim the overall Championship (beating the English Section Champions Bristol City reserves in a play-off) - on a wider front things were not so rosy. Mounting dissatisfaction in the coalfields led to widespread strikes and economic depression, that started in the Welsh Valleys. This heralded an era of unrest throughout the United Kingdom. Of the 11 teams who started the season in the Welsh Section, only seven completed their fixtures.

The six clubs who had fielded their first teams (Swansea Town reserves completed the numbers) were survivors, and all played within the 18 strong revised Western Section of the League during 1923/24. But it was now a tougher proposition, and Ebbw Vale could only finish fourth from bottom.

Another poor season followed before the club recovered to finish fifth (the top four being the reserve sides of League teams), and hence top of the decimated Welsh contingent which now numbered just four. By now a novel method of providing regular revenue had been devised whereby local miners had money deducted from their pay, which was given to the Club, and in return they gained free entry to matches. The 1926/27 season was even better, with one of the last home matches producing a 3-1 home victory over Bristol Rovers reserves at which there was a *"splendid attendance."* The team ending up fourth in the table after a final match 5-0 thrashing of Weymouth. A year earlier they had won the Welsh Cup, and the time had now come, the Club's officials decided, to make a bid for the (English) Football League. Although the team's success was somewhat tempered by the earlier death, in March, of 51 miners in a disaster at Marine Colliery at Cwm, near Ebbw Vale.

Whilst Ebbw Vale may have reached a (moderate) peak in their fortunes, and therefore the best time for an application, the grim economic situation continued unabated. Although the big town and city teams from Swansea, Newport and Cardiff - the latter, in the First Division, actually winning the (English) F.A.Cup that year - could report progress, for their smaller town compatriots it was a different story.

Aberdare Athletic departed from the Football League as Ebbw Vale made their bid, whilst Merthyr Town were to follow three years later.

But the heart ruled over commonsense, and after such a *"wonderful season"*, the locals were not going to let the economic situation dampen their enthusiasm. *"Ebbw Vale are applicants for entry into the Third Division of the English League, and hopes are entertained that a strong case will convince the authorities that they are eligible for higher honours"*, the local Press proclaimed. The case was clearly not nearly strong enough, and commonsense prevailed when the Club failed in their attempt; in fact it was a depressing showing, Ebbw Vale being the only club of the four who sought election who gained not a single vote.

Ebbw Vale never made another attempt at Football League status, but they continued playing in the Southern League for several seasons, although their successes on the pitch gradually declined. After two successive wooden spoon finishes, the Club - by now known as Ebbw Vale and Cwm - left the competition in 1932, to play solely in the Welsh National League (South), where they had also fielded their first team since 1919. A reformation in 1950 eventually led to the Club's admission to the National League, where they played for much of the 1980's and early 90's, becoming founder-members of the new competition in 1992. But they made a sudden and somewhat unexpected departure six years later, after a high final position the previous season in the National League.

ELLESMERE PORT TOWN

(1960)

Yet another 'one attempt' club, and one who eventually folded before further reincarnations at lower levels.

Although formed in the 1890's, the Club had only rare successes, their - albeit moderate - first being the winning of the Wirral Amateur Cup in 1899. But several disasters saw them fold and reform on several occasions. The first re-birth was after an inactive period during the First World War, and following a spell at the fairly minor level of the West Cheshire League - where they became Champions two years running - plus a short spell in the Liverpool County Combination, they were admitted to the Cheshire League in 1924.

For a few years the town actually had two representatives in this competition, for Ellesmere Port Cement Works had been members since 1921. The Cheshire League was of a far higher status than its 'County' title would suggest, for it was from this competition that Chester made their way into the Football League. Several League teams fielded their reserves, and the likes of Altrincham, Northwich Victoria and former Football League Stalybridge Celtic plied their trade. After a few poor to dreadful seasons the Club resigned from the Cheshire League, and now broke, they folded.

Meanwhile, it had been impossible to maintain two clubs at such a high level, and the Cement Works had already departed.

A successful period coupled with good crowds were insufficient to impress at their one attempt.

A short period back in the West Cheshire League for the reformed Ellesmere Port club again ended in oblivion, before the third revival - in 1935 - which saw the Club continue - apart from the Second World War period - for many years.

In 1948, Ellesmere Port was again admitted to the Cheshire League, and this time they held their own. They had, during the interim, played in the West Cheshire and the Liverpool Combination competitions. Of particular note was the support for the team which saw normal attendances of around 4,000 during the late 1940's and early 50's, and even more for F.A.Cup matches.

In 1956 the team finished in 5th place, and their short halcyon period was about to unfold. In 1958 they became League Champions, on goal average, and repeated this table-topping success in both the following two years. Even now, after the post-War boom period, crowds were occasionally exceeding 3,000, and the time was ripe to make a bid for Football League status.

In early April 1960, the Club was top of the Cheshire League, they were solvent - thanks in part to a supporters "Auxiliary Association" which had just handed over £1,000 to the parent club from the profits of its pools competition (in total £10,700 had been raised in three years) - and everybody was on a 'high'.

"To all these lads (the team), *who by their efforts are greatly enhancing our claim for League status, I think we owe a great thankyou",* voiced a supporter. The team clinched the title on Easter Monday when they beat Chester Reserves 2-0 before a crowd of over 3,000 at their York Road Ground. Having made a profit on the year, it was later announced, of £1,081 (albeit aided by £2,150 in donations) all looked on course for a hoped for success at the Football League re-election meeting.

One note of caution was expressed by J.R.Stockbridge, the Cheshire League Secretary, who reproached the Football Association, in defence of Ellesmere Port Town, when he stated that: *"Their application for full membership of the F.A. had consistently been turned down."* If the F.A. did not have enough faith in the Club, would the Football League clubs act similarly? With the Fourth Division now operating in the Football League, there was no regional applications, but Ellesmere had strong competi-tion for there were 18 applicants, plus the four re-election seekers.

Only six of the aspirants could be considered from the 'North', of whom the Port was the only representative from the Cheshire League. However, up against Lancashire Combination runners-up, and frequent applicants Wigan Athletic, plus the fast-rising Headington (later Oxford) United, and worst of all the all-conquering Peterborough United, realistically Ellesmere Port had little chance, unless of course all four re-election bidders were snubbed - an unthinkable outcome!

"Little Support For League Bid", announced the local Ellesmere Port Pioneer newspaper. *"Town Received Only One Vote."*

And that said it all. Peterborough United replaced Gateshead in the Fourth Division, Headington United with 10 votes and Wigan with six were no better than also-rans, and with their solitary vote, Ellesmere could only boast of beating Hereford United (who were destined for League status later), Kings Lynn, and F.A.Cup heroes Yeovil Town.

The outcome was a severe disappointment to the Club and its supporters, and this was reflected in the first home crowd the following season, when only 2,260 bothered to turn up for the visit of Stafford Rangers. A few years later, the team tumbled down the final league tables, the crowds disappeared, and for the last home game of the 1965/66 season there was a paltry 355 present at York Road. The Ground disappeared two years later, and is now part of the town centre development. The Club ended their days at the reasonably well equipped Thornton Road Stadium, which had been built around 1970, and located close to the M53 Motorway.

However they rose in stature again, being promoted to the Northern Premier League in 1971, but then dropped down to the Lancashire Combination two years later, before finally folding in 1975. A couple of attempts were made to field a Senior side in the town, but the latter incarnation, that of 'Ellesmere Port Town and Neston', became defunct in 1989. Later reformations of a football club in Ellesmere Port were that of 'another' Town club in 1992, followed by 'Ellesmere Port United', who survived for just a few years, but also at a fairly low level. Those heady days of high status championships and crowds of over 3,000 in Ellesmere Port are now only dreams of yesteryear.

ENFIELD

(1986)

For such a prominent club, at least in the post-War years, it comes as something of a surprise to find that, not unlike Dartford, Enfield only made one application for League recognition. That single attempt was in the last year before automatic promotion was finally introduced. Ironically, 1986 was, on paper, one of the best years for such an attempt, when there was no competition other than from the four Football League clubs who were seeking re-election.

Enfield is an old established club, having been founded in 1893 as Enfield Spartans, before they dropped the suffix in their name in 1900. Their beginnings were humble for they played in the local Tottenham and District Junior Alliance for two seasons from 1894, before a step up to the North Middlesex League.

Just one attempt, yet a year later they may have gained automatic promotion - but would they have survived?

In 1903, the Club was elected to the London League where they played until 1921, apart from two periods in the Middlesex League. Alongside their matches in these competitions the first team also played in the Athenian League from 1912, as founder-members, until 1963, being absent for only two seasons during this long period, apart from the War-time seasons.

Enfield were little more than an average Amateur team during the inter-war years, and really didn't come to prominence until 1962 when they became Athenian League Champions, a success that was repeated one year later. Success at this level earned them the chance of a move up to the Isthmian League, where they remained until 1981.

The mid-60's saw the Club really making their mark, for during the period between 1968 and 1981 they were Champions on no fewer than seven occasions, including a trio of Championships at the beginning of this era. Enfield F.C. was hence an Amateur club until this definition disappeared in 1974, and to add to their league honours they were also F.A.Amateur Cup winners in 1967 and 1970, plus European Amateur Cup winners in the latter year. Some good F.A.Cup runs had seen them reach the 1st or 2nd rounds on several occasions, including their best ever performances when they reached the 4th round in 1981, after beating both Hereford and Port Vale, before losing - but only after a replay - to Barnsley.

In 1981, the Club was invited to join the Alliance Premier League, which they readily agreed to, and there is little doubt that they were well deserving of this elevation to the brink of the Football League itself.

The team probably surpassed even the wildest dreams of its supporters, when after claiming the runners-up spot at the end of the first season (and winning the F.A.Trophy at Wembley), they went on to capture the Championship one year later. In the latter season it was a close run finish, with Enfield just pipping Maidstone United to the post - yet it was the latter club's name that was put forward to the Football League election vote! This would seem to have been a strange decision, for during the first four seasons of the Alliance Premier, Maidstone United came from 'nowhere' to claim their best finish - the runners-up spot.

The early years of the Alliance Premier League saw a not always cordial relationship with the Football League, and despite there now being only one nominee - from the former - there was still an element of the 'closed shop' within the latter. In 1983, the relationship had improved between the powers-that-be that ran the two competitions, as could be seen from Maidstone's votes which nearly ousted Hartlepool United from their League slot. This year it was agreed that the nominated club would relate to the best graded ground from the top five finishers in the Alliance. Within a few days of the end of the season the inspections commenced, and, unfortunately for Enfield, Maidstone came out on top.

Enfield had to wait another three years before they became a serious contender again. In 1986 they captured the GM Vauxhall Conference (as it was by now known) crown, and this time by a clear seven points above runners-up Frickley Athletic. On this one and only occasion Enfield were able to stake their claim for the League - but they failed dismally. They received only 6½ votes (the only time fractional votes came into the figures!), which was way down from Torquay United's 61, the lowest of the re-election candidates.

This apparent lack of confidence was probably due to several factors. The Football League had now agreed that from 1987, and subject to ground requirements, there would be automatic promotion and relegation.

Hence the voters now probably felt it would not be fair for one of their members to suffer being voted out on this last possible occasion! In addition the Southbury Road ground had been surpassed by Maidstone's home venue in 1983, and therefore there may have been doubts on its suitability.

Finally, Enfield F.C. would hardly have enhanced the Football League with its attendances, which during the past season had only averaged 767, and three years early was barely any better at 841. And so after a long wait to reach this position, the Club had failed at their only attempt, and one that could never be repeated.

Enfield were unable to claim the Championship again, and therefore the best chance of promotion was lost; if they had 'delayed' their last such GM Vauxhall Conference triumph, who knows, things may have taken a different path in the years to follow.

Relegation to the Isthmian League in 1990, followed by the loss of their Southbury Road Ground in acrimonious circumstances has left the Club having to struggle along with drastically reduced support, and with no long term headquarters. It is difficult to imagine Enfield F.C. ever being in a strong position to claim promotion to the ultimate goal again.

FAIRFIELD ATHLETIC

(1895, 1896, 1897)

Fairfield Athletic (the Club is also referred to without the suffix in a number of contemporary publications), is a now long-forgotten club, one from a bygone era when applications for Football League election were made from many unfamiliar names. In fact it takes a degree of diligent searching to even find where 'this' Fairfield is located!

In the late 1800's, the football 'map' was quite different from a century later, for the game, especially at a professional level, was based almost totally in the North and Midlands. Lancashire, and its surrounds was the hot-bed of support, with the likes of Preston, Blackburn Rovers, and Bolton Wanderers at the forefront, with the two Manchester clubs and Darwen in the wings. Professional non-League clubs, in the North-west abounded, with both the Lancashire League and the Lancashire Combination providing outlets for such clubs' endeavours, not to mention The Combination (founded in 1890) which catered for clubs in a wider geographical area.

The Lancashire Leaguers managed more votes than Tottenham, Millwall and Crewe - but never made the grade.

Fairfield (Athletic) F.C. was located in the area of their name, and is currently little more than a suburb of Droylesden, to the East of, and part of Greater Manchester. The Club was formed in the mid-1880's and first entered the Lancashire League in 1892. Their league career started in unremarkable fashion, with the team finishing ninth in the 12 team competition at the end of each of their first two seasons.

Their opponents around this time included the likes of Liverpool F.C., Bury (the Shakers attracting a crowd of around 2,000 for the Fairfield home game in January 1894), Blackpool (who later combined with South Shore) and former Football League members Accrington.

In 1894, Bury moved up to the Football League, and Fairfield became the surprise Champions at the end of the 1894/95 season, pushing Blackpool into second place. This was no mean achievement, for there were also a number of fairly prominent, at that time, non-League clubs in the league such as Nelson, Rossendale United and Stockport County.

Fairfield were a reasonable bet for the Championship for much of the season, although support at home was not always forthcoming, as was seen when the attractive Friendly match with Scottish club Johnstone - additional fixtures were necessary due to the relatively few league matches - drew only a *"poor attendance."*

Towards the end of March, it was announced that the Club would be allowed to play Friendly matches with Football League teams again. The Club had been boycotted by the League due to their alleged *"tampering with their* (League) *players."*

Although this was probably not the principal reason for Fairfield's later lack of success at the election meeting, trying to entice players away from these clubs no doubt did not help their cause! The first such match was against old foes Bury.

By early April, Fairfield lay in 3rd place in the Lancashire League, and a victory at Bacup would have taken them to the top, but a 3-1 defeat denied them this position. However, when Nelson were beaten 5-1 at home on the 15th of that month, before an unspecified, but quoted in the local press *"Record gate"*, this resulted in them heading the table, and virtually guaranteed the Championship. In addition the Club added to this major success with an appearance in the Semi-final of the Manchester Senior Cup that season, although their progress through to the 1st round proper of the F.A.Cup, for the first (and only) time, was probably best forgotten, for they lost 11-1 at Sunderland!

When it came to the end of season re-election meeting, the Club decided to apply, on the very slim 'record' of this one solitary Lancashire League Championship win, and no other feats of note. Three of the four clubs for re-election were comfortably voted back in (Walsall Town Swifts were rejected in preference to Loughborough), and although the failing clubs votes were not revealed that year, it is a safe bet that Fairfield, along with the only other aspirants Blackpool, gained little - if any - support; ironically with so few clubs offering themselves, this was a rare year when there was a good chance of acceptance - but only for the right club(s).

In August 1895, there was a crowd of 2,000 for the annual sports day at the club's sparse Gransmoor Road ground.

But it was later agreed, after the Football League Ground Committee inspected the venue, that should Fairfield entertain any further thoughts of applying for League status, improvements would have to be made. Although Gransmoor Road was properly enclosed, there was no *"accommodation"* (presumably stands or cover) for spectators, and the Local Council agreed to undertake this work. At the end of the season, despite no repeat success in the Lancashire League, another election attempt was made, with six other non-Leaguers, and although this was unsuccessful they did pick up three votes... one more than Tottenham Hotspur! The team managed to attain runners-up spot in 1897, and with seven teams again jostling for recognition, Fairfield again managed three votes... this time one more than Crewe Alexandra, and two more than Millwall (Athletic).

Although listed in the Lancashire League fixture lists for the 1897/98 season the Club folded during the Summer or very early into the season, a situation probably brought on due to financial reasons. From League Champions and three times aspirants to the Football League, Fairfield disappeared even faster than their rise to moderate prominence. There were two short periods in the early 1900's when 'Fairfield' entered for the F.A.Cup, but these refer to another, completely non-related club, in the Buxton, Derbyshire area.

The Gransmoor Road Ground had disappeared by the time of the First World War, with a school being built in its place. Currently the road is a mixture of turn of the century and modern housing, and there is nothing left to remind the passer-by that a now long forgotten Senior status football club had once played there!

FOLKESTONE

(1933-36, 1962, 1966)

Despite being a fairly large and well populated County, Kent has only ever had one sustained Football League club (Maidstone United had three seasons), and even that representative - Gillingham - were voted out in 1938, before their return in 1950. Yet there have been several other clubs that have made their bids, but all have failed.

Over the past century, there have been a number of reincarnations of Folkestone F.C. that have played under various names and at various levels. But these upheavals have taken place in comparatively recent times, following the almost inevitable problems with finance which has given rise to these rebirths. The latest club - Folkestone Invicta - have fought their way up through the ranks to the Southern League Premier Division, and they are therefore just two (big) steps away from the ultimate goal.

Founded originally in 1884, Folkestone became founder-members of the Kent League in 1894, and moved to the Cheriton Road Ground in 1914, the home of the various 'Folkestones' for much of the time since. In 1923, the Club were admitted to the Southern League, just a few years after the mass exodus of teams which became the Third Division in 1920. For the first few seasons in this company the team held its own, except for the disastrous 1926/27 season when they claimed the wooden-spoon. Four run-of-the-mill years followed, until the appointment of player/manager Harry Warren in 1931, following which the team were well and truly put on the football map. But this progress was only made after the Club almost folded at the end of the 1930/31 season. In February a public meeting was held when it was announced that £2,500 was needed to save the Club. Extra shares at five shillings each (25p) were made available, and this life-saver, plus the formation of a supporters club ensured their continuance.

A tight finish at the end of the 1931/32 season saw the team become runners-up to fellow Kentishmen Dartford.

No luck for another Kentish team - despite attempts over a wide period.

At this period, the Southern League (Eastern Division) was lacking in numbers, and for the 1932/33 season, with only eight competing teams, the Club had to look to the Kent League and the London Combination (Division 2) to make up the number of games. Although the team only finished third in the Southern League that season, their exploits in the F.A.Cup made the headlines. Their most notable victories were those played at Cheriton Road against the Third Division South leaders Norwich City (1-0) and Newport County (2-1). The third round took them to First Division giants Huddersfield Town, and before a crowd of 13,378 (including 434 Folkestone fans who came by special train), they were hardly disgraced in the 2-0 defeat...*"The greatest game in their history"*, reported the local press.

Just a week after their Cup defeat, on the 21st January, the Club announced, somewhat prematurely, that they would be applying for election to the League; *"A surprise to many"*, said the local scribe. At the time it was understood that locally both Dartford and Tunbridge Wells would also be applying, although in the event neither did. Folkestone's intentions caused a certain amount of ill-feeling with their two neighbours, for they felt that they had been upstaged by this early announcement, and rather than split the votes the pair had little option but to withdraw.

An appraisal was made of the Cheriton Road Ground at this time in relation to the bid for League status: *"Folkestone's ground is quite good... must be good accommodation for teams, and the installation of new baths in the Club's pavilion is a step in the right direction"*, the local press announced. Third place in the Southern League, 4th in the Kent and 5th in the London Combination was enough to give some hope, especially as Folkestone were only one of four aspirants.

It was felt that if Newport County finished in the bottom two then there was a very real chance that they would be voted out, and Folkestone could be in. A first meeting took place on Tuesday 9 May, and the result of this would be left to a final decision by the First and Second Division clubs on the 29th. Surprisingly there was always the possibility that other non-Leaguers may seek election at the last minute, for they could apply as late as two days before the meeting - but none did. The Chairman, Mr. H.Henley, along with the others seeking election, was given five minutes to state his case, and although he agreed he was *"given a fair hearing"*, he, together with Harry Warren who was also at the meeting, felt that there was insufficient time to convince the powers that be.

The first meeting recommended that the two re-election clubs be retained, and this was confirmed later that month. In any event it would have been Llanelly with 20 votes, who would have stepped up, for Folkestone could only come second with a paltry five. There was a glimmer of hope when it was announced that Clapton Orient were in severe financial trouble, and they were given one month to resolve their problems or they would be rejected from the League. Although this didn't transpire, if it had then a further election meeting would have been necessary.

Folkestone did well in various Cup competitions again the following season, but a final poor finish at 7th (of nine), meant that it was somewhat farcical for them to apply for League status again. The two clubs for re-election were very strong candidates to retain their membership (this was possibly the reason why no other club bothered to chance their luck) - Cardiff City and Bournemouth & Boscombe - and Folkestone received not a single vote. The end of the 1934/35 season produced a similar situation, when Folkestone ('The Wasps' as they were at this time known) - who finished 7th of 10 and Champions, of the Eastern and Central Divisions respectively - received one vote, as did Bath City - the only two to apply.

In 1936, Folkestone made their last bid for the Football League for many years. Ironically a good League table finish - runners-up - and a run through to the F.A.Cup second round was offset by financial problems which no doubt helped to deter support at the re-election meeting. Folkestone once again upset Dartford, who also stood for election and hence split the votes.

Although the Darts finished one place below the Cheriton Road club, Folkestone's last match 5-0 defeat at Watling Street could hardly have boosted their confidence! Bath City had the greatest credibility with nine votes, whilst the two clubs from Kent managed just one each. Sensibly, Folkestone refrained from any further Football League applications for nearly thirty years, due in no small part in their decision to drop back down to the Kent League in 1939, where they remained until 1959. The Club's return to the Southern League was well justified, for they were immediately promoted to the Premier Division, only to drop back to the First two years later! Somewhat ludicrously, in view of their relegation, they and virtually all of the Premier Division applied for election to the League, and like most of the 25 clubs, they received no votes.

After promotion again, in 1964, they held their own in the upper division (despite a trading loss of £2,000 in the first season), and in 1966 - but only a moderate 15th final placing of 22 - made their sixth and last bid for glory. Folkestone, along with nearly half the Southern League Premier Division decided to stake their claims, in another farcical year when no fewer than 15 clubs (plus three who had their applications turned down) applied for election.

A run through to the 3rd round of the F.A.Cup helped their cause, although at one time in the New Year they lay 3rd from bottom in the Southern League. But a new spirit of optimism prevailed, resulting in the formation of a supporters club and a 'Team Building Fund' which raised £400 from local businesses in just a few minutes at its first meeting. There was a multitude of League applications, due no doubt to this announcement: *"The formation of a super league for the top clubs in the Football League is a possibility... this might lead to the opportunity for the top clubs in the Southern League to join a re-organised Fourth Division."*

It was to be nearly thirty years before a 'super league' evolved, and at the 1966 re-election meeting all four League clubs easily retained their places, whilst the hopefuls could only manage a handful of points between them. Folkestone were one of only four that received none. Relegation the following season, followed by several years of indifferent form ensured that the Club never made another attempt.

GLOUCESTER CITY

(1956, 1958, 1959, 1964)

Although formed in the 1880's, it was not until 1939 that the Club finally made it to the Southern League, joining the War-time competition, after their Birmingham Combination fixtures came to an early and abrupt end that season. This first season consisted of just 14 matches in a much reduced Southern League, Western Division. Gloucester City had made a slow move up the football 'ladder' starting in the Bristol and District League (later Western League) and after folding and then reforming they had to start again at grass roots level.

The Gloucester and District, North Gloucester, and - as founder members - The Gloucestershire Northern Senior Leagues were traversed. On turning professional they joined the Birmingham Combination, a somewhat quirky geographical choice. With a pre-War population of over 50,000, and not many clubs nearby in competition for support it is strange that the path they trod took so long to accomplish, although part of this can be explained by the fact that Rugby has always been popular in the area.

Although the Club has maintained a continuous membership of the Southern League since 1939, they have rarely hit the headlines in this competition, in fact they have often been in the bottom half of the lower division, winning promotion only in 1969 (finishing in third position of the First Division), but relegated two years later. The team's only Championship was in 1989, when they were promoted from the Midland to the Premier Division, and two years later they were runners-up in the higher section.

Geographically, Gloucester must have stood a chance - but with representation now from nearby Cheltenham, the future looks bleak in this direction.

Since then the Club has slipped back into the sectionalised lower (Western) division, and therefore they have never really experienced a purple patch in their history.

Despite such an unimpressive record, the Club's name is familiar in non-League circles, and they surely must be regarded as one of the Country's under-achievers at this level. Even so the Club have considered it worthwhile to make four attempts at the Football League.

In 1956 they were part of an 11 strong band of optimists, with all but three coming from the Southern League, who were making a bid to join the Third Division Southern Section. Gloucester City had enjoyed quite a good season, finishing 7th of 22, and were one of only two clubs to receive at least a consolation vote (meanwhile Peterborough United were in the middle of their long term struggle to gain recognition, and they gained eight).

Two indifferent seasons followed, but even so another attempt was made in 1958. This was the first season when an elevation to the new Fourth Division was on offer, and in total 12 clubs tried their luck.

Peterborough United made their last but one unsuccessful attempt (they achieved their goal two years later), and with 15 votes they were streets ahead of the competition. Gloucester City were one of four teams that received not a single vote, in what was again a futile attempt.

But the Club wouldn't take the hint, for a year later they were at the League's re-election meeting again, despite a poor season which had seen them finish well down the bottom half of the Southern League North-Western Zone. Three of the teams for re-election saw their votes of confidence reduced, Peterborough United only missed out on replacing Aldershot by five votes. The voting thus left more to be shared amongst the other 13 hopefuls. Despite being the lowest placed team in the Southern League seeking election, they at least gained one vote, which was more than four of their higher placed league compatriots. Obviously the representative from one club thought they deserved a chance, but this was still a long long way from Football League acceptance.

Despite being now confined to the First (second level) of the Southern League, and the five poor to indifferent seasons that followed, Gloucester City made one more futile attempt at the League, although there was some particular justification on this occasion. By early April 1964, the team was reasonably placed in their division, and when they lost 1-0 to Crawley Town, this was their first home defeat since the previous November. On April 18th the Club lost their last home game, to Yiewsley (later Hillingdon Borough), and this was noteworthy as it was the last competitive match at their Longlevens Ground. Despite the significance of this match at the ground that had been 'home' since 1935, no special arrangements or ceremony were made, *"We shall just be out for a good win"*, remarked Tommy Casey the Player/Manager.

On Friday 15th May, the local Press announced that amongst the other candidates, neighbours Cheltenham Town, plus Bath City, would also be applying for Football League status, but at the re-election meeting, this pair in fact did not appear alongside Gloucester City. Despite their indifferent playing season, Gloucester City were able to put a good case in view of their imminent move to a new Ground.

Originally, the large site that had been purchased in Horton Road, which was conveniently situated fairly close to the City centre, was to be ambitiously developed, but when the projected costs reached £100,000, a more modest design was the compromise. At an expenditure of around £36,000, the Horton Road Ground provided seating for around 500, covered standing for - supposedly - 4,500, with an overall 10,000 capacity.

It was surprising, perhaps, that there were not more clubs applying for League membership - there were 13 hopefuls - since a proposal had been put forward to reconstitute the Football League into new Premier, First and Second Divisions, with those in the Fourth - plus additions from the non-League world - forming a new two (geographical) divisional 'Alliance'; although many years later, a not dissimilar reformation did of course take place. However, this plan was defeated at the June 6th meeting of the Football League, as was a slightly different alternative of having five divisions each with 20 clubs, which would have embraced eight new clubs into the League. Therefore the hopes of those applying at the re-election meeting were dashed, and only Wigan Athletic with five votes came anywhere near to ousting one of the clubs seeking re-election - Hartlepools United comfortably retained their place with 36 votes, the lowest of the four. Gloucester City at least received one vote, whilst three applicants got none.

This was to become the last bid by Gloucester City, and although they have come close on a few occasions they have yet to reach the next 'steeping stone' - the Alliance/Conference. With a brand new Ground that has been occupied since 1986, the club and its supporters can always live in hope, although it must have been particularly galling to see near neighbours Cheltenham Town rise to League status in 1999.

GOOLE TOWN

(1975)

Goole Town were one of many clubs that suddenly emerged to make an application for membership of the Football League, failed, and sensibly never tried again!

The Club chose 1975 to make their applic- ation, although there is no overriding reason why that particular year was chosen. Playing then, in the Northern Premier League

Although no lesser person than the Foot- ball League Secretary himself gave the club a 50/50 chance, in reality they didn't stand a hope!

(they started as founder-members in 1968), at the turn of the year they only lay in a modest 9th place, and in fact their 4-3 victory over Buxton on the 4th January was the first home victory since November. And support around this time was not particularly good, with only 750 turning up for the F.A.Trophy victory over Brereton Social. Even the visit of Champions-elect Wigan Athletic drew only 1,000 to the grandly named Victoria Pleasure Grounds. The Club finished in a healthy, but hardly an election-worthy 8th (of 24) in the league, to equal the best position of their seven years in this competition.

The 1974/75 season was, however, the Clubs most notable in the F.A.Trophy, for they won through to the quarter-finals. It was perhaps the support that was there for the right match that encouraged Goole to make their later bid to enter the League.

Romford's visit in the 3rd round attracted 1,850, and in the quarter-final, an encouraging 3,200 turned up at the Pleasure Grounds for Matlock's appearance, which resulted in a 1-0 defeat. Although this was dwarfed by the record crowd of 8,700 in 1950 who were present for the local derby with Scunthorpe.

This did show that there was la- tent support out there, if only it could be encouraged for the run of the mill matches.

There was no doubt that Goole were to make a determined bid, for on the 11th April, the Football League Secretary - Alan Hardaker - arrived at the Ground to give his opinion on the Club's chances.

Hardaker, together with the Grimsby Town Chairman, spent one hour with the Senior Committee of Goole Town, and gave the Club a somewhat surprising chance of, *"fifty-fifty"* of them gaining admission. Clifford, the Goole Town Chairman said of Richards after the meeting: *"He was highly delighted with the playing area and the changing facilities, both of which would be the envy of many clubs".*

However, Alan Hardaker cautiously advised the club that the lynch-pin of Town's application was based on the success of the proposal to regionalise the Fourth Division, and hence allow the ingress of more clubs. *"This is unlikely for two or three years"* he added.

To make their case stronger it was agreed that there should preferably be more covered accommodation at the Pleasure Grounds, plus some other minor improvements. In view of the fact that the Club actually proceeded to make an application that year, Clifford's statement was somewhat strange: *"Under the present set-up, Town would not be interested in Football League membership."*

Although he did add that if in fact there was a reformation of the Football League, and hence the likelihood of a weakened Northern Premier League (14 clubs had already intimated that in these circumstances they would be applying), in order to safeguard the Club's interests he wanted to ensure that they would not be left behind.

Therefore when Goole Town's name was included in the list of clubs applying for League membership that year, this was probably no more than 'testing the water' to see what support they would get.

There were 14 hopefuls in 1975, of which five were from the Northern Premier League, and based on their final positions, Goole Town had the second least chance of success. Therefore up against the likes of Wigan Athletic and Yeovil Town, Goole's two votes - better than six of the other aspirants - could be considered quite successful.

Of course such a reformation in the League never took place, and by the end of the following season, Goole Town had slipped down to 10th in the League. Realistically they could never have sustained a Football League team, especially as they represented the second smallest population of the clubs in the Northern Premier.

Although originally formed in 1900, they closed during the Great War and folded in the mid-1920's. They reformed soon after but did not win any major honours until the late 1920's, by which time they were playing in the Yorkshire League. In the early post-War years they joined the Midland League and then the Northern Premier as founder-members, in 1968.

Since the late 1970's, the Club's fortunes have somewhat mirrored the local industry, as they first slumped to the Northern Counties League, and finally folded around 1995. Reformed as 'Goole A.F.C.' in 1997, the Club still play at the Pleasure Grounds, and are members of the Northern Counties East League once more.

GRAVESEND & NORTHFLEET

(1947, 1961, 1962)

In several respects Gravesend and Northfleet can be regarded as an under-achiever in the non-League world. Geographically (North Kent), they are well situated with a good catchment area - albeit with Gillingham F.C. not far up the road - and they have at Stonebridge Road a Ground which could probably be brought up to Football League standards without too much effort and expense, yet their three attempts at the League have produced woeful results. Whilst overall, on the playing front, they have done themselves no real favours.

The story of football in the area started with two clubs, that of Northfleet F.C., founded in 1890, and Gravesend United who first saw the light of day three years later. The earlier club evolved from the Invicta Cricket Club (that had been founded by teenagers in the town), from which was formed a football section, in October 1890, initially under the name of 'Northfleet Invicta'. Home games were played at Portland Meadow (now the Blue Circle Cement Works), and the 'Invicta' was soon replaced by 'United'. With a roped-off pitch and pay box, spectators were charged admission at their next Ground - at Wombwell Park Estate (which no longer exists) from 1892, but after one season they moved on to Collins Meadow, which was later overlayed by Huntley Avenue. This later venue was an enclosed Ground, with a clubhouse and changing rooms. By 1895, the Club were running a professional team, the players being paid between 10 and 12 shillings (50-60p) per week, but with home crowds averaging only around 500 during the early 1898/99 season, they folded, the last match being played on the 5th November 1898.

Another club from Kent who arguably have (or had) the right credentials, but never made it.

The Club's first match was played on the 8th November 1890, and in 1895 they were competing in the Kent League, becoming Champions and also being awarded the Kent Senior Cup that season. In 1896 they were elected to the Southern League, along with neighbours Gravesend United, but it soon became apparent that the two closely located clubs were vieing for the same support. Northfleet reformed in 1901, due principally to the efforts of founder-member Joe Lingham, who was to remain loyal to the Club until his death in 1943.

Meanwhile, just up the road, Gravesend United (an amalgamation of Gravesend F.C. and Gravesend Ormonde) became founder-members of the Kent League in 1894, their second season. The early years saw the Club play at Overcliffe (close to the current St.James Avenue) and then on the site later occupied by the Grammar school for Girls in Pelham Road. With both clubs struggling for the same support, an amalgamation was mooted early in 1898, a suggestion that was not entertained by Northfleet, unwisely since they folded a few months later. If the amalgamation had gone ahead, then this would probably have been a vastly different story! Gravesend gradually faded away, first dropping down to the Kent League in 1901, followed by many years at a lowly level. The Club eventually rose again, albeit only to the humble Kent Amateur League, in 1932.

After their resurrection in 1901, and in contrast to Gravesend's sorry state, Northfleet United soon progressed upwards, first to the West Kent League, and then the Kent League itself in 1906.

Many Championships and County Cups were won in the inter-War years, and during the 1930's they acted as a 'Nursery Side' for Tottenham Hotspur, when players of the ilk of Vic Buckingham, Ted Ditchburn, Charlie Buchan and Ron Burgess wore the United's colours.

Now very much the 'poor relations', Gravesend United plodded on in the Kent Amateur League at their new Central Avenue Ground. At last, in 1946, commonsense prevailed, and the two clubs combined to become 'Gravesend and Northfleet' with the latter's Stonebridge Road as the home Ground. The way was now cleared for a single representative team in the area, that was immediately embraced into the Southern League.

On August 31st that year a large crowd of over 5,000 (it would have been more had it not been for local transport problems) was present for Hereford United's Southern League visit (a 3-0 victory). At the end of the season, which transpired to become a moderately successful one, the 'new' Club first applied for Football League membership, like many other hopefuls that year. But no votes were taken for it was seen as only fair that the four lowest placed members should be given another chance after the turmoil caused by the War.

The next decade or so produced indifferent to poor final finishes in the Southern League (including the wooden spoon in 1955) with not even a decent F.A.Cup run to enhance the Club's claim as a prominent non-League outfit. But eventually their heyday came when they won the Championship in 1958, and followed this with the runners-up spot a year later. Perhaps these were the years when a serious bid for Football League membership should have been made. However, having earlier experimented with employing full-time professionals which did not lead to the hoped for success, it was probably considered wiser to consolidate rather than be rash.

By 1961, the Club were once again employing full-time players, and despite a poor season in the Southern League Premier, when they finished fifth from bottom following a disastrous end of season run, a second - which was to prove ill-timed - bid was made for League recognition. With Oxford United capturing most of the non-League votes, there were few left for the 'also-rans', and Gravesend and Northfleet - along with four other clubs - received none. The third, and final, attempt was made a year later, but with only a marginal improvement in Southern League form (a rise of four places), and still with no F.A.Cup run of note, they failed once again. Oxford United swept up most of the votes, and they were comfortably elected in place of Accrington Stanley who had resigned. Once again, this time within a ludicrously enormous group of 25 hopefuls, and together with the majority, the Club found themselves with not one vote of support.

Some very poor seasons followed for Gravesend & Northfleet, and after relegation they could barely make the grade even in the lower division of the Southern. It wasn't until the mid-seventies that the team began to realise its true potential and after a decade or so of moderate to good seasons, they were 'promoted' to the new Alliance Premier League as founder-members in 1979. After an initial good season, the Club slumped and were relegated to the Southern League in 1982. Since that time they have hovered between the top and second levels, and hence have never had a realistic chance of rising at least to the Alliance Premier League again.

A 'horizontal' move across the Pyramid to the Ryman (Isthmian) League has not had the desired effect, and despite moderately good attendances at this level, plus a Ground which even in the safety-conscious turn of the century years can still boast of covered accommodation for over 2,000 and seating for 600, there appears to be no realistic chance of eventual promotion to the Football League, at least in the short term.

GUILDFORD CITY

(1932, 1947, 1960 - 65, 1967, 1968)

Guildford City were one of the reasonably few clubs who, if they had gained admission to the League, may very well have made a success of it. With a pre-Second World War population of around 30,000 - not dissimilar to that of neighbours Aldershot - which has since risen to around double that number, and with a semi-urban surrounding area with an estimated catchment of one third of a million, support for a League team may well have been forthcoming. In fact, at their first attempt in 1932, it is debateable that they may very well have been given the o.k. that year rather than the Shots! Conversely, the area has since become, to a degree, a 'London stockbroker belt' environment, and hardly that associated with support for the local football team! This has been verified by the fact that after folding, in 1974 (and all vestiges of the original club disappearing ten years later), there has not been, since then, a Senior club in the town; one of the largest in the country without such represent-ation.

Founded originally as Guildford United, in 1921, they immediately became professional and were accepted into the Southern League from the outset, where they remained until their demise over 50 years later. Just up the road, Aldershot had a similar start and finish as Guildford, although they were formed six years later, and eventually folded around two decades later than City. A premature attempt at Football League status was intended to be made in 1923, but since the Club does not feature in any official records for that year, they obviously abandoned the attempt.

Guildford generally struggled in the Southern League until 1932, when they finished third, whilst Aldershot - who had had a far better time in the Southern - ironically finished second from bottom in the year that they were elected to the Football League!

Aldershot were comfortably welcomed in with 35 votes (and effectively replaced Thames Association), and Guildford received a respectable eight. However, this preference for Aldershot was met with dismay at Guildford, not least the money-spinning local derby gates would disappear.

They were mostly lean years for Guildford City leading up to the Second World War, except in 1938, when they became the surprise Champions, and a year later when the runners-up spot had to suffice. Yet surprisingly on neither occasion did they apply for election to the Football League. The first year can probably be explained by the dramatic climb to the top by Ipswich Town - well supported and 1937 Champions - who were unopposed in the election stakes. In 1939 both Champions Colchester United and Chelmsford City unsuccess-fully applied.

Guildford City were one of the many who made an application in 1947, which did not even go to the vote as the re-election candidates were voted in en masse.

The preference for Aldershot was met with dismay in Guildford.

Once again the Club's lack of success was greeted with dismay by the supporters, who had agreed to raise £1,000 should they have been successful, and the club officials who were confident that they could have attracted gates of 8-10,000!

It wasn't until 1960 when The City made their next attempt, the first of six consecutive years. The early post-War years had seen some good and some indifferent performances before the Club's second Championship success in 1956, yet they made no application for the League that year. Several generally poor seasons followed, and in 1959 they were effectively relegated to the new First Division of the Southern League.

Yet despite finishing only fifth in the second tier, they decided to make a bid for League promotion. Although they only received two votes in 1960, this was a better showing than four Southern League Premier Division teams. Promoted to the top division that year, at the end of the 1960/61 season the team finished a dismal 15th in the final table, hardly giving their next bid a realistic chance. Not a single vote was cast in their favour, which could hardly have come as a surprise for the Club; the 'new' Oxford United were undoubtedly the top Southern League team, and their 'promotion' was only one year away. Ludicrously the following year saw a record number of 26 clubs apply, and once again Guildford City received no support (despite finishing third in the final table) along with 14 other teams.

Guildford had another good season in 1962/63, finishing fourth in the Premier Division, and with Oxford United now out of the way, and no obvious successor to the top non-League club 'crown', the voting was expected to not greatly favour any one team. But with 12 clubs vieing for League status, and the 'old pals' act of re-electing their own well to the fore, there was no way in for any ambitious non-League team. Guildford City did manage three votes, the third best of the hopefuls, but this was scant consolation.

The next two years followed in very similar fashion - good final Southern League placings for the City... no outstanding non-League team worthy of Football League status... and the re-election of the bottom League clubs by huge margins over the nearest hopefuls; Guildford received two and three votes respectively. At least the Club had not been barred from applying in 1964, when a number of fellow Southern Leaguers had - as a punishment for signing Football League players on free transfers!

No application was made in 1966 - a poor year in the league for the Club - and a recovery the next season led to the Club's penultimate bid in 1967. But the re-election meeting of the Football League continued in the same vein as it had throughout the 1960's, for there was still no dominant non-League club at this time, and Guildford City had to scrap with 14 other clubs for the few votes, just 20 in total.

This represented around half the total that the lowest re-elected club Rochdale received; City, along with four others received no votes, although amongst this group was Cambridge United, who were to find that patience would prevail eventually.

The Club's tenth, and last, bid for Football League status was made in 1968. Fifteen clubs in total tried their luck, and yet again with no outstanding club, either form the North or the South, the re-election candidates had no trouble in maintaining their status. In fact the top non-League bid came from Cheltenham Town, their only application, but with three votes this was hardly cause for optimism! Guildford City managed one vote, poor perhaps, but one better than Yeovil Town and Nuneaton Borough.

Guildford's frequent Football League applications may have been enhanced had it not been for their continual financial struggles, for although their home gates compared well with their contemporaries, they often tended to overstretch their resources, particularly with the signing of ex-Football League players - including a squad of 16 in one season - who no doubt were on high wages. The Club's fortunes continued to slump from the end of the 1960's, and heavily in debt they had little option but to sell the Ground, which was officially announced in 1972, in order to cover their debts. A complicated arrangement allowed the Club to continue using their Josephs Road Ground for a few years and they were also to benefit from the proceeds received in the eventual development of the site, a sum that was in effect used up before it was received!

The local Council promised to assist in finding the Club a site for a new Ground, but despite a patient wait over several years this never materialised. Eventually Guildford City had to groundshare with two different clubs, and their financial viability continued to plummet. Internal turmoil eventually split the Club, and after a merger with Dorking F.C., the new organisation soon floundered too. The final attempt at retaining the identity of the City club was made with another merger, to form that of Guildford and Worplesdon, but this club also had but a short life. Josephs Road became a housing estate, and to this day there is no Senior football club carrying the Guildford name.

HASTINGS UNITED

(1956)

Hastings is the only club (apart from Brighton and Hove Albion) in Sussex to have applied for membership of the Football League, which in view of the relatively small populations of the County's main towns is perhaps not surprising, although there is, and always has been, a thriving non-League football structure in this area. Hastings United was a mere 'babe' when they made their single application, although football - at varying levels of seniority - had thrived in the coastal town since the end of the 19th century.

Although some of the formation dates and amalgamations of the early clubs are at variance between different reference works, the broad development of Senior football in this Sussex town can be summarised. Hastings and St. Leonards F.C., formed in 1894, was the first major club, and four years later St. Leonards F.C. came on the scene. The latter club were soon to turn professional and, as St. Leonards United they joined the Southern League Second Division in 1905.

A year later there was a sensible amalgamation with the Hastings club, and under the new name of Hastings and St. Leonards, they remained in the Southern League until 1910. At this time they had their best season and finished as Champions of the Second Division Section (B). Somewhat incongruously Stoke (the potteries club) were section (A) Champions, and the Sussex club were the losers in a play-off to decide promotion. If the Hastings club had been promoted they may well have gone on to help form the new Third Division of the Football League (in 1920), but instead they slumped to near obscurity!

Just one attempt made by the only Sussex team to try, and fail.

For a few years, St. Leonards Amateurs (founded in 1907) became the major team in the area (although Hastings and St. Leonards F.C. did make a single season Athenian League appearance in 1913), but they too soon disappeared, in 1924. The Amateurs demise may have been brought about by the reformation of the earlier St. Leonards club, who in 1923 took over the newly created Pilot Field Ground. This local Council inspired venture cost an enormous sum, in excess of £40,000, to develop, and uniquely provided two grounds, backing on to each other, but at greatly different levels.

As well as enormous embankments, a 1,000 covered and seated Stand (which still remains today) was erected on the better developed lower Field. The team remained as Amateurs for many years, but eventually after changing their name to Hastings Town around 1976, they eventually 'rejoined' the Southern League in 1985.

Between times, the club that is the subject of this Football League application was formed, in 1948, having had no predecessors unlike their near neighbours. The club's formation immediately created problems for it was they that gained the use of the better - lower - Pilot Field, that had been the home of Hastings and St.Leonards, whilst the former occupants were 'relegated' to the upper Field. Hastings United took the local football support by storm when they immediately adopted professional status, and were elected into the Southern League for the 1948/49 season.

The new Club's progress was not as they would have wished, for after an uneasy start - two seasons around mid-table - they then endured two years when they finished bottom. But the Club fought through this unhappy period, and in the 1953/54 season won their way through to the 3rd round of the F.A.Cup - including a 4-1 defeat of Swindon Town - and it was only a replay defeat to Norwich City that prevented further glory; the home tie attracted an all-time near 13,000 record gate to the Pilot Field. One year later the Club finished third in the league, and again reached the 3rd round of the F.A.Cup. At Sheffield Wednesday they held a half-time lead, and it was only a late final controversial goal that took the First Division club through.

Although the 1955/56 season was something of an anti-climax, the decision was made by the Club to make a bid for Football League status. By early January the team were handily placed 5th in the table, and the 5-2 thrashing of Kidderminster Harriers attracted a crowd of 3,651 to the Pilot Filed, proving that there was support for a successful team. Conversely a slump saw the team drop down the table, and despite some more good home victories in February and March, the crowds dropped to the 2,500 mark. Even so the last home game saw 2,683 come through the turnstiles for the scoreless draw with Cheltenham. Ironically the Reserves became the Metropolitan League Champions, and their home match with Brighton's third team in the Semi-Final of the League Cup attracted a crowd of 2,432.

The impetus for many clubs seeking a higher standard was probably generated by a Southern League Management meeting on the 17th April, when representatives from the leading non-Leagues discussed the formation of an association of professional clubs from without the Football League. There was also mention made of a National challenge cup, with the Final to be played at Wembley - but the F.A.Trophy did not follow for more than a decade.

Eleven of the clubs from the South made a bid for League status that year, but even the up and coming Peterborough United could only muster eight points; Hastings United along with seven others received none.

The Sussex club were determined to make a strong bid the next time, and as well as engaging several new full time professionals, improvements were made to the Ground. The pitch, which in the past was excellent, had deteriorated, due in the main to there being no full-time groundsman. But a next time never came, for United began to find that running a fully professional team was an expensive business.

Whilst several promotions (and consequent relegations) were experienced in the later, two division, Southern League competition, the Club were never in a strong enough position to make another bid for League status. It was ironic that the team's last promotion in 1982, was to see their demise just three years later, and whilst still a member of the higher division. With debts at the end of £92,000, Hastings United folded, and therefore, despite a Ground which could have relatively easily have been improved to Football League standards, became the home venue, once again, of Hastings Town. With the demise of United, the Town in effect took their place in the Southern League, albeit in the Southern Division.

Changes and additions have continued around the Pilot Field, and by the dawn of the 21st century, although Hastings Town remained at their Ground, the latest new Club, 'St.Leonards' (formerly works team Stamco and then Stamco St. Leonards), were occupying the upper pitch, 'The Firs'. Realistically, despite the several Senior clubs that have, and still do represent the seaside towns of Hastings and St.Leonards, there would seem to be little chance of Football League representation in the near future.

HILLINGDON BOROUGH

(1970, 1971, 1972)

The former Hillingdon Borough club, in reality, was one of the least successful of the long list of Football League aspirants, yet Football League matches in fact at one time came close to being staged at the Club's Leas Stadium in Falling Lane.

Although a very old-established club, having been founded in 1872 as Yiewsley F.C., the actual later name did not come about until a century later, when it was decided to adopt the somewhat more up-market name, following the creation of the London Boroughs that now surround the Capital, in the mid 1960's - and the creation of the London Borough of Hillingdon.

Falling Lane nearly became a Football League Ground, but not with Borough as the host!

Although only playing in the First Division (the second tier) the Club finished 6th in 1965, when their opponents at this level included Hereford United and Wimbledon, before the runners-up place a year later, and promotion to the Premier Division. Three years later, when the team claimed second spot, average crowds were hovering around the 1,500 mark. But all earlier attendances were eclipsed in the F.A.Cup when they entertained Luton Town in the second round in December 1969. A massive crowd of 9,033 packed into the Falling Lane Stadium, and the minnows stunned most people with their 2-1 victory, yet they fell to fellow non-Leaguers Sutton United in the third round.

Until this time the Yiewsley club had been little more than a small town Amateur organisation located West of London, close to Heathrow Airport. Until 1919 the club played at Junior level, then they moved up to the Great Western Suburban League, but were soon back at a lower level. However, they gradually made the upward move again, and in 1945 were elected to the Spartan League.

It wasn't until they became members of the Corinthian League (in 1954) - having previously played in the Delphian - that they met with any real success. A few good years saw the Club fix its sights on the Athenian League, but when this did not come to pass, they made the extreme transition of turning professional, and were accepted into the Southern League for the 1958/59 season.

Three years earlier, there was a serious suggestion that Falling Lane would become a Football League Ground! But rather than Hillingdon Borough hosting this level football, it was to be Brentford F.C. The League club, in a financial crisis, it was reported, were intending to sell Griffin Park and move about ten miles West (the area from which much of their support came and still does) to Yiewsley. The plan never got off the Ground, but the Bees still nearly saw the end of their home, when Queens Park Rangers came close to moving in (with no place for the incumbents), in January 1967.

Meanwhile the Borough achieved perhaps their most memorable feat when they were Wembley finalists in the F.A.Trophy - in only its second season - in 1971.

Although with nothing more than a moderate performing team, the Club chose this period for their unsuccessful bids for Football League status.

In 1970, there was a rare chance for a club to join the elite, for after four successive re-election bids, Bradford (Park Avenue) were finally discarded. But Southern League Champions Cambridge United reached their peak at the right time, and comfortably achieved sufficient votes for the move upwards, and from the North, Wigan Athletic - who gained 18 votes - came second. There was no support for most of the also-rans, including Hillingdon Borough.

A year later, it was the turn of Hereford United to carry the banner of the non-League contingent, although even they had to wait another year before achieving Football League status, when they just pipped Barrow in their re-election bid but only after the voting went to a second round. On both occasions there was no place for the Middlesex side, and their bids again received no votes.

By 1973, the Southern League had embraced additional clubs such that the competition was now split into three divisions. That year the Hillingdon team could only finish below mid-table, and a year later they were rock bottom. This signalled the start of the end for the club that never really stood a chance of League status, and now had only a decade of existence left.

However, even with support now only in the mid-hundreds, the team did manage to claw their way back into the Premier Division after just one season's absence, and maintained an around mid-table final finish during the next few years. In fact, at the end of the 1978/79 season, they came very close to gaining a place in the new Alliance Premier League.

But financial gloom was now to the fore, and after a few more years of gradual slump, the Club was finally wound up in 1983.

But this was still not the final end, for a reformation under the name of plain 'Hillingdon F.C.' saw them retain their place in the Southern League, albeit the regionalised Southern Division, in effect a joint second tier. But crucially, to ensure the continuance of the Club, the Falling Lane Stadium was sold.

Two years later the season ended in near farce, for with their very survival staring them in the face, they played their last match lying second in the table, but achieved a total of only two points in this and their last two away matches, and instead of promotion celebrations, extinction was the final outcome!

The name of the club did not disappear immediately, for an amalgamation with Burnham F.C. (just West of Slough) saw the birth of 'Burnham and Hillingdon F.C.' But this was little more than a cosmetic exercise which allowed the lesser club achieve rapid 'promotion' to the Southern League. Within two years the 'Hillingdon' was dropped from the new title, and for some years the 'old' club disappeared completely.

However, the name of 'Hillingdon Borough' does appear on the football fixture lists once again, although with little or no connection to the former club, for a team of this name took over the Ground of the former 'Ruislip F.C.' in Breakspear Road (in the North of the Borough). But playing only in the Spartan South Midlands League, the chance of eventual Football League status is even more remote than that of their predecessors!

KETTERING/KETTERING TOWN

(1900, 1927-29, 1957-62, 1967, 1969, 1971, 1973-76, 1979)

Apart from Yeovil Town, there are only two other clubs that can equal the number of attempts that the Northamptonshire club made to gain election to the Football League, but neither can match this record over such a long period. Although the name was changed (in 1924 when the former Kettering F.C. became a Limited company and added the 'Town' suffix to their name), the Club was one and the same.

Of all those who have striven to gain Football League status, Kettering Town are without doubt one of the most deserving of this elevation. Their longevity at a high level, and accompanying honours - including many later appearances in the F.A.Cup - their Rockingham Road Ground which is deserving of such status, and their catchment area for support, should all one day translate to eventual 'promotion'.

Many attempts over many years, by a well 'qualified' club..... will they ever make the final goal?

Formed in 1872, it was well over twenty years (after eight years in the Midland League, which culminated in the Championship for the second time) before they reached the highest level outside the Football League itself, the Southern League, in 1900. Notably they were immediately placed in the First Division, alongside 14 other teams, all of whom bar one would eventually become members of the Football League (at this time both Brentford and Fulham languished in the Southern's Second Division).

A satisfactory first season at this level saw the Club finish below mid-table, when their first election bid was made. With few teams making the attempt around this time, they managed to receive two votes of support.

But their stay at this level lasted just three more seasons, for after finishing bottom of the table in 1904, they slipped down to the United Counties League before re-appearing in 1909 - in the split Second Division this time. After another short period, they drifted away again, before their next appearance in 1923. Being run on a very professional level from 1924, their conversion paid dividends for they soon became a leading team in the Southern League, and in 1927 they made their second bid for a higher status. Despite only four clubs staking their claim in the South Section, Torquay United were overwhelmingly favoured, and Kettering received just one vote.

The Championship of the Eastern section a year later led to their third attempt, but with a paltry two votes they surely deserved better, when only three clubs applied, especially since one aspirant - The Argonauts (who received the most votes of the non-Leaguers) - existed in name only! Despite retaining the Championship in 1929, their third successive bid for the League received virtually no support, although financially the Club could barely have afforded such a 'promotion', with home attendances often not even reaching four figures. The financial situation got worse - only 296 spectators were present at Rockingham Road for one match in the 1929/30 season - as did the team's playing record after a mass exodus of players to Crystal Place.

After this slump the inevitable happened, for the Club had to opt for a lower level from 1930, and did not make another appearance in the Southern League until 1950. A few years of consolidation was followed by the Club's best, to date, season of 1956/57.

Their success, the Championship of the, by now, single division by eight clear points, was almost inevitable with the appointment of Tommy Lawton as player/manager, who signed on a number of prominent professionals to aid him. Despite this achievement, the Club's plea for Football League status fell upon deaf ears, for only the rapidly improving Peterborough United captured any real support (only seven votes), whilst Kettering and four others received none.

The departure of the charismatic Lawton (to Notts County) after just one season soon led to a decline in the Club's fortunes, and just three seasons later they finished bottom of the Premier Division although they immediately bounced back again, and the early 1960's were moderately successful. Although not the best of times to continue their quest for Football League status, especially since this period heralded an unprecedented number of hopefuls, Kettering Town continued to make their bids, and not surprisingly were rebuked on every occasion from 1958 to 1962, receiving just one vote each year, and none at their last attempt.

Several somewhat lean seasons followed, including relegation to the Southern League First Division and the next election attempt was not made until 1967. However, even this was futile for apart from finishing in fifth place in the table - of the lower division - there was not the slightest chance with so many others clamouring for a place. Kettering received no votes. Promotion a year later, and a good run in the F.A.Cup one season on plus a creditable 9th in the Premier Division, was sufficient for the Club to try their luck yet again. Whilst coming nowhere near gaining a place in the Football League, some encouragement must have been gained with their three votes and coming second from top of the non-League contingent.

Somewhat ludicrously their next try was two years later, when they finished second from bottom in the Division and were once again relegated - it surely came as no surprise when they had no support at the re-election meeting. After so many years of trying the Club at last were on the verge of a short successful period, and for once stood a real chance of elevation.

Promoted back to the Premier Division in 1972, they capped this with the overall Championship a year later. At last they made a real inroad with a total of 12 votes at the election meeting, just two less than Yeovil, but still woefully short of the number claimed by the four re-election candidates. A year later and Kettering Town came the closest ever to Football League recognition. Workington had consistently struggled in the Fourth Division, and were making their second consecutive re-election application. Many felt that enough was enough, but in the virtual closed shop that existed within the Football League around this time they were given yet another chance. Polling 28 votes, the Cumbrians clung on, having obtained just eight more than Kettering.

After a somewhat poor, below mid-table, finish and a worsening financial situation at the Club, another attempt was made at the League, and although they slipped to second in the pecking order (Workington still managed to hang on!), 14 votes was perhaps more than could reasonably have been expected. Financial constraints were probably the reason for no more attempts during the next few years despite their generally good playing record. At last, in 1979, one last try was made. The runners-up spot in the Southern League provided the credentials, and with only one club each from the North and South in competition, this should, perhaps, have the best chance. But unfortunately - for Kettering - the four re-election candidates really did deserve another chance, and the Club received just 12 votes (Altrincham managed one more), whilst Halifax Town were comfortably re-elected with 37.

This is really where the story ends. Members of the Alliance Premier League from its inception the following year (1979) meant that in most years only the Champion-winning team would be seeking election. Kettering Town have never quite made it, although four runners-up finishes illustrates how close they have come. With crowds hovering around the 2,000 mark, and 5,000 plus for the local derby with Rushden and Diamonds in the 1998/99 season shows that if the occasions demands it a winning team could command support.

KINGS LYNN

(1956-1962)

With little serious competition, football-wise, in this part of the Country it could be argued that Norfolk deserves another Football League club. Handily placed to the west of Norwich (the County's only League representative), and East of Peterborough, the only other town of reasonable size is nearby Wisbech. Whilst the population of the town itself is around 40,000, it is a relatively barren area for additional support; the situation is not unlike that of Scarborough, and although that club survived a number of years in the League, attendances were never great.

The Club was founded as Lynn Town in 1879, and for many years were a strong Amateur side, reaching the F.A.Amateur Cup Final in 1901. They were founder-members of the Eastern Counties League, in 1935, but after the Second World War and briefly flirting with other Midland competitions they returned in 1948. Real success at last came at the end of the 1953/54 season when they won both the Championship and League Cup, which signalled the desire to move upwards.

Unfortunately the town is not ideally situated, being neither in the South and too far East to be considered as being in the Midlands. However, they chose, and were accepted into the Midland League for the 1954/55 season, and after four moderately successful years they became members of the enlarged Southern League from 1958.

By this time the Club were already in the middle of their run of Football League application bids. The first attempt was made in 1956, although there appears to have been no particular reason or indeed any chance at this time. Nearby Peterborough United were coming into their stride and beginning to pick up worthwhile votes, and in addition the likes of Bedford Town and Chelmsford City - all broadly in the East Anglia region - had reasonable hopes.

Finishing fifth in the Midland League, a clear 19 points behind the all-conquering Peterborough, they clearly stood no chance at the election meeting, and accordingly received no votes. Although finishing way down the table a year later (just within the top half, at 11th), the Club again tried their luck, and despite only seven teams making a bid in the Southern Section (with neighbours Norwich City having the indignity of applying for re-election), again no votes were cast in Lynn's favour.

Room for another representative from Norfolk - but would support be sufficient?

In 1958, King's Lynn fought back to finish 6th in the League, although this time 24 points behind Champions Peterborough. With the formation of the Fourth Division there was no regional split in the voting, and with 12 clubs countrywide applying, it was somewhat surprising that the Norfolk team actually managed to receive two votes.

The Club's venture into the Southern League was reasonably successful, but a final finish of seventh in the regionalised table, hardly merited a further Football League application, especially when it is considered that several clubs placed much higher were not even seriously considered. However, by virtue of their top half of the table finish, the Club were placed in the new Premier Division of the Southern League for the 1959/60 season, and were now to play in the strongest competition outside the League itself.

A very respectable 8th final position in the table counted for little when it came to the election voting, for the Club once again received no support.

A mid-table finish a year later did little to enhance the Club's chances for their sixth assault on the League, especially as the 'new' Oxford United had taken over as election favourites after Peterborough had at last achieved their deserved admittance (at the expense of Gateshead), which left few votes for the also-rans; King's Lynn, with two others, received no votes. At the end of the 1961/62 season, the Club made their seventh (and final) consecutive attempt.

A poor season in the Southern League was only counteracted by an excellent F.A.Cup run, which also no doubt gave them the encouragement to try again. Chelmsford City, and more notably Coventry City were both beaten 2-1 on their own grounds in the first two rounds, which led to a money-spinning visit to Everton. Their £4,341 share of the 45,000 gate at Goodison Park (which included around 1,000 from Norfolk) represented unprecedented riches for the Club, allowing them to clear their debts and clear the remaining mortgages left on the Club's houses.

A 4-0 defeat resulted in the team having to come to terms with their league match performances, which were not helped in their next match, a 3-2 home loss to high-flying Bath City. The attendance was an encouraging 1,779, but less encouraging was the team's drop to bottom of the table (in contrast the Reserves, at this time, were top of the Eastern Counties League). Perhaps to boost spirits, an official announcement from the Club was made in early March that: *"Though the threat of relegation still casts a shadow over the club, the board have very much in their minds the prospect of League football for Lynn."*

With talk of an extension of the Football League for the following season, there was to be a record number of applications in 1962, and Kings Lynn - after their repeated attempts - felt they must stand a good chance of success this time.

"We have good facilities, are financially sound, have good gate potential, even if they are low at present", a spokesman said. On the subject of floodlighting (which the Club did not have), the Club's official line was a little off track: *"The novelty of floodlighting is past, and under present conditions we can do as well without it,"* then a little more realistically, *"but in League football it would be a great asset."*

The team recovered for a while then slipped back again to leave them second from bottom by late March. The Cup run had left the team with a fixture pile-up, which required 12 games to be played in 27 days. But a reasonable run was not enough to prevent relegation, and the last home game, a 3-2 victory over Tonbridge, drew an equally depressing gate of only 882.

Despite the prospect of lower division football the next season, the Club announced they would be employing full-time players (as were Cambridge City, Chelmsford City and Oxford United). On 22nd May, the Club announced that they would be, *"making an application for League status and have circularised the chairman of the clubs in the hope that we may be considered fully capable of meeting all the requirements that are necessary for the Fourth Division."*

The club's credentials were spelt out: Facilities at the ground are the finest in non-League football, full-time playing staff, plans for floodlighting, no Bank overdraft, and geographically well placed (Peterborough 35 miles distant, Norwich 45 miles). A population catchment within a 16 mile radius of 125,000 was claimed, and this was expected to rise by 10,000 in the next two or three years. Such impressive claims convinced just one voting member at the election meeting!

Despite their credentials, it is only a winning team that can claim the pot of gold. Since the early 1960's, Kings Lynn's record has been far from impressive, but who knows, instead of seven annual attempts - and virtually no support - a good run, and one final Championship could just clinch a place for the Linnets one day.

LANCASTER TOWN

(1921)

The Club was formed in 1902, as plain Lancaster, the name they bore until 1910, after which time they added 'Town' to their title. Playing at their unusually named 'Giant Axe' Ground, they were admitted to the Lancashire Combination (Second Division) in 1905, the competition they remained within until 1970.

The first few years in the Combination - the First Division of which was, around this time, the strongest non-League competition in the North-west - were moderate ones. Yet despite a far from disastrous final place of 14th of 20 in 1910, the Club's name did not appear in the Combination the following season, but when it did - in 1911, it was as Lancaster Town. Presumably the return was as a reformed club, but the regrouping hardly led to immediate success, for two dreadful seasons followed, when the team finished bottom of the table on both occasions, and was lucky to retain its place in the Second Division.

A moderate recovery was made in the 1913/14 season, and the transformation was complete a year later when they took the runners-up spot behind Rochdale Reserves, who claimed one more point. Unfortunately the Club was denied the chance of automatic promotion, for the Great War intervened, and for the next four years only subsidiary Wartime competitions were played.

However a team by the name of 'Lancaster United' (probably the nucleus of the 'Town' side) were highly successful in the 1918/19 season, taking the title of the 'Auxiliary' competition.

Having missed out eighty years ago, the chances today of making it to the League are very slim.

With the post-War demise of the Second Division, Lancaster Town were in any event 'promoted' to the First Division of the Lancashire Combination, and proved themselves to be worthy members, with the Runners-up spot in 1920, and 5th a year later. With the extension of the Football League for the coming 1921/22 season, the chances of election looked quite favourable for the team that had come good at the right time.

By mid-March, the team lay 8th in the Combination, and with healthy crowds, including over 5,000 (a gate of £210) present for the visit of Dick Kerrs from Preston. Another game around this time also *"attracted a big crowd"*, but this was a Ladies match, and one suspects a degree of voyeurism was the attraction as it was reported that the large number was due to, *"the novelty of seeing a number of girls in knickers"* !

Lancaster Town had been undefeated for 12 matches when they entertained Leyland on Good Friday, but lost the game 5-3, and dropped to 5th. The match receipts amounted to £153, a far cry from ten years earlier when these rarely exceeded £10. With only two defeats since New Year's day, the curtain came down on the season at home to Beccles United, which was drawn.

In preparation for their assault on the Football League, the suggestion of becoming a Limited Company the previous November was finally ratified at a special meeting at the YMCA Rooms on the 3rd March. At the meeting it was announced that, *"an effort is to be made to secure admission to the newly formed Third Division (North)"*.

The Club had been well supported since Christmas, and this gave them confidence for their application, but more money was needed, and of the required £500 quoted, £150 was raised at the meeting.

The Club's representatives travelled down to London a few days later for the 7th March election meeting in what must have been an optimistic frame of mind, with no less than 20 new places in the Football League up for grabs. Fourteen clubs already had their places booked, including Accrington Stanley, who had finished one place below Lancaster in the Combination! Lancaster, although admittedly not having much of a prolonged track record, could argue that they were well supported (better than Stanley), were favourably located and had a reasonable Ground (with serious intentions to improve it) - whilst Accrington were surrounded by other Football League clubs and, in Peel Park, had at this time, one of the worst grounds of the newcomers.

But Lancaster Town were all but shunned at the Election Meeting with an almost derisory three votes in their favour, whereas the almost unknown Castleford Town came close to being accepted, albeit from a 'political' standpoint rather than from their footballing ability! It must have been a dejected Lancaster Town party that returned North that day.

Yet by the start of the 1921/22 season steps were being taken to make their case stronger, with the announcement of the intention to enlarge the small Stand, complete with cover, and the taking out of a five year lease on the Giant Axe Ground, rather than the Annual arrangement that had previously been made.

The season was highly successful for the Club not only became Champions of the Lancashire Combination, three points clear of runners-up Chorley, but also completed the double with their League Cup Final victory. Just to emphasise their prowess at this time, a year later the top and second positions were reversed. Yet surprisingly the Club made no further application for membership of the Football League, whereas New Brighton, who finished third in the Combination in 1922, made a bid and received seven votes of support.

Perhaps it was financial considerations that held them back, and as several indifferent seasons followed they may well have not been up to the task in any event. The Club soon fought back and became a prominent Combination team in the late 1920's and early 30's, before changing the suffix in their name to 'City' in 1937. Since those heady days, Lancaster City have continued at a reasonably high level, keeping their place in the Lancashire Combination until 1970, when they joined the Northern Premier League. For a few years the standard then dropped and the Club were demoted to the North-West Counties League, but they regained membership of the Northern Premier in 1987.

Lancaster is an interesting old town that has maintained an 'olde world' appearance, with even some cobbled streets still remaining. Unfortunately in keeping with this atmosphere, the football ground also shows signs of old age, and although only two theoretical steps away from the Football League, the Giant Axe would have to undergo giant improvements for acceptance.

LIVERPOOL CALEDONIANS

(1892)

This club's solitary effort for Football League membership was one of the most bizarre, and the circumstances provide some unusual facts. Without doubt their application was so relatively obscure, that the facts set out here would appear to be the only acknowledgement given to the club, since other relevant references appear to have ignored them entirely!

Look in any reference book, and no record of membership of any league will be found, quite simply because at the time of the election meeting the club had never played a match, and even after their rejection they had only one part season of playing experience before they folded and their record was expunged!

Caledonians were given the chance, when Liverpool F.C. weren't good enough!

Until the early 1890's, football in Liverpool was dominated by two clubs, Everton and Bootle. One hardly has to relate the career of Everton, their history having been well documented, suffice to say that the club were founder-members of the League in 1888, and during their long history have never had to seek re-election. The history of Bootle F.C. has obviously not been so well publicised, and details of their career as a member of the Football League will only be known to the serious football historian. However, around 1890, they were a force to be reckoned with and for a time vied with Everton for football dominance in Liverpool. Their ability was recognised when they were elected to the League, in 1892.

1892, was a very significant year for the Football League as a whole, for it signalled the first major change in the set-up with the formation of the Second Division and hence the doubling of numbers of clubs in the competition.

The year was also significant for football in the City of Liverpool, when big changes and big ideas abounded. Everton F.C. had been in dispute with their President, Mr.Houlding, who owned the Sandon Hotel (the club's headquarters at this time) and also owned the concession rights for the refreshments at Anfield. The Club decided to move away from their 'home', and they set up shop - across the other side of Stanley Park - to Goodison Park - which soon became regarded as arguably the best Ground in the country.

Meanwhile, Bootle F.C. (founded in 1878, a year earlier than Everton) were at this time playing their home matches at the Cricket Ground in Hawthorne Road. The two leading teams were in opposition as early as 1880, and although of equal ability in the early years, by 1885, Everton were gaining the upper hand, especially for support, and this was emphasized when the latter became founder-members of the Football League in 1888.

But Liverpool was a big city, and quite big enough to sustain two leading clubs (as history will confirm), and four years later, Bootle were on the brink of the big time with their own admission to the Second Division.

With Everton removed, Anfield became unoccupied, and Mr. Houlding - no doubt principally in a show of pique - decided to form his own football team. And so Liverpool F.C. was born. But this all came about within a very short time, and almost on formation (in 1892) the club applied for admission to the First Division of the Football League.

With no track record whatsoever, it is little surprise that at the Football League meeting on the 11th May at the Queen's Hotel, Fawcett Street, Sunderland, the Liverpool F.C. postal bid (most of the other aspiring clubs sent representatives), was not even considered, although it is most likely that this decision was influenced by Everton F.C.! Liverpool had not considered applying for the new Second Division, and instead satisfied themselves with membership of the Lancashire League for the 1892/93 season. Elected to the League the following year, the rest is history as they say.

There was mention of a 'Liverpool Association' (football club) back in 1880, who significantly played the first game at their new ground at Wavertree on 1st October 1881 - against Bootle, and lost 1-0. Although the almost complete absence of fixtures between the Association club and other top teams from the area suggests they were not a very high profile club, it was at the probable same venue that the later Liverpool Caledonians played their home games. Liverpool Caledonians were formed in 1891, from a group of exiled Scotsmen, in much the same way as their counterparts, London Caledonians, who were formed in 1886.

The Liverpool club immediately set themselves up as a professional organisation, becoming a Limited Company from the outset, and during their first season, 1891/92, entered the Liverpool Senior Shield - which they won - and the Liverpool Senior Cup, where they reached the Semi-Finals. Their fixtures that season included Friendly encounters with Cowlairs and Airdrieonians - inevitably from Scotland - plus Southport Central (two games during April in the two Liverpool competitions).

The Club played their home games at Woodcroft Park, Wavertree, and like the new Liverpool F.C. they only applied in writing for membership of the Football League, in 1892. Also like their neighbours they were turned down, although one suspects not so conclusively, for they were allowed to try for the new Second Division. However, with no track record, unlike the other 12 applicants - and again without a vote being taken - they were the unlucky 13th candidate.

Not deterred, they did gain admittance to the Lancashire League, and from the 3rd September played seven matches of which three were won, and two drawn, albeit only a single fixture was played away. Reasonably good crowds heralded the new team's arrival with 2,500 present for the second match (versus Blackpool) and 5,000 when Fairfield were the visitors in November. A good run in the F.A.Cup was enjoyed, notably three victories - 7-1 versus Wrexham, 3-2 over Bootle and the same score at home against Chester. Support appears to have drastically collapsed, as the latter match attracted only some 1,000. Despite an enthusiastic campaign to attract the crowds for the 4th qualifying game - at home to Northwich Victoria - a match billed as *"The Event Of The Season"*, by *"The Club of Great Promise"* (neither of which materialised), a 3-2 defeat ensued.

This was destined to be the Caledonians last match, for shortly after they went into liquidation, following a brief life which had seen the Club try to grow too big and too quick. Their Lancashire League record was removed, and the only official results that season of this very shortlived club that remain, relates to their mini F.A.Cup run.

LLANELLY

(1922, 1923, 1929-1933, 1947, 1950, 1951)

This club from South Wales was one of a group of teams from the principality who made unsuccessful bids for the English League in the boom days of Welsh football in the early 1920's. However, unlike their compatriots, their bids continued during two further periods, at times when they could well have joined in competition with the likes of Cardiff, Swansea and Newport County.

The Club has been recorded as being founded in 1896, however, at the meeting of the South Wales League in Cardiff on the 5th June 1893, when it was agreed to form the South Wales and Monmouthshire F.A., one of the elected vice-presidents for the new organisation was a Mr. Buckley, from Llanelly!

Despite sustained pre-War bids, and three during the post-War period, did the club ever stand a realistic chance?

One of the fourteen clubs who joined this new F.A. was Llanelly, therefore a club certainly existed in the town at that time, which may have been a shortlived forerunner. In any event, Llanelly were not amongst the very first surge of Clubs in South Wales that first challenged the power of Rugby which had been dominant from about 1870. As early as 1890, saw the first season of the 12 team South Wales League, and notably Llanelly were not members. In fact it would appear that the Club did not come to any sort of prominence until their election to the Southern League Second Division in 1912.

By this time football had really taken off in South Wales (the North was a different story where the round ball version of the game had always been the more dominant), and Llanelly were one of ten teams from Wales within the 13 club league.

Their debut was greeted enthusiastically by the locals when a crowd of 6,000 turned up at Halfway Park (where they played until 1923) on the 14th September. Unfortunately for the majority present, it is was a bad day, as the homesters lost 3-1 to Croydon Common, and they were also defeated in the return match in London a week later. But overall a successful start was made with a final mid-table position, which was repeated in both of the following two years.

After the enforced four year break due to the First World War, Llanelly returned to the Southern League and recorded a good finish of third in 1920, but a disappointing third from bottom the following year. In 1919, the Second Division had become effectively the Welsh Section of the League, and for no obvious reason (although economics was the norm), the Club decided to field just a team in the independent Welsh League for the 1921/22 season.

It was at the end of this season that the Club made the somewhat strange decision to first apply for Football League membership. Strange since Cardiff City, Newport County, Merthyr Town and Swansea Town became members in 1920, followed by Aberdare Athletic a year later, and slightly more prominent clubs Abertillery and Pontypridd had already tried their luck (the latter in 1922 in fact coming close to success). There really was no room for any more South Wales clubs, especially as the economic situation was already beginning to bite, and consequently Llanelly received no votes.

Although there was an extra club trying their luck in 1923, Llanelly actually received nine votes, one more than Pontypridd. But by now the local industrial situation, and in particular coalmining, had worsened further, and the professional Welsh clubs, both in the Football and the Southern Leagues were really struggling badly. Sensibly Llanelly held back from further applications for some years, having during the interim returned to the more diverse Western Section of the Southern League for two seasons, before probably fading away from Senior football (or indeed possibly closing down).

In 1929, they received no votes, and after yet another try with the Southern League the following season, they surprisingly gained four supporters from the League, albeit it had been a poor campaign in this competition which saw them finish third from bottom in their section. However they did win the Welsh League 'double' (Championship and Cup) which had never been accomplished before, and they were confident that attendances could increase, with a catchment of around 300,000 within a 12 mile radius of the town.

The Club decided to field a team in two sections of the Southern League in the 1933/34 season, and during the early part of the decade, slightly better performances transpired. Then they decided on playing in just the Welsh League once again from 1934! The Club's roller coaster ride both in the competitions they entered and their Football League applications then took another strange twist, for after receiving no votes in 1931, they came close to election a year later with an incredible 25.

It would seem that if only they could have put together a consistent run of good seasons, and preferably in the Southern League, there were plenty of clubs in the Football League that would have been willing to support them.

The last attempt for some years was made in 1933, and after having won the Welsh League for the second time, they received 20 votes, only six less than Newport County who managed to retain their place with the elite.

Llanelly's next attempt at the League was in 1947, when a host of clubs were all denied even the satisfaction of a vote, for the four incumbents of the North and South Divisions for re-election were given another chance. In 1950 there were four places up for grabs with the extension of the Football League about to start, and Llanelly were one of the many hopefuls.

But their bid was a forlorn one as they received not even one vote for their effort, and in any event - although their application was considered - the fact that the ground was also used for Greyhound Racing, was frowned upon. A year later, their last attempt, produced the same result, although the Club had re-entered the Southern League, and in fact had enjoyed a successful season which saw them finish in fifth place, amongst some high ranking opposition.

The end of the 1951/52 season saw the team slump to third from bottom in the final table, and after no fewer than ten unsuccessful bids for recognition, they decided enough was enough, and their name was never again amongst the re-election hopefuls. After a period of generally poor seasons, Llanelly returned to the Welsh League in 1957, and even at this level they have only occasionally given their supporters something to cheer about. However, talk of Football League membership can never again be an option for Llanelli (they chose to adopt the Welsh spelling in the 1970's), or indeed any other Welsh League clubs after the ruling of the Welsh F.A. which came about, not without its critics, in 1992!

LOVELL'S ATHLETIC

(1948)

Within the 100 year plus history of Football League elections, involving around eighty clubs that unsuccessfully applied, and the 100 plus clubs that made it at some time, Lovell's Athletic are unique. For the club from Newport in South Wales, are the only works team that ever made the attempt (ignoring the claim that Prescot Cables F.C. could make). Works' teams in senior football are not unknown, although those at a high level are somewhat thin on the ground. A.P. (or Lockheed) Leamington of the Alliance Premier was one, and Sankey's (Wellington) who played in the Cheshire another, although at lower levels there have been plenty. Lovell's claims for the limelight went further than making their single application, for a few years earlier, it could be argued, they actually played in the League for several seasons!

The Toffee-men were unique in the annals of clubs making an application to join the League.

The Club was formed towards the end of the boom period of Welsh football, in 1918, and came from the Manufacturing Confectioners factory of G.F.Lovell and Company, makers of the famous (well at one time), 'Toffee Rex', 'The King of Toffees' as they became known. The club started at a purely amateur level in the Rexville district of Newport, Monmouthshire. Founded by the company owner, Mr.George F.Lovell, his son, Harold, played in the team's first ever match, but a tragic injury resulted in this also being his last ever game, although he was to become a prominent figure in Welsh football circles.

Starting at a local level, Lovell's soon became a powerful force and in 1923 were admitted to the part-professional Western League, becoming Champions at their first attempt.

Even more dramatic was their acceptance into the Southern League (Western Section) in 1928, and they competed well, but two years later they resigned, and opted, amazingly, for the London Combination. Just two unsuccessful seasons were spent in this 'foreign' competition, for the Western League was by now again preferred, and the first team also competed in the Welsh League around this period.

When War was declared in September 1939, the Southern League ran a Wartime competition, in which Lovell's were invited to enter, and where they promptly became Champions of the eight team Western Section, overcoming the likes of Worcester City, Hereford United and Cheltenham Town.

Newport County (new members of the peacetime Second Division) ceased to play after one War-time season, and near neighbours Lovell's Athletic - never the best of supported clubs at their level - not only enhanced their playing staff with some of the County players 'guesting' for them, but were also able to attract bigger crowds to their fairly basic Ground which was directly opposite the parent company factory.

Reminiscent of a fiction novel the improbable continued after two seasons (in the Western Regional League), when the Club was invited to join the Football League (West) for the 1942/43 season. The fairytale continued with the works team becoming Champions over the likes of Second Division Swansea Town, plus Cardiff City and Bristol City! *"Rexville is the home of first class football in Newport, with many games with notable teams. A remarkably successful season"*, the local Press proudly proclaimed.

The team also comfortably qualified for the final rounds of the League Cup, where they finished on a par with Liverpool and well above Manchester United! A year later the situation was similar with them topping the local League table again, and once more playing in the final rounds of the League Cup. The third season of this astonishing period saw the team only finish third in their six team league.

In common with virtually every club, Lovell's support was inevitably poor at this time, and Harold Lovell dipped deep into his pocket to ensure that the Club should carry on. The home games with Cardiff City usually guaranteed rare good attendances, normally between 5,000 and 7,000, but in March 1945, for a League Cup match, the record crowd for a match at Rexville was vastly exceeded when an estimated 10,000 crammed into the little enclosure.

The situation was summed up graphically by a local reporter: "*A packed ground, rosetted spectators, the crowds breaking through the touchline fences, a player collapsing insensitive in the last minute, the police calling for a loudspeaker van to guide home the crowd - all this was not a dream of pre-war cup-ties but what happened at Rexville where Lovell's Athletic beat Cardiff City 1-0 in the War Cup qualifying competition. How is it done then? Guest players? Partly, but mainly because Lovell's handle a football team with a spirit and experience unique for a non-League club.*"

For years Lovell's Athletic had achieved unprecedented fame. They had fought with, and had often come out on top of established Football League clubs, albeit in the somewhat surreal world of Wartime football. But with near normality returning in 1945, the Football League clubs regrouped and played in their own near normal divisional groupings. The fairytale had come to an end for the Newport works club, and now with the guest players, as well as their elite opponents gone, they made the drop down to the Welsh League for the 1945/46 season.

But the glory days were not quite over, for in the two-legged first round F.A.Cup-tie that season, Bournemouth were thrashed 4-1 at Rexville (although the Welshmen were defeated 3-2 on the South coast), and then after beating Bath City, they met Wolverhampton Wanderers in the third round.

Another crowd of around 10,000 was present for Billy Wright, et al, but the bubble burst at this time with a 4-2 defeat, even then it was only after the homesters had first taken a two goal lead (however, the second leg ran true to form with an 8-1 defeat).

There was no stopping Lovell's in the Welsh League for two seasons, and it came as no real surprise when they took their place in the Southern League again for the 1947/48 season. But Newport County were of course back in business again, and therefore the mighty Lovell's Athletic had to once again don the mantle of 'the little non-League club'.

Even so at the season's end the team finished a very creditable sixth. Fed on exotic fare during the War years, and wanting more, the time had now come when the Club made their unique bid for Football League status. Perhaps it was their past record that let the powers-that-be allow Lovell's to apply for election, although if the unimaginable had happened and they had achieved the necessary votes, the Football League would hardly have been willing to allow a mere Works team to join the elite! The situation never arose, for the Club, along with most of the other hopefuls, received not one vote.

Although the Club held onto their Southern League status until 1959, with little support, they were at that time forced to rejoin the Welsh League. Eventually, in 1969, the football team folded, and there were only the memories left by those who had witnessed the halcyon 'Football League' days.

MANCHESTER CENTRAL

(1929, 1930, 1931)

There is little doubt that the City of Manchester is big enough - both geographically and from a population standpoint - to support more than two Football League clubs. Although it can be argued to what extent does greater Manchester truly extend, for Bolton Wanderers, Stockport County, Oldham Athletic, Bury and Rochdale, have all been long-term members, although ask supporters of those clubs and they would probably not wish to be considered as being fans of a 'Manchester based' club!

Despite, being England's third City, Manchester was somewhat slow in adopting football in a big way, especially as the earlier development of the sport started on their doorstep, around the Bolton area. There were of course many football clubs in the area during the early days around the 1870's, but the Manchester pair, United and City, were not formed until 1878 and 1880 respectively and it was to be some years before they became prominent.

United (as Newton Heath) joined the League in 1892, and City (as Ardwick) became members a year later. But it was to be some years before any real success came to either team, and no other club from the City, or its immediate surrounds, made an approach to join for many years.

Even when another Manchester based club applied, it was not a recognised and well established outfit, but one which suddenly appeared and at a Senior non-League level (and after three attempts were to disappear as quickly).

From nowhere, Manchester Central burst upon the scene when they were accepted within the Lancashire Combination for the 1928/29 season. There is little doubt that the Club was formed with big ideas in mind right from the outset, and as a home base they used one of the two stadiums at Belle Vue. This was a large venue, albeit probably better suited for speedway racing for which it was also used, with a curved roofed enclosure around most of the oval perimeter. The Stadium was set within the Zoological Gardens - a vast outdoor entertainment centre, with funfair, exhibition halls, and a zoo, etc. - not unlike the Crystal Palace, at this time, in South London.

A good record, good gates, and a good Ground... but not good enough for the League!

The Stadium was situated just to the East of the centre of Manchester in the Gorton area and notably Manchester United's Old Trafford Ground was about five miles to the West whilst the Maine Road base of City was even closer, being about three miles South-west.

Whilst it may seem ludicrous to think today that a new, ambitious, non-League club would pose a threat to either United or City now, in the late 1920's there was a danger that the newcomers would prise away some of the support for the established pair were far from the dominant forces they are now. United had finished well down in the First Division in 1928, whilst City had just been promoted after a couple of seasons in the Second. Admittedly the pair were two of the best supported clubs in the country, but evidently there was still the perceived risk that some football fans may be enticed to drift East to Belle Vue.

Central's first season was moderately successful for they finished 7th in the 20 team Lancashire Combination, only five points below runners-up Horwich R.M.I. Within a year of entering Senior football, the Club decided to make a bid for Football league status. It came as no real surprise when the Club was rejected, attracting just two votes, albeit Chester, Rhyl and Workington all received none. Just a few miles away, fellow Combination club Prescot Cables - who during Central's short life became their main rivals - had also made a bid but they received just one vote. It was the Prescot team that halted the Central's progress in the Lancashire Junior Cup. Another team, who played in the Harpurhey area a few miles North of Belle Vue, was Manchester North End, who were well supported and could command crowds of over 3,000 for their Cheshire County League matches.

For the 1929/30 season, the Club's reserves were admitted into the Cheshire County League. This situation emphasizes the ambition and respect that Manchester Central were already able to command, for the only other second teams playing in this strong competition - which to many was on a par with the Lancashire Combination itself - were those of Football League clubs.

The season was a very successful one for the Club for they finished as runners-up in the Combination, just one point behind Champions Lancaster Town. The F.A.Cup was entered for the first time, and after a good 2-0 victory at Mansfield Town, they only lost 1-0 at home to Wrexham in the second round. The latter match attracted a big crowd of 8,500 to the Belle Vue Stadium, almost certainly a record figure.

The Club made their second bid for League status, and after such a good year (and being run on such professional lines for they were a Limited Company), their chance of success was considered to be very good , and it was reported that they *"anticipated good support."* But this optimism - repeated over many years in all parts of the country by countless teams - was shattered when the Central managed to claim only 13 votes.

There were only two other rivals for support, neighbours Prescot who were rejected with no votes, and (ironically) Mansfield Town who received 15 and were accepted a year later - but to the Southern section of the Third Division!

Central faltered somewhat during the 1930/31 season and could only finish well down the Combination table at ninth, whilst the Reserve team had a torrid time, finishing seven points clear at the bottom of the Cheshire County League, after conceding 140 goals in 42 games! Such records were hardly impressive for another application for 'promotion', but one was made, and the Club failed dismally, with only four votes. Nelson were voted out and deservedly Chester took their place. But notably Wigan Borough - founder-members of the Northern section - although apparently safely placed in the table, were having severe financial problems. With pathetically low home attendances (just 600 for the last game of the season) this had resulted in the selling off of all their good players.

After such a poor overall season, Manchester Central decided to cut their losses, and withdrew from the Lancashire Combination, opting to play their first team in the Cheshire League and the reserves in the more locally based Manchester League. Wigan Borough threw in the towel on the 26th October 1931 and became the first club ever to resign mid-season from the Football League.

Manchester Central immediately stepped in and offered to take over Wigan's fixtures, but aided by the objections from both Manchester United and City (they obviously perceived a threat from these local upstarts), the option was not taken up.

This proved to be the Club's last bid for League membership, for although finishing in a respectable 5th in the Cheshire League they realised that any attempt would be futile. In fact at the end of the season, the Club resigned from the Cheshire League, and they disappeared as quickly as they had appeared, never to be seen again.

MID-RHONDDA

(1925)

Look for 'Mid-Rhondda' on any map and you will find no town of that name, for the football club bearing this title was based in the town of Tonypandy. Laying in the Rhondda valley, just to the West of Pontypridd, Tonypandy was host to one of several clubs in this area of South Wales that made attempts to join the Football League, most of whom not only failed but were soon to fold after their abortive efforts. Aberdare and Merthyr were the only two that made it to the League (for a few seasons), whilst for the likes of Mid-Rhondda there really was never a chance.

Fairly detailed accounts referred to regarding the Club's progress (or more accurately lack of it!), reveal some elements of similar problems that were no doubt encountered by the other clubs in South Wales that floundered. In this light it is quite amazing that any attempt should have been made by Mid-Rhondda to join the Football League when they could barely exist in the Southern or even the Welsh League.

Founded in 1912, the Club incredibly played their first game within one week of formation; springing up so fast, this lead to their nickname - 'The Mushrooms'! The home Ground (which has been demolished and is now a Car Auction site) lay alongside Primrose Street in Tonypandy and was previously used by the Mid-Rhondda Rugby Club in 1908, who played in the Rugby League but for only one season. Earlier that year, The Athletic Ground had hosted the first ever Wales versus England match under Rugby League rules, when 12,000 packed into the large oval shaped enclosure which had just one small covered Stand.

One of several clubs in this area of South Wales, that made an attempt, but failed dismally.

The football Club were immediately admitted to the Southern League, playing their first match at Newport County, and they finished just below mid-table in the Second Division.

But two years later they had dropped to second from bottom, suffering one defeat by 8-0 at the hands of Stoke (formerly and later of the Football League). After the long break due to the First World War, the team hit back with a vengeance, winning both the Welsh and the Southern League Second Division titles; in the latter they were undefeated, with much of the credit accorded to former Aston Villa player, Secretary/ Manager Haydn Price.

That season was undoubtably the Club's best, and support was good, including a stagger-ing crowd of around 20,000 for the F.A.Cup match versus Ton Pentre. However, it soon became a financial struggle, not helped by coal strikes in 1921, and for the following season the club had to pay £140 for the rent of the Ground, and an enormous expected outlay of £1,200 on wages. The Club already had an overdraft, and £1,500 was required to complete work on a new Stand. During the Summer an appeal for funds was made, which was especially aimed at younger supporters.

With no automatic promotion the Club continued in the two leagues, and in the Southern they slipped down to 5th place, due in part to the loss of several disgruntled players, which came to a head when one, Egerton, successfully sued the Club for unpaid wages.

The expected home gates of £200 were not being realised, especially as the coalmining industrial problems worsened, and for one match in April free admission was allowed for a Welsh League match. The club resigned from the Southern League in 1921, and in November the Club was suspended by the F.A. of Wales while their financial records were investigated. Eventually they were allowed to continue playing, but only after a new board of directors was appointed and a guarantee of £1,000 was given to the F.A.

The financial plight was revealed at a public meeting on the 21st November when a dire story was told. The 1919/20 season had shown a loss of £98 which increased to £2,831 a year later, and to that date there was an additional shortfall of £450. The new Grandstand had cost £2,500, which was being paid by installments, and the top home gates of around £160 only equalled the players wages! On February 11th, the Club went into voluntary liquidation. In April 1921, Haydn Price was accused of not handing over to the Club the full transfer fee received from Grimsby Town for a player, and he was also summoned to Court for non-payment of £66 for goods acquired from a local Sports Outfitter.

In June 1922, Mid-Rhondda F.C. was allowed by the F.A. of Wales to reform, but they were too late to apply to rejoin the Southern League, and Welsh League fixtures and Friendly matches had to suffice. This caused immediate financial problems due to poor home attendances, which were not helped by non-paying spectators viewing from the adjacent railway embankment. The Club were not re-admitted to the Southern League, in the 20 strong Western Division, until the 1924/25 season, when they performed well to finish 5th. Yet despite being in a far from secure financial position - with economies which included making players travel long distances to fixtures and back in the same day - they applied for election to the Football League.

It must surely have been expected by everybody (except presumably by the Club's Directors) that they would fail. Despite being the only candidate for the Southern Section they received not one single vote.

The Club, and the problems, continued, and during the A.G.M. in the summer it was revealed that further financial irregularities were suspected, and so another F.A. investigation was started. By April 1926, £113 was owing in players wages, and it was revealed that £150 was needed urgently in order for the Club to finish their fixtures.

Appeals were launched and a benefit match was played (which raised less than a quarter hoped for), but the Club nonetheless survived. Just! For the 1926/27 season - with the worsening coalmining situation - much revenue was lost from subscriptions from miners, and so the Club became all amateur, with ground admittance halved to sixpence (2½p).

Yet at the end of the season (after finishing bottom of their Southern League section) and still not having learned the lessons of the past, there was talk of the Club becoming a Limited Company, with the obviously ludicrous expectation of 2,500 season ticket holders, and average home attendances of 5,000!

As early as November 1927 a public meeting was called over the possibility of Mid-Rhondda closing down, but one again they managed to struggle on. It became so desperate, that the Club was suspended for not playing a match at Weymouth, as they couldn't afford the travelling expenses. At the end of the season - as wooden-spoonists again - the Club folded (in March) for the final time, leaving debts of £1,400.

(MITCHELL) ST. GEORGE'S

(1889)

This Birmingham based club has the dubious distinction of being one of the three clubs who applied for election to the Football League at the end of the competition's first season, and never subsequently became members (the other two being Sunderland Albion and South Shore, although the latter subsequently merged with Blackpool F.C.).

Football became popular in England's second city in the mid-1870's, one of the earliest clubs being Small Heath Alliance who were formed in 1875, and much later became the current Birmingham City club. Amongst the myriad of other teams in the city, most of whom are now long forgotten, were Birmingham Excelsior (who were based in Witton) and St.George's, whose home ground, at that time, was in Fentham Road (quoted in 1881 as in 'Buckfold', but more likely referring to 'Birchfield). In the 1881/82 season, St.George's made their debut in the F.A.Cup, but it was not an auspicious occasion as the team lost 9-1 at Wednesbury Old Athletic in the first round.

St.George's were not a very successful club, and these perennial strugglers merged with Mitchell's - a Birmingham Brewery team - in the mid-1886, to become Mitchell St. George's, after the former club had all but disbanded earlier, in April, that year The Club President was Mr.H.Mitchell, who was quite probably the owner of the Brewery. In the late 1880's, by which time professional football had been recognised - albeit reluctantly in many quarters - the idea of forming a 'league' (emulating a similar arrangement that was being practised in cricket) was proposed by J.J.Bentley.

One of the first batch to apply to join the League, and one of only three that never eventually made it.

The instigator was the President and Secretary of Turton F.C. (from the Bolton area), who later became President of the Football League. Mr. Bentley drew up a list of eight teams that he considered should form the first league, five of whom became eventual members, and three - Halliwell, Old Carthusians (a surprise choice since this club stuck rigidly by its principals of Amateur football) and Mitchell St. George's.

William McGregor, a Scotsman who moved South in the 1870's, became a leading figure with Aston Villa and the so-called 'Father of the Football League' disagreed with some of the clubs proposed, stating that in his opinion there should be only one club from each town. He doubtless saw the conflict of interest should both Villa (who were quoted in this context as being 'petulant') and St. George's both becoming founder-members of the League!

After an initial meeting in London, the formation of the 12 club Football League for the 1888/89 season was decided upon on the 17th April 1888 at the Royal Hotel, Manchester. Meanwhile, Mr. Hall of Crewe Alexandra proposed the formation of an alternative competition, 'The Combination', in which his club plus others, including St.George's, would participate. On the 27th April this was ratified, and the 'Second League', as it was often referred to came into being, with Mr.H. Mitchell of Mitchell St. George's becoming the President.

Although run on similar lines to the 'First League', The Combination was not run with the same discipline - for fixtures were often cancelled at late notice.

Therefore it comes as no surprise to find that the season was never full completed. The competition finished in disarray, and based on known results at this time - 5th April 1889 - St.George's were placed 10th of 20 clubs, having made a bright start which saw them nearer the top earlier on.

During, or at the end of, the season, the Club changed its name to the more upmarket 'Birmingham St. George's F.C.', and at the Football League's first ever re-election meeting, on the 5th May at the Douglas Hotel in Manchester, when the bottom four clubs of the twelve, in theory, had to resign, St. George's applied for a place. Alongside them were eight other clubs, six of whom would eventually gain a coveted place in the set-up. Those seeking election were each given five minutes to stake their claim (except Grimsby Town and Walsall Town Swifts who applied in writing only), before the voting took place.

All four clubs for re-election were voted back in - even after this first season a closed shop could be detected, a situation which became known as the 'old pals act', and there was no place for St. George's, although they did gain five votes (the best of the hopefuls) and only two less than Notts County.

A better organised alternative to The Combination was created for the 1889/90 season, 'The Alliance,' which soon became more commonly known as the 'Second League'. Birmingham St. George's joined 11 other clubs in this new league, including Sheffield Wednesday - who finished as Champions - Newton Heath (later named Manchester United) and Nottingham Forest; St. George's were placed 7th in the final table.

Despite their near miss a year earlier, the Club did not apply for election in 1890, although on this occasion, Stoke - who had finished bottom of the table in both seasons - were thrown out, with Sunderland taking their place.

The following season was better, and the Club moved up to 4th in the final table, but again no place was sought in the Football League, although by now the Club was experiencing financial difficulties, due - almost inevitably - to poor gates, and they probably realised that their elevation to the League would incur even greater expenditure. This reason would not be one to deter many non-League hopefuls in the years to come, but at this stage the fledgling Football League had still to prove itself as 'the' competition to be in. This reasoning was well illustrated two years later when Accrington F.C. lost out in the end of season 'Test Matches' which had been introduced, and rather than be demoted to the Second Division they chose instead to resign and join the more local Lancashire League!

The 1891/92 season became the last recorded campaign for Birmingham St. George's. A miserable season which saw them win just five and draw three of their 22 fixtures resulted in them claiming the bottom place in the table. Just to add insult to injury they were also deducted two points for an infringement of the rules. Although this was the beginning of the end for the club, ironically, if they had so wished, the Club may well have gained admission to the Football League that year, for the First Division was extended and the Second Division formed; all the Alliance clubs (bar Birmingham St. George's) won a place. And so ended an inglorious life of a club, which is by now all but forgotten.

MORECAMBE

(1957 - 1966, 1970)

If persistence guaranteed a place in the Football League then Morecambe would have become members years ago! Ten consecutive applications (plus one a few years later) but a total of only eight votes (plus one in 1970), on the face of it a hopeless case, but in reality a Club deserving better perhaps.

The current Morecambe F.C. was formed in 1920, yet 23 years earlier there had been attempts to establish the sport in the seaside town on the North-west coast, in Morecambe A.F.C. (an important suffix since there was already a 'Morecambe F.C.' - who played the rugby code).

When the Rugby team folded in 1906, efforts were made to improve the status of the local football team, who until that year had only played in local football leagues. But the club never realised their ambition and rose only as high as the West Lancashire League, before they folded in 1912.

Many futile attempts in the past, but Football League membership could now become a reality !

Post-First World War surge of interest in football also came to Morecambe, and at a public meeting on the 7th May 1920, at the West View Hotel, the first discussion was held with regard to forming a new club. Sharing the Woodhill Lane Ground with the local Cricket Club (to which there was probably an attachment), the team gained entry to the Lancashire Combination, and finished the season in a reasonably satisfactory position in the table. A move was made the next season to Roseberry Park in Lancaster Road.

After a few indifferent seasons, the team claimed the Championship of the Combination in 1925, became a Limited Company in September 1927, and had the Ground donated to them the next year.

A period of generally indifferent to poor seasons followed up to the Second World War. After the hostilities, the first few seasons were reasonably good on the field with moderately encouraging attendances, usually in the low thousands, but the 1950's brought a mixed bag of results.

1957 heralded the start of the Club's marathon of attempts to gain entry to the Football League. Whilst undeniably having good credentials for this elevation off the field - a good catchment area for support and a reasonably equipped Ground - on the pitch their performances for the first few years hardly warranted this effort, and correspondingly they received little support.

That first year they finished third in the Lancashire Combination and their attempt was reasonably justified, especially since the Champions - Prescot Cables - made no move to better themselves nor did runners-up New Brighton who had only departed from the League six years earlier. A 'closed shop' meeting in respect of votes gave none to Morecambe, and the best performers, Wigan Athletic and Burton Albion, received only one each.

The next four seasons produced somewhat disappointing final finishes in the Combination table between fourth and seventh, and therefore their chances of Football League membership were very slim.

During this period the likes of Peterborough United, Headington (later Oxford) United and Wigan Athletic left little chances for Morecambe, and despite their persistence their best showing was just one solitary vote in 1960.

The Club's second Championship of the Combination in 1962, coupled with their best run in the F.A.Cup which took them through to the third round - after the beating of Chester - when they lost 1-0 at home to Weymouth before a record attendance of 9,383, gave the Club cause for optimism. But this year wasn't the best for non-League hopefuls, when no fewer than 26 clubs made the attempt. This large number was caused by Accrington Stanley's resignation from the League and the consequent definite place that was left open. But Oxford United had the right credentials for they dominated the voting and were duly elected.

After such a successful season all that Morecambe could hope for was a few good seasons to give them added credibility. The Club's wish was granted a year later with their second successive Championship, although home attendances were somewhat disappointing with figures generally around only two thousand plus. But their achievements brought only a modicum of recognition at the election meeting, when they obtained two votes.

The sixties produced a period when there were no outstanding non-League clubs who warranted a place in the Football League, and equally a 'closed shop' situation regarding those who had to apply for re-election. In any event Morecambe F.C. did themselves no favours with final positions in the Combination of 10th, 3rd, and 7th for the corresponding years of 1964-1966.

By now home crowds often didn't reach 1,000 and therefore the Club's persistence in trying to gain a place in the League inevitably resulted in failure. The best year produced two votes (in 1966) and one in each of the other two.

Declining to apply for Football League status in 1967 was strange after so many abortive, 'no hoper' earlier attempts, for that year would surely have produced a vague chance of success.

The Club swept all before them in the Lancashire Combination, becoming Champions again and finishing six points clear. Although the home support improved considerably, it still only rarely reached 2,000, but a three match F.A.Cup epic with York City brought the team to national attention. Even more surprising was that no attempt was made the next year, despite another Championship victory, however with home support barely any better, it may well have been the financial considerations that probably wisely prevented a move in this direction.

Founder-members of the newly formed non-League 'super league' in the North, the Northern Premier, produced an initial third place, followed by a very disappointing 15th of 20 teams. Yet quite inexplicably the Club chose the latter year, 1970, to make their next and final attempt at the Football League!

With Bradford P.A. likely to be voted out, which they were, a place was left open. Hereford United were possibly the most popular of the candidates, although it was Cambridge United that finally made it, and Morecambe's single vote was perhaps better than they deserved in the circumstances.

The whole of the 1970's and 80's gave no reason for optimism, for the Club rarely finished in the top half of the final table, and consequently no further election bids were made. However, with a series of ground improvements, and eventual promotion to the GM Vauxhall Conference in 1995, there is at last a very real chance of attaining membership of the Football League.

At least the Club will not have to depend on repeated attempts, for now it is in their own hands. One Championship, perhaps a tall order, but then they should make it!

NEWCASTLE CITY

(1912)

From the early 1880's, football was popular in and around the City of Newcastle. The two clubs that became the most prominent were Newcastle East End and Newcastle West End, and the story of the former (and in which the latter was also heavily involved) is under a separate heading.

However, the name of 'Newcastle City' was once mentioned, perhaps only casually and only by a local supporter, in relation to the move of the East End team to the ground of the former West End club at St. James' Park in May 1892: *"I trust the name of the new lessees of St. James' Park will adopt the title of Newcastle City."* They didn't, preferring instead the name of Newcastle United.

Newcastle City first came to notice in 1909, when the club of this name joined the Northern Alliance. This League contained clubs now long forgotten, but also a few which would later attain some prominence, those such as Ashington and Blyth Spartans, plus interestingly 'Newcastle East End', a name that had disappeared in 1892 at the birth of Newcastle United!

There was undoubtedly room for other Senior non-League clubs in and around the City, and it would have been thought plenty of support, for Newcastle United from modest crowds soon rose to become one of the best supported teams in the country; the first Second Division club to average 10,000 plus (1897/98 season), and the first to average over 30,000, in 1906/07.

Just one attempt was made, but there was no place in the Football League for another Geordie club.

Yet history has shown, especially in later years, that this fanatical support did not spread outside the City boundaries for the later struggles of Football League clubs Gateshead, Ashington and Durham was principally due to poor gates.

From the relatively humble Northern Alliance, Newcastle City soon progressed into the part professional North-Eastern League, but without picking up any major honours on the way. By now their status was such that they entered for the F.A.Cup, but lost their first match in the preliminary round by 2-0 at Blaydon United in the 1910/11 season. A year later the same opposition was defeated 2-1, in Newcastle, but the City lost in the second qualifying round.

The Club's home Ground was at Brough Park, Byker, about two miles to the East of the city centre, which much later attained dubious fame as the district in which a teenage TV series was set! The North-Eastern League was the most Senior of competitions in this part of the country and was generally dominated by the reserve elevens of Newcastle United, Middlesbrough and Sunderland. Therefore this competition was not an unreasonable one to use as a stepping stone for access to the Football League, the route in fact used a decade later by Ashington, Darlington, Durham City and Hatlepools. By April 1912, the Newcastle City team was reasonably placed at 8th in the league, after suffering a surprise defeat to Gateshead Town before a crowd of 2,000 at Brough Park.

There was then a build-up of fixtures over the Easter period which saw the team play no fewer than four matches in five days! Seaham Harbour were first visited on Good Friday, when before a *"very large attendance"* a 3-1 victory was gained, followed by a scoreless draw with Spennymoor at home. After a one day break, the return with the Seaham team produced an emphatic 5-0 victory at Brough Park, but only before a *"small gate"*, a match played in high winds throughout.

Finally another victory was attained at North Shields Athletic, at Hankey's Lane, before a 2,000 crowd on the Tuesday. But even this set of good results could do little to lift the team up the table, and they finished a final 7th.

But more importantly, steps had already been taken to try to gain a place in the Football League. On the 15th April, the Club reported via the local newspaper: *"Since issuing the circular letter to the League clubs a few weeks ago, the East End club* (sic.) *have received encouraging letters from members of both divisions of the League. The Brough Park executive are doing everything possible."* The incorrect reference presumably was a mistake by the reporter for although a club by this name did exist at this time (in the Northern Alliance), the application was definitely from the City club.

One of the most encouraging replies came from Tom Watson the Liverpool F.C. Secretary, who was a Tynesider, and a great supporter of football in this area. *"One of the main factors is the support, and we hope this can be maintained for the last three games"*, the report continued; a 1-1 draw resulted with North Shields at Brough Park before a *"poor crowd"*, a 1-0 defeat followed at West Stanley, and finally a 0-0 draw was played a home to Carlisle United. Efforts continued to be made to impress the voters at the forthcoming re-election meeting.

Due to the local strikes in the coal-mining industry, there was plenty of free and willing labour, and this was used to build-up the embankment on the side opposite the Grandstand. *"Big crowds will in future be able to view the match with ease and comfort"*, it was reported.

But all these efforts came to nothing, for Leeds City and Lincoln City were convincingly re-voted in, and of the six applying clubs, Gainsborough Trinity fared best with nine votes (one third the number gained by Lincoln), whilst Newcastle City managed just one.

It really could not have been a surprise that the Club had been rejected for they had hardly impressed during their short career, and no further attempt was made. The team was never able to challenge for honours in the North-Eastern League, and in fact there was a regular regression down the table, with finishes of 11th, 15th and 18th in the succeeding years. The Club rarely progressed far in the F.A.Cup, and emphatic defeats were more the norm, including a 5-1 loss at home to South Shields in the 1912/13 season, and 4-0 at Blyth Spartans two years later.

By 1913, South Shields were making a determined effort locally for Football League membership, and at great expense their employment of quality professional players ensured they dominated the North-Eastern competition. Ironically, Shields once considered moving to Brough Park, a venue which was later destined to house greyhound Racing, but which was unable to attract crowds to City's matches; on the 17th March 1915, for a Wednesday afternoon league match, the official attendance was just 13 for the visit of South Shields!

The Newcastle City name never reappeared after the Great War, and the Club which had existed so briefly, and had tried to flirt with the big-time, was banished to history.

NEWCASTLE EAST END

(1892)

It is debateable whether this club should be included within this section of non-League clubs that 'never made it', for shortly after their attempt for membership of the Football League their name was changed to Newcastle United. However, since just before their election attempt there was a 'loose' amalgamation with the rival West End club, this inclusion has been considered valid.

Football really commenced in the City with the formation of Tyne Association (formed by the ex-Public schoolboy sons of leading families in the area) in 1876, and Newcastle Rangers two years later. By 1883, there were many clubs in and around Newcastle-upon-Tyne, notable inclusions being Newcastle East End (following the amalgamation of the 1880 formed Stanley club and Rosewood) and Newcastle West End that had been formed a year earlier. West End had evolved from a cricket club, and played their matches on the Leazes. From the outset, East End had the financial advantage of being supported by well known influential men.

One of the founders of West End, William Neasham, arranged for the team to play on a few acres of land that he leased, which had previously been used for sheep grazing before the animals went to slaughter. Although the site had a pronounced slope to one end it was transformed into a proper enclosed Ground and later became known as St. James' Park. At the first match the princely sum of seven shillings and eleven pence (40p) was taken at the gate, and the spectators included just one women, the wife of Tommy Watson the Club's Secretary/Manager.

East finally joined with West, and United was the eventual result!

East End, who played at Chillington Road, Heaton (to the east of the City centre), managed to entice Tommy Watson over to them, before he moved on to Sunderland where he helped to create the all-conquering 'Team of all the Talents'. Great rivalry was struck up between the two clubs, each winning the Northumberland Cup twice, and for the 1889/90 season they both became founder-members of the Northern League, by which time the pair were employing professional players.

Around this time, West End set about establishing themselves as the top Newcastle team by appointing additional directors and encouraging thirty supporters to donate £5 each to pay for improvements to St.James' Park, principally for the provision of wooden duckboards around the pitch. They also introduced a number of Scottish players to the team, including International Ralph Aitken from Dumbarton.

This ploy by West End initially paid off, for they finished their first league season as runners-up, two places above East End. Not to be outdone, the Chillington Road club became a Limited Company in March 1890, and £800 of share capital was soon taken up. They too looked to Scotland for talent and became generally more successful in this respect than their Western neighbours, offering (in addition to a day job), fifteen shillings (75p) for a win, ten shillings for a draw or defeat, and one shilling for every goal scored. East End soon overtook West End in superiority, and this showed in the next two seasons final tables, when East End finished 6th (albeit with only eight teams) and 4th, whilst their rivals slipped to 7th and 8th (of nine).

The competition between the two clubs became fierce, each having expended large sums of money, and hence having to recoup this principally at the gate. It soon became apparent that at this time Newcastle could only support one fully professional team. East End in broad terms had the team, whilst West End without doubt had the superior ground.

Newcastle West End just about completed their season before folding, and just to rub salt into the wound, their many defeats that season included two versus East End, by 7-1 and 8-1. East End meanwhile finished their league programme at the end of April with a home gate of 3,000, but a 1-0 defeat to runners-up Middlesbrough, to mark their end of football at Chillington Road.

At the end of the season, six officials of the two clubs met at the house of East Ender Joseph Bell and agreed that the surviving club would take over the lease of St.James' Park since its location near to the City was a great attraction, in addition their future at Heaton was uncertain. There was no formal amalgamation, but several of the West End directors and three players joined East End. Former West End men, founder-member William Neasham and James Telford, who switched their allegiance, were to later become Newcastle United Chairmen.

In early May the newspapers announced that East End was about to amalgamate with West End. This brought the retort next day that *"West End is defunct in every sense."* Another fan wrote: *"I read with astonishment in today's issue of your paper that East End are going to remove to St.James' Park."* Things do not change for obviously this fan was horrified that his team should abandon their Ground, and play on that of their bitterest rivals!

East End's ambitions were obviously high, for despite not being one of the top finishers in the Northern League, they applied for election to the Football League that year of 1892.

Newcastle East End's Mr Turnbull represented the Club at the Football League A.G.M. which was held at the Queen's Hotel, Fawcett Street, Sunderland on the 11th of May, and he, with all the other applicants presented their cases for admission to the League, each pledging to honour it should they be elected. Although the League was to extend from 12 to 16 clubs, one place was offered to West Bromwich Albion, who were given this opportunity by virtue of their winning of the F.A.Cup (a possible controversial move which was never repeated).

The two clubs for re-election were voted back in, although newcomers Nottingham Forest and Sheffield Wednesday received more votes, and Newton Heath (later Manchester United) completed the quartet. Newcastle East End, together with Middlesbrough Ironopolis and Burton Swifts received just one vote each.

East End then declined the invitation to apply to join the new Second Division (as did Ironopolis), preferring instead to continue in the Northern League, and a year later they duly finished 2nd and 1st respectively. But the two teams both came to their senses in 1893, applied for election (to the Second Division), and were duly elected; East End under their new name of Newcastle United.

But this was not the end of either Newcastle East End or Newcastle West End for the names appeared again in the fixture lists. East End were active again by 1896, and for two seasons, a club with this title were playing in the North-Eastern League in the 1932/33 season (formerly known as 'St.Peter's Albion' they reverted to this name on their move down to the Tyneside League in 1934).

Meanwhile West End were members of the Tyneside League from 1933 until the outbreak of the Second World War.

NORTH SHIELDS

(1947 - 1955, 1957, 1962)

North Shields were founded in 1896 as North Shields Athletic, changing to Preston Colliery and finally back to North Shields, first joining the North-Eastern League after spells in the South Shields and District League, the Northern Combination, and the Northern Alliance. They remained within this semi-professional competition almost continuously until 1964, but in all this time they were only very rarely amongst the honours, winning the League Cup and the League's 'Non-Reserve' medal twice each, plus a single Championship in 1950 (plus a similar table-topping success in 1961 in one of two seasons when they and most of the former North-Eastern clubs joined the shortlived Northern Counties League).

Perhaps it was this almost complete lack of real success that dissuaded the Club from making any attempts to join the Football League between the two World Wars, despite their semi-professional status, unlike several of their neighbours and others in the North-East. But there again most of this selection of clubs achieved their elevation not through any spectacular performances. Ashington, Durham City and Hartlepools United were all members of the North-Eastern League when they made it by the 'easy route' - being part of the block admission - to the Third Division North on its foundation in 1921, despite none of the trio having ever won the Championship. Blyth Spartans and West Stanley were also in the North-Eastern in 1921, but their applications received insufficient votes. Even Carlisle United who were voted in, in 1928, had only one league Championship to their credit.

An eminently suitable Ground, was insufficient to gain election, in an area already well endowed with League clubs.

However, North Shields didn't even apply in 1921, nor did they for nearly thirty years - clearly they appreciated they stood no chance, or quite simply were not interested!

Despite the Club's belated attempts to gain a place in the Football League they had a very colourful life in the meantime! In October 1917 the Club folded after suffragettes burnt down the uninsured Stand at their Hawkey's Lane (Appleby Park) Ground, but the Club reformed after the War as North Shields Athletic and in 1928 were renamed North Shields AFC.

The Appleby Park Ground had been built over former mine-workings, and during a match in 1947, a player bearing down on goal suddenly disappeared up to his waist, which was the result of the sudden re-appearance of a one metre deep hole in the penalty area! The hole became known as the 'McGarry Hole'.

But this misfortune did not stop the Club from making their first application for membership of the Football League that year. However, due to the re-election of the four clubs required to re-apply, without even going to the vote the Club and the other hopefuls were disappointed. There then followed a period when after so many years without trying, North Shields made continuous bids up to and including 1955.

Whilst their record on the pitch was not remarkable, in other respects the Club were worthy candidates.

They boasted a Ground which had a record attendance of 12,800 (set in 1936 versus South Shields), and for the first floodlight game - as early as March 1955 - the visit of Middlesbrough Reserves attracted 4,500. There was a 850 seater Stand, and the Ground was terraced virtually all round with several areas under cover. The Club had run a professional team for much of their life and therefore they would have presumably had no illusions regarding the extra demands of Football League football. But results counted first and foremost, and to a degree location - just ask neighbours Gateshead who later, in 1960, were, in the view of many, unjustifiably dumped!

It was only at their fifth attempt did the Club receive even one vote of support, and this transpired to be the only one in their first marathon nine applications. Yet the Club were not deterred, and after missing one year, they were back in the fray in 1957, but again to no avail. The Club's last bid came in 1962, the year when Accrington Stanley resigned which left one definite vacancy, and no fewer than 26 clubs trying to fill the place. With no support yet again, North Shields probably created the lowest number of votes pro-rata to applications - 1 to 11!

Not only did the Club decide never to apply to the Football League again, but most unusually, during this period, they actually changed to formal Amateur status in 1963. With Appleby Park then having a claimed capacity of 15,000, total seating for 1,000, and cover for 3,500, they undoubtedly had one of the best non-League enclosures in the Country.

In addition North Shields could boast a spacious Social Club (opened in December 1962) plus modern, centrally heated, changing rooms within the same building.

The way was open from the 1964/65 season to join the much respected Northern League, and the Club started in fine form winning their first match 7-1 at Shildon. The team became an immediate success in their new surroundings, something previously denied to their supporters, and in 1969, they not only won the Northern League Championship but in capturing the F.A.Amateur Cup at Wembley (beating Sutton United 2-1) they became what is generally regarded as the only former professional club to achieve this feat.

This level of achievement was never repeated, but the team could usually be found lying in the top half of the league table. Then, in the early 1990's, a bombshell was dropped when it was announced that the club were heavily in debt, the sum being in six figures.

The Ground was sold, but did not realise as much as hoped for, and after a period of ground-sharing the club eventually moved to a new ground. But gone were the large seated Stand, the covered enclosures, and the impressive Social Club, and now playing at a lower level in the 'Pyramid', it would be fanciful to expect North Shields F.C. to rise high enough again to make a serious challenge for a coveted place in the Football League.

NUNEATON TOWN/BOROUGH

(1923, 1933, 1950, 1968, 1969, 1973-76)

Nuneaton Town, and their successors, Borough, have over many years made a number of attempts to join the Football League, but these have been almost totally unsupported. Yet, despite an existence that has seen many ups and downs, the Club - its Ground, its support and its catchment area - could, quite possibly, one day reach this ultimate goal.

The early days of football in Nuneaton were full of turmoil. Founded in 1889 as Nuneaton St.Nicholas, there followed the use of several different grounds, a name change to Nuneaton Town, their collapse due to mounting debts and finally a re-emergence as Nuneaton Juniors, then back to the 'Town' suffix - and all within a dozen or so years! By the end of the First World War, Nuneaton Town had become more stable, and with the purchase of an area of land at Wash Lane Farm - which was later to become known as Manor Park - they embarked on a career in the Birmingham League. This followed a period spent in the lesser Birmingham Combination.

They have the Ground and the support potential, yet have failed dismally in the past - can Boro make it in the future?

The Birmingham League, was, not unlike the Cheshire County League, a competition that offered a higher standard of football than its relatively local name would suggest. This competition (which later became the West Midlands League) offered, during the inter-War years, a geographical alternative that was almost on a par with the Midland and Southern Leagues, and the likes of Kidderminster Harriers, Shrewsbury Town and Wellington Town (later Telford United), all progressed via this route.

Nuneaton Town were unable to make any real impression on this league, and in fact eventually reverted back to the Combination in 1926. However their fourth season, 1922/23 had culminated in a final third place in the table (behind Champions Shrewsbury Town and Bilston United), and they marked this achievement with their first Football League election bid.

It is a surprise to find that there were so few applicants - just four - considering the Third Division Northern Section was extended by two that year. However, there was no support whatsoever for Nuneaton Town. Possibly with a view to raising their profile for another attempt, the club entered the Southern League in 1924, but two very poor seasons in the Eastern Section dictated a move down to the Birmingham Combination, and a long period before they made another Football League bid.

It was to be another ten years before the Club's second, and final attempt was made. However, playing now only in the Birmingham Combination - albeit successfully with two Championships and a Runners-up place to their credit - there really was very little chance of advancement from there to the Football League.

In early January 1933, the Club lay second in the table, behind the leading Birmingham 'A' team, trailing by only three points and with four games in hand. But a poor run, sparked off by a 5-4 defeat to Redditch, saw the team slipping behind.

After an 8-2 thrashing of Market Harborough, there were hopes of a revival, but it never came. Then, on the 3rd March the following statement was made by the local newspaper: *"It is understood that the Directors of Nuneaton A.F.C. (sic.) are shortly to consider the question of better class football for Manor Park, and in this connection the 3rd Division of the English League is being mentioned."* Although, as a word of caution, the report emphasized this would only be possible if there was better support for the remaining matches that season.

The entertainment value (despite the goals) in the 3-3 draw at home to Darlaston that followed was so poor that there was little chance of additional support! The team had dropped to 4th by mid-March, and things got worse with a 4-0 defeat to Birmingham's third team at Bedworth's ground. There were some victories, but the season finished with a 5-1 defeat at Dudley Town. Many felt that the poor results were due to insufficient back-up, by the absence of a reserve team. Nuneaton Town finished 4th in the table, hardly a 'promotion' position from this lesser league, but the Club went ahead with their application to the Football League at the Meeting on the 29th May, and actually managed one vote of support. Interestingly their bid on this occasion was made to the Southern section.

A return to the Birmingham League was made in 1933, and in August, the Club *"hoped that supporters will rally round the club this season so that the directors can again apply for admission to the Third Division next season."* Two reasonable seasons followed but no further election attempt was made, then a pair of poor campaigns followed. At an extraordinary shareholders meeting after the end of the 1936/37 season the Club folded, but within a few days a new club rose from the ashes, that of Nuneaton Borough. After a season in the Central Amateur League, the club turned professional and, like their predecessors they joined the Birmingham Combination. After the War, the Club were very successful, finishing as runner-up in the Combination and this led to another unsuccessful bid for League status in 1950 - with no votes in the Southern section.

After a spell in the Birmingham League (winning the Championship in 1952), the 1966/67 season was one of the best for the Club, for they finished runners-up in the Southern League Premier Division (having joined the competition in 1958). They also reached the 3rd round of the F.A.Cup where a massive, and record, attendance of 22,114 was at the Manor Ground for the visit of Rotherham United. This memorable season could have given a slight chance for a successful election to the Football League, but the Club delayed this bid until 1968 - when they again received no votes!

Some good seasons followed up to the mid-1980's, including two spells in the Alliance League, but their several bids for the League all resulted in emphatic failure, Although their last attempt, in 1976, did produce a record two votes. The season had seen reasonable crowds at the Manor Ground, typically 1,640 for the 2-1 victory over Dunstable in January, which took the team to third in the table, and 1,452 for Burton's later visit. But running with a squad of only 19, a cash crisis resulted in this number being depleted by two, and had shades of the failures of 1933.

After a goal drought, two excellent victories were obtained at Weymouth and at Champions-elect Wimbledon, both by 4-1, but by early April the Championship was conceded to the London team and the Southern League runners-up spot had to suffice.

Although two runners-up spots were taken in the Alliance, the Club was demoted in 1987 due to problems with their Ground, and they then tumbled down through the Southern League. In 1991, the Club was on the point of extinction, but a consortium of Businessmen took over, and gradually Nuneaton Borough have clawed their way back.

With the Ground now sorted out and an established place back in the Alliance - with gates often topping 2,000 - there is at last a real chance that the Club could make it to the Football League.

PONTYPRIDD

(1921, 1922, 1923)

Yet another of the South Wales contingent who tried their luck around 1920. In modern day terms, it would be ludicrous to consider the inclusion from the Rhondda Valley and adjacent area of four clubs in the Football League (plus Swansea), plus six more that were anxious to gain such recognition. Yet this was the situation during the inter-War period, however, the social and economic situation was far different then. The sudden expansion of the coalmining industry and the consequent employment of 'imported' workers and their families from far and wide, ensured a population explosion in the Valleys.

One bid came surprisingly close for the ambitious Welshmen - but subsequent events showed they would have been unsuitable.

With relatively plenty of money around, and limited pleasures on which to spend it, the growth of football at this time was almost inevitable. Pontypridd, like most of their contemporaries never made it to the League, but on one occasion they came very close, and in this respect they had far greater success than those other teams.

The first club of any note in the town was Pontypridd United, formed probably around 1900, but by 1906 they were in financial difficulties, and they finally folded after acrimony within the team, due to the introduction of new players who had arrived in the district - ironically 'immigrants' were one of the reasons why several clubs in the area flourished! But the sport soon returned to the town and by 1911 'Pontypridd F.C.' was ambitious enough to apply for, and gain election to the Southern League Second Division. Finding a suitable Ground was easy, for a private company built Taff Vale Park, initially for the use of athletics and cycling.

But anxious to increase revenue the owners readily let the football club rent the venue. However, there were complaints by visiting teams regarding the concrete cycle track which came very close to the pitch.

Pontypridd made a very satisfactory start in the Southern League, finishing 5th of 14, alongside a mixed bunch, with the likes of Portsmouth, Cardiff City, Southend United and Walsall. Additionally they reached the Welsh F.A.Cup Final in 1912 (and a year later), only losing to Cardiff City and Swansea Town respectively after replays. The next three seasons were not so successful, then, in common with most of the Welsh clubs, football was discontinued during the First World War, and re-convened for the 1919/20 season, but at this time there was some unrest within the Club.

In September, the Supporters Club stated that they wished to take over the running of Pontypridd F.C. The Club's Directors at the time were naturally unwilling, unless the supporters could show that they had the necessary financial backing. This was not forthcoming, but equally the Supporters Club could hardly be ignored, and eventually both parties came to a compromise, whereby two seats on the Board were offered (although four were asked for), in view of the shares that were held by the fans. The supporters stated their intention to eventually buy up all the necessary shares in order to control the Club, which does not appear to have happened. But the season was quite successful with an eventual place of 4th in the 11 strong Second Division.

By October 1920, the Supporters Club had bought up £250 of the shares (the Club were valued at £355 in 1921) and had hopes of obtaining another fifty pounds worth. However, there were some unsavoury incidents during matches, for in that same month the referee was hit by a missile at Taff Vale Park, and the Club were ordered to put up warning notices around the Ground, and in December there was a pitch invasion at the end of a match following a hotly disputed goal. A large crowd swarmed around the dressing-rooms, but were eventually persuaded to disperse peacefully.

Obviously football in the town was now being taken very seriously, and the Club demonstrated this with their first application for Football League status at the end of that season. Their credentials were hardly perfect, for they only finished fourth again in the table, and Aberdare Athletic (who showed they had the all-round requirements), were elected, having finished as runners-up in the Welsh Division. Bath City's claim was, on a geographical basis - if not on their playing performances - stronger, and they exceeded the five votes obtained by Pontypridd.

The situation was far from perfect at Taff Vale Park, for the Club reported a loss on the previous season, and in December a Public Meeting was called to discuss the financial situation. But there was a welcome boost for the funds when Cardiff City of the Football League 1st Division was entertained in the Semi-Final of the Welsh Cup (the same club had been beaten a year earlier but then they fielded a reserve eleven).

Although a 3-0 defeat was the result, there was a crowd of 12,000 present (probably a Pontypridd record), although a full house had been hoped for; the Ground capacity was claimed to be 30,000, but included only 300 in the seated Stand. Although there were only nine teams in the Southern League Welsh Division, the Dragons as they were now known, only finished 5th, but they were determined to join the Football League, and they made another bid in 1922.

Surprisingly they nearly reached their goal, for at the meeting in June they obtained 21 votes, albeit nine short of re-elected Exeter City.

But obviously at this time the League were keen to gain greater Welsh representation (although a year later both Newport County and Aberdare Athletic finished at the foot of the Third Division South!) This near acceptance spurred the Club on, and a year later, despite only receiving eight election votes, they bought Taff Vale Park and vowed to build a new 2,000 seater Stand and dressing-rooms at an estimated cost of £4,000, but still running at a loss, this appeared to be somewhat ambitious.

The Club were determined to attain their ultimate objective, and despite a worsening financial situation, they announced in December 1924 (having completed the new Grandstand) their intention to terrace all the banking and provide cover for much of these areas.

But football in South Wales was already on the decline, and only 4,500 were present for the Welsh Cup Final that season that was played at Taff Vale Park. After a year's absence, the Club announced their intention to try for the League again, in 1925, but their application was not even considered - no doubt due to their precarious financial situation - despite them finishing third in the Southern League Western Section.

In early July 1925, at a Public Meeting, following their continuing financial losses, the Club was closed down by the Directors, who were unable to raise the £200 required to commence the approaching season. But a new club was immediately formed, albeit the wages bill was to be only £40 per week (two years earlier it was £160), but immediately the old problem of finance rose again, and by March 1926 only Amateur players were used, which no doubt contributed to the Club's second from bottom final place in the table.

In June the F.A. of Wales suspended the Club (for accounting irregularities) and they were not allowed to reform until debts had been paid, but this never came to pass. The Ground was first sold to the new Pontypridd Rugby League Club, and was subsequently purchased in September 1927 by the Greyhound Racing Association.

POOLE TOWN

(1962, 1964)

A good example of 'how the mighty have fallen'! Perhaps referring to Poole Town as 'mighty' is something of an exaggeration, but the Club was certainly a Southern League force to be reckoned with at one time, had a large well equipped Stadium, and a catchment area that could conceivably have attracted gates worthy of the Football League. The Ground still exists - Poole Stadium in Wimborne Road - still hosting Speedway and Greyhound meetings (and there is talk of the football club's return), and so does the Club, but now well down the Pyramid, playing at a Recreation Ground and competing in the lowly Hampshire League.

The Town's original club, 'Poole F.C.' was formed by the merger of Poole Rovers and Poole Hornets in 1890. This team originally played at a Ground that was located immediately adjacent to the local harbour, and was so close that the pitch was frequently covered in seaweed! The current Club has returned full circle for these predecessors spent much of their early years in the Hampshire League, before progressing up to the Western (in 1923) and finally the Southern League in 1926. By now they were playing at a Ground in Breakheart Lane (later Linthorpe Road). The team shot to fame through their run in the 1926/27 season F.A.Cup, which saw them start in the preliminary round, later beat Newport County at home, followed by a 2-1 victory at Amateurs Nunhead, and finally record a very creditable 3-1 defeat at Everton. Two years later they were drawn at home with near neighbours Bournemouth & Boscombe Athletic of the Third Division South, a game which was lost 3-1, but before a record 7,000 attendance.

"Will the soccer citizens of Poole and district grab the chance of bringing the Football League to the town?"

Despite moderate performances in the Southern League, they folded during the 1929/30 season, but reformed soon after as an Amateur club adding 'Town' to their name. The new Club gained admission to the Western League, but soon they too came close to folding, when they were left homeless after losing their Breakheart Lane venue. Fortunately they were given, rent-free, the use of a suitable field, before finally settling in at a brand new Stadium in 1933. Right from the start, Poole Stadium offered facilities far better than the previous venues, and many years later underwent further developments which included floodlights in 1954, and a 1,400 seater Grandstand seven years later.

In 1952, the Club turned professional, and - emulating the route of their predecessors - were accepted into the Southern League in 1957. In 1962, the team were playing in the second tier, First Division (albeit their runners-up place secured them promotion), when they made the first of two bids to obtain Football League status. Well before the end of the season, the decision to apply had been made, and in January the local newspaper asked the question: *"Will the soccer citizens of Poole and district grab the chance of bringing the Football League to the town?"* However, it was recognised that support at home matches was one of the biggest factors, for attendances rarely topped 2,000.

That year, it was hoped, would offer the best opportunity for 'new blood' into the Football League set-up since 1920, for plans had been discussed relating to a reformation of the Fourth Division into two new regional sections.

This, it was planned, would allow the ingress of eight new clubs. The Club (along with a record number of 25 other hopefuls) decided the time was right and set about preparing a brochure to accompany their application. In addition plans were announced that the Ground was to be purchased by the Club. On the 24th January there was a further boost to their aspirations, when the brand new £7,500 floodlights were turned on for the first time for the match versus Yeovil Town. This, it was felt, would be another factor to boost attendances, which it was admitted by the Club were poor for such a large catchment area.

From 3rd in mid-January, the team jumped to top of the table after their 2-0 defeat of Tunbridge Wells a couple of weeks later, but a later shock 4-0 home defeat to Canterbury City dented their Championship hopes. The last three matches had to be played within five days, and a thumping 8-0 defeat of Ramsgate confirmed the Club's finish of second, and hence promotion. The reformation of the Fourth Division never came to pass, and the one vacancy (caused by the resignation of Accrington Stanley) was taken by Oxford United. Poole Town, as with the majority of the 'also-rans' received no votes.

Although the Club had expressed their aspirations, they also recognised that it was difficult enough to make ends meet in the Southern League, let alone the Football League, and economy measures were announced for the coming 1962/63 season - hardly a financial statement to impress!

A profit had actually been made on the previous season, although with the home gate money amounting to £3,363, this represented a slight drop. From 23 professional players, the Club stated that they would only be engaging 18 for the following season.

After a fairly bright start to the season, the team gradually slipped down the table, and eventually were unable to hold on to their Premier Division status. A year later, in the First Division, a reasonable season saw them finish 9th of 22, and despite only being a 'second tier' Southern League team, the Club decided to make another bid for the Football League. Vieing with 13 other non-Leaguers, all of whom it could be argued had a better case, it really could have come as no surprise when the Club received no votes of support.

This was to be Poole Town's second and last attempt at the Football League, and events since suggest that the Club will never again be in a position to consider this possible. Despite hovering between the top and second levels of the Southern League, after the team played their last match at Poole Stadium in 1994, their fortunes took a nosedive.

Groundsharing and other factors have seen the Club slide down the Pyramid, and with no new Ground on the horizon, their main hope can only be that they may be able to occupy their former home again.

PRESCOT CABLES

(1929, 1930)

Works' teams reaching Senior level football are rare. Of those few clubs that have actually applied for election to the Football League there are just two. Lovell's Athletic's attempt was unique in that this club was a complete Works team, the name referring just to the company and not a place, whereas the independent Lancashire club added the 'Cables' to their name at a later date. However, Prescot Cables can also claim a unique record for they made two attempts (Lovell's made only one), and on one occasion actually received one vote of support, unlike the Welsh toffee making team.

Prescot F.C. was founded in 1884 and played their first match when they entertained the second eleven of St.Thomas' from nearby St.Helens. The match was played on the local Cricket Ground, and *"was watched by a good sprinkling of spectators"*, the result being 3-1 in favour of the visitors. The 'Watchmakers' (referring to the town being a centre for this industry), soon moved to a separate field adjacent to the Cricket Ground, which eventually became known as Slacky Brow, named after a colliery spoil heap that had formed a small hillock, just South of the Ground. In non-spectacular fashion the Club rose through the ranks, from Friendly and local cup matches, via the Liverpool and District League, the Lancashire Alliance (in 1895), to the Lancashire Combination which they joined in 1897. But this proved to be too big a step, and after just one poor season they found their niche again, back in the Alliance.

Three years later the Club moved up again, joining the Lancashire League, which was broadly on a par with the Combination.

Their applications for League status were unique - but they were never serious contenders.

This move was all the more remarkable since the team had finished bottom of the lesser rated Alliance! The Lancashire League at this time included the likes of Barrow, Workington and Southport (Central) who were all destined for a move up to the Football League, and subsequent rejection!

Despite only a moderate campaign, the Club decided to continue in the same competition for the 1902/03 season, complete with no less than 40 players. However, a dispute with the Cricket Club with regard to access to the Football Ground, got completely out of hand, and unable to play on their pitch, in these most unusual circumstances, the Club had no choice but to disband.

For a short period, the Wire Works team acquired the title of top town team, but this role was soon taken by Prescot Athletic, who were formed in 1906 and played in the Liverpool League. Their home was the Athletics Ground in Hope Street, but it was not until after the Great War that they aspired to a higher level, when, in 1918 they joined the Lancashire Combination, having dropped the 'Athletic' from their title by this time.

But Prescot, due to financial considerations (not least the travelling expenses), decided to move to the more localised Liverpool Combination in 1920. At least the Club was being run economically, and in 1922 work was carried out on building up the embankments at Hope Street in order to provide a claimed capacity for 15,000 despite the Club's moderate status.

Although not always meeting with great success in either league matches or cup games (for some years the F.A.Cup had been entered), crowds at home matches were very good, and with a number of other clubs groundsharing at different times, the finances continued to be buoyant. This money also allowed the continued improvement of the Ground, with new fencing, turnstiles, pitch drainage renovations, and covering to the terrace. Around the mid-1920's the Directors of the local wireworks (the cable factory) took an increasing interest in the Club - their own football team was a Groundsharer at one time - and all were invited to the opening of the new covered accommodation in January 1928.

That season (1927/28) was unusual to say the least, and probably unprecedented in British football! The season was well past the halfway stage, Prescot were heading for a possible Championship in the Liverpool County Combination (they eventually finished as runners-up), when - in February - Fleetwood of the Lancashire Combination resigned with only 16 matches of 38 left to play.

The Prescot Management approached the Lancashire Combination committee and offered to take over Fleetwood's fixtures at this late stage in the season. Amazingly it was agreed, and so the Prescot team, after a frantic rush to sign on a complete new team of players, finished the season playing two first teams in the two competitions. Although somewhat irrelevant Fleetwood/Prescot finished 16th of 20 in the final table.

By now there were several Cable Company men involved in the Club, and in what must have been one of the first large scale sponsorship arrangements the name of 'Prescot Cables F.C.' was adopted that Summer. Now bona-fide members of the Lancashire Combination a very good season was completed, with a final finish of fourth.

The start of the season had seen the opening of an impressive Grandstand on the West side of the Ground, and the Club now considered they had all the credentials for a try at the Football League, as did six other hopefuls. Manchester Central, who soon became seen as the Club's deadliest of rivals, managed two votes whilst Cables received just one. However, this was one more than Chester and Workington!

In October 1929, the second phase of the West Stand - a gift from B.I.C. the Cable Company - was formally opened by Charles Sutcliffe of the Football League, giving a seating capacity for 1,000. Another good season (5th in the Combination) prompted a second try at the League, but with only three new applicants in the Northern Section, and arguably in a more consolidated position, the Club received no votes; particularly galling was the fact that Manchester Central managed 13! Despite the three runners-up spots that followed the Club made no further attempts at election, and for a brief period the Club moved over to the Cheshire League, but without any real success.

Back in the Combination in 1936, Prescot Cables remained in this company up to 1975, but earlier, in 1964, and now named 'Prescot Town', the Club's fortunes began to slide, on and off the pitch. Four years later, irregularities with regard to the Social Club led to a mass walkout by many members, and with this financial lifeline cut, the Club were later forced to change to Amateur status. A further financial crisis evolved, not helped by home attendances which sometimes barely reached three figures, and the Club - now named simply 'Prescot F.C.', struggled to carry on.

Rejected from the Lancashire Combination in 1975, the team currently play in the North-West Counties League - as 'Prescot Cables' once again!

RHYL

(1929, 1932)

It is quite surprising, when Wales is looked at from afar, how different the North is from the South - at least in footballing terms. For in the North, football was established in the earliest days, around the same time as the game was taking a hold in Lancashire; rugby never was and still is not a serious threat. Conversely, in South Wales, football did not really 'take-off' until around 1900, in a rugby dominated environment.

Yet strangely, there is, and only ever has been one Football League representative from the North - Wrexham - whilst the South have had (at least from the early 1920's), anything between two and five teams. But perhaps it is not so strange, for those in the more densely populated South were far more dependant on Industrial matters, and in particular coalmining (with the addition of many workers from afar), whilst their counterparts belong to a more rural community, with only a scattering of reasonably populated towns.

A good period in their history led to two futile attempts by the only club from North Wales to (unsuccessfully) try their luck.

When it came to election bids for the Football League, there was a similar repeat of numbers, with around eight from the South, and just two from the North, Bangor City and Rhyl. Like so many non-League clubs, Rhyl F.C. have gone through a number of transformations, reformations and name changes - technically different clubs but in many cases enthusiasts who have perpetuated the team. Just to add to the confusion, in the early days there were several clubs operating from the town at a reasonably high level!

Originally formed way, way, back in 1870 (as Rhyl Skull and Crossbones it is said!), by early into the 20th century the town's probable principal club had become Rhyl Victoria. By the post-First World War years the club, who reformed in 1922, became Rhyl Athletic, and finally plain Rhyl F.C.

The principal football team in Rhyl graduated via a number of leagues, notably their first - the North Wales Coast League (which was formed following a meeting held in Rhyl, on 24 March 1893), as Rhyl Town at this time. Over the years other leagues of which the most prominent club of the town was a member included The Combination, the Welsh National League and the North Wales Football Combination. Over many years various local cup competitions were won, and although the ultimate goal, the Welsh Cup, was not first captured until 1952, the Final was reached on several occasions from 1927.

Without doubt the Club's rise to fame occurred in the 1926/27 season, when - as Rhyl Athletic and members of the Welsh League - they surged through to the third round of the (English) F.A.Cup, beating Stoke City (in a second replay) and Wrexham, before narrowly succumbing to Darlington. Another run was made through to the second round a year later (losing at New Brighton by 7-2 after being two goals up), and the first round in 1928 (albeit a somewhat disappointing exit to Midland League Grantham).

Although the Club had been unable to repeat their Welsh National League Championship of 1926, they considered the time was ripe for an attempt at Football League status in 1929. But that year was not the best choice, for seven clubs vied for the Northern votes, led by Mansfield Town (who gained 16) and along with Chester and Workington, Rhyl received none.

The 1929/30 season was the last for the Welsh National League, and Rhyl became founder-members of the short-lived North Wales Football Combination, moving on to the somewhat strange geographically chosen Birmingham League a year later. Although no particularly notable achievements came their way for some years, at least the Club could consider their chosen competition was a better stepping stone to the Football League, and another attempt was made in 1932.

By the 1932 New Year, the team was making a good challenge for the Birmingham League Championship being handily placed in 4th, and their hopes were reinforced after *"one of the best games of the season"*, when Cradley Heath were beaten 6-3, *"before a large number of spectators"*. A variety of results followed before an unexpected 6-0 thrashing to Kidderminster Harriers in late March, but a defeat which saw the Lilywhites (as Rhyl had been known for many years) maintain a 4th place. But by the end of April the team had slipped to 7th, and finally 5th after beating Bilston 3-2 in the last game of the season.

By now the Club had announced its intention of making another League election bid, and to reinforce their claim a run through to the Welsh Senior Cup Semi-Final (losing only after a replay to Wrexham after a 3-3 draw), *"will go a long way to assist them into the 3rd division"*, the local newspaper considered, *"their chance can be described as 'rosy'."* At the re-election meeting in May, Councillor Edwards, a Director of the Club, represented Rhyl F.C.

He told those present that the Club, formed ten years earlier, had always managed to pay its way, and the Belle Vue Ground - with a then capacity of 7,000 - would be extended to hold 15,000, including the addition of a new Stand, should their application be successful. But the attempt was fruitless, for as the local Press lamented: *"At a meeting in Manchester of the clubs of the Northern section, Rhyl applied for admission to membership of the Northern Section but failed to secure a single vote."* This statement was incorrect, for in fact they received two votes! This lack of support was unfortunate, for 1932 was a year when an excellent chance of 'promotion' was possible, for Wigan Athletic were the only other non-League applicants, and they received no votes.

Realistically speaking the chance of Football League status for Rhyl was always remote, for although they had no real competition for support, the population of the North Wales coast town was only around 14,000 at this time, with an extended catchment area that embraced just a few other small towns and villages. The Club never reached the heights in the Birmingham League, and in 1936 they tried their luck at the more suitable Cheshire County League. The early post-Second World War days were without doubt the best for Rhyl F.C., for they became Champions twice, and runners-up three times, in five consecutive seasons.

But the Club never made another attempt to join the Football League, and despite a poor end to their Cheshire County League record, they moved on to the Northern Premier League in 1983, after one good year in the North-West Counties League. With the radical changes that were forced upon clubs by the F.A. of Wales in the early 1990's, the Club are currently members of the Welsh National League. Whilst the chance of playing in Europe is realistic, the chance of playing near at home in the (English) Football League has gone for ever!

ROMFORD

(1960 - 1967, 1969 - 1972)

Romford F.C. made a prolific number of applications to the Football League (12 in total) during the 1960's and early 1970's, but only received a moderate number of votes in total, yet on one occasion they received the most of the non-Leaguers, albeit many short of that required. In some respects they had the qualifications, being a stable and generally successful club with an impressive Ground. Yet from a location viewpoint, an election to the League could have been disastrous, for laying just to the East of London, their broad catchment for support also included those of Leyton Orient and West Ham United, with Southend United not far distant, plus of course a myriad of other established non-League teams; and Thames Association's brief encounter during the early 1930's was far from a success!

A good Ground would not have been sufficient for an area already well served by football clubs.

The later Romford, founded in 1929, eventually folded in 1978, and therefore their 50 year life was in fact shorter than the 'Romford F.C.' that preceded them! The original Romford were formed in 1876 and reached the Quarter-Final of the F.A.Cup in the 1880/81 season (when they lost 15-0 to Darwen!) They also met Blackburn Rovers four years later, when the Lancashire team were on their way to winning the competition for the second time, of - eventually - three consecutive seasons.

An unimpressive career in the South Essex League followed, until the 1909/10 season, which was a disaster, for the team never completed their fixtures. The club either folded or possibly reformed, for around this time both 'Romford United' and 'Romford Town' came upon the scene.

The former, the more Senior, competed in the Athenian League for two seasons up to the Great War, but soon after the hostilities had ended both clubs faded from the scene. Earlier, 'Romford Victoria' were playing matches at Brooklands, the Ground that was to become the 1929 Romford's home venue, and also during the pre-War years was that of 'Romford Town'.

When football recommenced after the war, Great Eastern Railways (G.E.R.) Romford donned the mantle of the most senior local team for a decade and played in the Spartan League, but they folded in 1931.

In 1929, a Mr. Gurney wrote to the local newspaper suggesting that a true Romford (town) team should be formed, and he was supported by a number of prominent businessmen in the area. After an initial meeting in February, the new Romford F.C. was created on March 18th. Support at the meeting was phenomenal, such that police were required to control the crowd which had spilled out into the street. An ingenious item of publicity had been circulated, designed to intrigue, which had boldly announced *'Romford v. Aston Villa'*, referring to a fixture that may come about if a new club was formed!

Taking over the Brooklands Sports Ground, the Club was admitted to the London League for the 1929/30 season. Romford were soon 'promoted' to the Athenian League, where they were very successful, and finally the top Amateur competition - the Isthmian - in 1939, but fixtures were suspended after just one game due to the second World War. The Club reconvened after the War, and continued their membership of the Isthmian League until 1959, when they turned professional.

By this time they had reached the F.A.Amateur Cup Final (in 1949), although their league record in the post-War years was far from impressive. The 19 seasons in the Southern League that followed (most years were spent in the top division), were also not particularly flattering, although the Championship was won in 1967, a period when the club was at its best. In the F.A.Cup, during this professional period, the team had some memorable matches, reaching the 1st round on five occasions, plus the second three times, yet they were never able to overcome a Football League club.

Quite well supported, and with the use of the well developed Brooklands Sports Ground, which once held a crowd of 18,237 for an Amateur Cup match in 1953, the Club embarked on their marathon of Football League submissions in 1960. It was not the ideal year for there were 18 non-League aspirants, but Peterborough United were overwhelmingly favoured to replace Gateshead, and Romford's two votes were as good as could have been expected. The following year the scenario was similar, with Oxford United the clear and deserved favourites to move up into the League (but they would have to wait another year), and amongst a host of other hopefuls, Romford managed just one vote.

The 1961/62 season saw the Club at least finish in the top half of the Southern League table, but this was not enough to impress, and with a record number of applicants - 26 - Romford received no votes. Sanity returned a year later when a more sensible number of twelve clubs staked their claim, but the incumbents were comfortably re-elected, and with no particular team deserving of selection the votes were fairly evenly spread. Even so the Essex club received only two, and in 1964, when the team had their best finish in the Southern League to that time (fifth), they received the confidence of four votes, still woefully short of election, but the joint second best.

The mid-1960's was a period when there were no outstanding non-Leaguers, but plenty wishing to try their luck, and in 1965 and 1966 Romford managed two votes.

Romford became the Southern League Champions at the end of the 1966/67 season, and this achievement it was felt offered their best ever chance. But there were still many clubs vieing for the opportunity to move up, and despite finishing top of the hopefuls, Romford's five votes were nowhere near enough. By now the Club, along with most others, was beginning to suffer financially. Home gates were dropping annually - even the Championship season saw an average well below 3,000, and the 1967/68 campaign produced only around 2,000. A drop to sixth in the League and financial worries precluded the Club from applying for Football League membership that year.

But a year later the Club were back at the re-election meeting, although they could only muster two League supporters, and one year later after a very poor season in the Southern League, their bid really was pointless, although they still managed to get one vote. A final finish of third in the table gave the Club officials renewed hope in 1971, but just one vote was their reward again. The 1971/72 season was another disappointing one, although the team did fight through to the second round of the F.A.Cup, but in this, their last bid for 'promotion', they could not even gain one vote of confidence. The immediate future guaranteed that there would be no more re-election meetings to attend!

The next six years were generally poor ones on the pitch, and with ever increasing financial worries, it was decided that they must sell Brooklands in order to guarantee their survival, and this was not helped by the withdrawal of Romford Bombers speedway team whose rent contribution had been a godsend. Once the team had dropped into the Southern League First Division South in 1975, it became obvious that there would be no way back, although they struggled on through the 1977/78 season, having by now sold Brooklands (most of which money was used to pay their debts) and playing 'home' matches on a number of other grounds. The club folded that Summer, but were re-born some years later. The first match of the new Romford was, ironically, a Challenge match against Aldershot Town, who had also just been resurrected.

ROSSENDALE

(1894)

Look for the town of Rossendale on any map, and you won't find it! Rossendale (United) F.C. are one of those rare clubs whose name does not relate to a town. Rawtenstall, South-east of Accrington, is the Club's base, and the Forest of Rossendale defines its broad location. The town, and nearby Waterfoot (where the Ground is situated), with some turn of the century buildings and cobble streets, have to a degree defied modernisation, and can be identified with the days when this Club decided to apply for election to the Football League.

Just one attempt made over 100 years ago, but what chance was there for the club from 'nowhere'?

On the fringes of the great explosion in football that occurred in the Bolton area during the early 1870's, Rossendale F.C. owed its existence to two Scotsmen, Sandy Lamberton and his brother Wally, who migrated to the area around 1868 and were employed at the Jam Works of Samuel Whittaker in Waterfoot. They showed the locals how to play this new game - football - and from these basic beginnings, Myrtle Grove F.C. (based in the Hareholme district) was formed; the forerunners of the Rossendale Club. Later, as Rossendale F.C., the Club took over the Rugby Club's Dark Lane Ground.

However, at this time, the Club was not without competition, for apart from a myriad of teams (generally any group of eleven men or boys!), Rawtenstall (founded in 1885), became Rossendale's greatest local rivals. Rawtenstall played on an enclosed Ground just North of the town, whilst in nearby Waterfoot, Rossendale's enclosure boasted a large pavilion. But it was Rossendale who became the Senior of the two clubs becoming founder-members of the Lancashire League in 1889.

Meanwhile their rivals, whose early fixture list included games against the likes of Burnley, Accrington, Blackburn Olympic and Grimsby, joined the lesser North-East Lancashire League. But even in this competition the club employed professional players, the wage bill totalling £72 for the 1893/94 season.

Rossendale F.C. first entered the F.A.Cup in 1883, and beat Irwell Springs 6-2 in the first round, only to be disqualified from the competition! In their early days in the Cup, the team had their highs and their lows (including an 11-0 thrashing by Accrington in 1887), but their greatest triumph - still talked about in the area today (so they say!) - was the hammering of Bury F.C. during the 1892/93 season.

Having won through two rounds, the Club were drawn at home to Bury (whose pair of matches in the competition had netted them 17 goals), but realising the monetary potential, they agreed to switch the tie to Gigg Lane for £80. Bury had already beaten Rossendale 6-3 at Dark Lane (before a crowd of 4,000) in an earlier Lancashire League fixture, and Bury were therefore overwhelming favourites for the Cup game. Yet defying all the odds, Rossendale romped home with a 7-1 victory (but lost the next round 2-1 at Blackpool).

The Club's competitive career got off to a bad start, for they finished bottom of the Lancashire League table at the end of the first season, gaining just 11 points from their 24 fixtures, eight points behind next placed Fleetwood Rangers.

However, although finance was always an ever-present problem, at least support rose from the pre-league Friendly game days of several hundred to around 2,000. Steady progress was made, with final finishes of 7th (of 11) and 4th (of 12) in the next two seasons. Even more encouraging were the attendances, with 6,000 being present for the visit of Bury in October 1891. The following two seasons were not so good, with another 7th place and then 10th of just 12 clubs in 1894, by which time attendances had slumped to around 1,500, and finally barely 1,000.

At least the Club received an honour that season, when they became the League Medal Winners (the only season it was awarded), with each player receiving a gold medal. The financial struggle had continued, and after a turnover of £1,027 (lower than most other clubs in the league), and the payments to players and trainers of £498, an overall loss on the season of over £95 was recorded.

In the circumstances, 1894 hardly seems to have been the right year to try their luck for a Football League place, but with the rumours of a Second Division split into two sections, the Club decided to apply: *"At the present time it is a speculative measure."* Powerful Lancashire League rivals Bury also applied to join - despite being in a parlous financial state - and they were successful. But Rossendale really stood no chance, especially as Blackpool (Lancashire League Champions) received only eight votes, far less than the number required. At the League's A.G.M. held at the Boars Head Hotel, Withy Grove, Manchester on the 21st May, Rossendale received not one vote of support.

This attempt was destined to become the Club's one and only, for their fortunes both on and off the field rapidly deteriorated. They managed to struggle through to the end of the 1896/97 season in the Lancashire League, and then folded. Meanwhile, up the road at Rawtenstall things were no better.

After their brief career in the North-East Lancashire League, the club was accepted into the Lancashire Combination for the 1894/95 season, and finished in a very respectable 5th position. Then things turned for the worse, and after managing a lowly third from bottom a year later, Rawtenstall, dropped a further position in 1897, gaining only nine points and conceding 113 goals in 28 games. The team was not re-elected to the Combination, and like their neighbours they did not operate during the 1897/98 season.

After one season with no Senior football in the district, a meeting was held at the Royal Hotel, Waterfoot on the 6th of July 1898, *"to consider the advisability of forming a football club for the Borough of Rawtenstall"*, from which Rossendale United came into being Those attending included former members of the Rawtenstall and Rossendale clubs, although members of the Bacup club, who were also invited with a view to an amalgamation, were absent.

The Burnley Road Ground of Rawtenstall had been taken over for development, but Mr. Lord, the owner of the Dark Lane enclosure, agreed to let the new club rent the venue, and he *"would not be hard on them about the price of the ground."* A Committee was formed with six members from each district, and therefore it is fair to say that the new club were, to all intents, an amalgamation of the two old ones.

After a disastrous first season in the Lancashire Combination, Rossendale United moved into the Central Lancashire League, before a move back to the Combination in 1901, where they remained until 1970. Later periods have been spent in the Cheshire, the North-West Counties and the Northern Premier Leagues, and the Club really are no nearer - nor further - from being promoted to the Football League than their predecessors were over a century ago.

RUNCORN

(1968)

Sandwiched awkwardly between Rugby League strongholds and not far from the Merseyside duo of Liverpool and Everton, football success in Runcorn is always going to be difficult. Although with a population of around 70,000 the town is big enough to support Football League football, in view of the above alternatives, enticing spectators down to the Canal Street Ground in sufficient numbers was a problem. It remains to be seen if their groundsharing arrangement with Widnes Rugby League (after Runcorn's Ground was sold for redevelopment in 2001) proves any better.

Formed in 1918, the Club originally became part of the Highfield and Camden Tanneries Recreation Club, the Canal Street Ground being bought by the football enthusiast owner of the Tannery itself. The Ground had been used by Runcorn Rugby League Club who were formed in 1876 (as a section of the local Y.M.C.A. Athletic Club), and moved there in 1879. In 1900 a record crowd of 15,000 was present for a match versus Oldham. The Rugby Club was known as 'The Linnets', and unusually the same was adopted by the new football team.

Runcorn started their career in the 1918/19 season Lancashire Combination (wartime) Liverpool section, finishing 5th in the table of 12 teams, which notably included Liverpool, Everton, Bolton Wanderers and Blackpool (who were wooden-spoonists). Runcorn's first campaign saw them capture the Lancashire Junior Cup with a victory at Anfield in the Final.

Successes in the early 1960's, but a slump later - a strange year to try for election to the League!

But their stay in the Combination was short-lived, for on the formation of the Cheshire County League on the 25th April 1919, they became founder-members of this new competition. At the end of the season they were surprise Champions, finishing 11 points ahead of runners-up Mossley having lost only three matches. Already support for the new club was surprisingly good, when crowds of around 4,000 were seen at Canal Street.

The Club kept up their winning ways, finishing third a year later. After such a tremendous start to their career it would not have been unreasonable for them to have a stab at joining the Football League at this time in view of the formation of the Third Division North in 1921. But both the Club and the League itself were newcomers - the former having not established itself for the powerful non-League force it became in later years - and therefore perhaps discretion was the better policy. It was just as well, for the 1921/22 season ended in disaster, Runcorn finishing in bottom spot!

The Club retained their place in the Cheshire League and gradually recovered, generally maintaining a mid-table position. Then at the end of the 1936/37 season they suddenly shot to the fore again with their second Championship, scoring 156 goals in 42 league games. They maintained this good form for the two seasons leading up to the Second World War with a Runners-up spot and another Championship win.

But the return in 1945 after the hostilities saw a downturn again in the Club's fortunes, and although attendances in the post-War boom seasons were generally good (up to the 7,000 mark), they again became a mediocre mid-table team. Despite winning no major trophies, the home crowds were still in excess of most of their Cheshire contemporaries, albeit they had slumped to around 2,000 by the late 1950's, but without an exceptional playing record, an application to join the Football League would obviously have been fruitless.

The early 1960's was a morale-boosting period, with a third place and another Championship to show for their efforts, with support up again - having dropped to a barely four figure average at one time. Once more consistency was not maintained, and on this basis, 1968 seems to have been a strange year in which to make their one and only application for an enhanced status.

During their career, Runcorn had rarely achieved notable results in the F.A.Cup, the yardstick by which many clubs based their decision on when to make an application to the League. They reached the 3rd round in 1939, when the Linnets lost 4-2 at home to First Division Preston North End before a record 10,111 attendance; Aldershot were notably beaten 3-1 at Canal Street in the previous round. But the team only managed two more appearances in the second round, although significantly the latter success was in the 1967/68 season, after Notts County had been beaten 1-0 at Canal Street.

Perhaps this relatively minor triumph motivated the Club into making their single application to join the League. With no outstanding non-League clubs vieing for the honour at this time, there was always a chance, but matched up against 14 others, many of whom had better overall credentials, the chance was a slim one.

In the event Runcorn managed two votes, joint second best with six other clubs, whilst Cheltenham Town managed three, which was still woefully short of the minimum required.

At least their past season was sufficient to earn them a place in the newly formed Northern Premier League for the 1968/69 season, and eight years later they claimed the Championship of this competition. In 1981 the Club's achievements eclipsed all others when they won the 'treble' (League, League Cup and President's Cup), and were rewarded with 'promotion' into the Alliance League. In previous years this may well have been the spur that was needed to encourage another application to the Football League, but a year earlier the decision had been made that only one non-League club would be allowed to try, and in any event such a team would inevitably come from the new Alliance League.

Even now this was not the limit of the Club's achievements for at the end of their debut season they claimed another Championship (by seven clear points), which begs the question - why did the Club not put themselves forward for a Football League place? Financial restraints may have been the reason, or possibly the suitability of the Canal Street Ground, but without doubt that year offered their best chance of success. In the final event third place in the Alliance Telford United were given this honour - and failed fairly dismally!

Events since those halcyon days have not been so good, for apart from three visits to Wembley to contest the F.A.Trophy Final, it has been an overall downward slide. Ground problems caused by a serious fire and then the closure of Canal Street (but on a positive note a virtual rebuild of the venue), plus relegation to the Northern Premier League has left Runcorn with an uphill struggle to regain their place at the top of the non-League pyramid.

SALFORD UNITED

(1907)

Why Salford United F.C. ever made an application to join the Football League is something of a mystery! A team which had achieved nothing of consequence, played in only moderate grade Senior football, did not even finish in the top four of their league, and was located in a Rugby League stronghold (which was probably one of the reasons for their effort).

Although seen now as little more than a suburb just to the South-West of the centre of Manchester, Salford was at one time on a par with the current third city of England. Going back to 1801, the population of Manchester and Salford (note the joint reference) was only 84,020 - perhaps a large town even then, but a district that went on to have an enormous population explosion over the next two centuries.

A mediocre team, in a mediocre league, and in competition with rugby - a forlorn hope!

The reason for the phenomenal growth was cotton and its ancillary industries. There had been plenty of encouragement to develop football in the area, for after a number of other earlier efforts, in 1890 the 'Manchester, Salford and District Elementary Schools' (note still the name pairing) was formed, and within two years fifty schools were associated with this organisation; in 1914 The Manchester Parks Committee provided the free use of 60 football pitches for Salford youngsters.

Yet despite this apparent enthusiasm for the game at a minor level, there does not appear to have been any particular moves towards the formation of a Senior club in the Salford district. In fact, relative to other larger Lancashire towns (and many smaller ones), football was fairly slow taking off.

Meanwhile, Rugby - and particularly in Salford - became the more popular of the two sports. The first Rugby team of note was Cavendish, who were formed in 1873, changing their name to Salford in 1879. This Rugby club's formative years saw a number of Ground changes, until 1901 when they finally settled at The Willows, Weaste, which is located North of the M602 Motorway, and just to the West of Salford centre. The fact that their first game attracted a crowd of 16,891 serves to illustrate the potential for the oval ball sport in the district. Salford United F.C., was formed it is believed in 1905, for no Club of this or a similar name has been traced prior to then. There was, however, a Salford and District League that started around 1895 until at least 1898, and also the Manchester Federation which existed around the turn of the century, but there was no club by the name of Salford United attached to either.

The first traced reference is in 1905, when the Club entered the Manchester League, and played alongside the likes of Altrincham, Witton Albion, Sale and Macclesfield - note despite the competition's title these were all clubs based in Cheshire! United's baptism was hardly a great success, for in the final league table they could only attain 14th place of 16.

At least the Club could claim to have a Good ground on which to play their home matches, for in 1905, the well established Salford F.C. (Rugby) had abandoned their Reserve team in order that they might groundshare with the new Salford United F.C. (Football). However, rather than being a neighbourly gesture, this arrangement was no doubt due to the extra revenue for although popular in the area, the local Rugby club was struggling to make ends meet.

The Willows Ground in Weaste was at this time elliptical in shape with a cycling and running track surrounding the playing area. The facilities were doubtless better than the Club's contemporaries, for there was a timber and steel framed Grandstand with an ornate facia to the roof, of near pitch length, with seating at least in the central portion.

Opposite, the 'Popular' side had a half pitch length covered enclosure with an uncovered stand of similar length alongside. In addition there was the obligatory Pavilion, which was shared with the adjacent Cricket Club, plus banking at the four corners to give elevated viewpoints.

"The Reds" as they became known improved considerably the next season, and by mid-March 1907, they lay in 8th place in the table after 19 games. But there was hardly any encouragement from the Salford Press, since they reported extensively on Rugby ('Northern Union' as it was known then), the two big Manchester clubs (City and United), plus the local minor Salford League, with barely a mention of poor old Salford United. A good run-in during the final few weeks of the season saw them finally finish in 5th spot, after drawing 2-2 in the last match with Champions-elect Altrincham.

Yet what can only be described as still a fledgling club, who had finished in a modest place in the table of only a moderately Senior league, decided to make an application to join the Football League at the meeting in May 1907. Whilst their credentials as a top rating club were sorely lacking there were two factors that probably acted as an encouragement. Firstly the Club were in a Rugby stronghold, and around this period in time the Football League were keen to encourage election applications from such outfits in well populated areas. Leeds City a year earlier had strolled into the League on this ticket, as did Oldham Athletic in 1908 and Huddersfield Town three years later.

The second reason for a bid was no doubt due to their location, close to and just North of the centre of Manchester, with an enormous catchment area, and not encroaching upon the League's two representatives, City and United. But Salford United's bid fell on deaf ears, and it probably came as no surprise when they did not receive a single vote.

Rather than aim for a higher league, the Club were content to remain in the Manchester League (perhaps their ambition of Football League status had already disappeared), but the 1907/08 season was a poor one, for the team could only finish in 13th place. A year later there was a vast improvement which saw Salford rise to 8th which must have given encouragement for the 1909/10 season. At last real success was achieved when the team topped the final league with Hurst (and with a better goal average), and were declared 1910 Champions after winning the deciding play-off.

However, during that campaign another, unsurmountable, factor evolved that was to see the rapid downfall of Salford United. On 19th February 1910, Manchester United moved across the City to start life in their brand new Old Trafford Ground. Unfortunately for the Club, Old Trafford was located less than two miles South of Salford. For the first match at this brand new venue an enormous crowd of 45,000 was present, including *"several thousands who had walked the road in from Salford."* Salford United struggled on for another year, but slumped to second from bottom.

In contrast Manchester United were crowned the Football League Champions, and the support for the other professional club nearby had all but disappeared. The Club disbanded that Summer, and Salford remains today as arguably the largest City in England never to have had a Football League club!

SITTINGBOURNE

(1962)

Sittingbourne are probably the only club that made a single 'no hope' attempt to join the Football League, yet in the few years since automatic promotion has been available, they really looked - for just a brief period - as if they could possibly make it. Kent has only had two League representatives (currently Gillingham and for just three seasons Maidstone United), and although there have been five other aspirants over the years, on paper Sittingbourne were always the least likely to achieve this goal.

Not many clubs, at least in the South of England, can trace their formation back as far as Sittingbourne F.C. having first seen the light of day in 1881 as Sittingbourne Un-ited. They first played home matches on the newly opened Recreation Ground, and five years later the club was reformed and renamed, when the 'United' was omitted. A further two years on, in 1888, one of their principal rivals in the town, who rejoiced in the amazing name of 'Nil Desperandum' (loosely meaning 'do not despair'), merged with the Club. By now football had become very popular, and the Recreation Ground was becoming increasingly overcrowded with football teams, therefore Sittingbourne F.C. - clearly the local club with the greatest ambition - moved their home venue to Gore Cricket Ground.

No-hopers in 1962, in with a realistic chance of promotion 30 years later, but currently in a slump!

In 1892 a further move was made to Vallance's Meadow, a field behind the Bull Hotel in the centre of town, and this venue was taken on a five year lease. The Meadow became 'The Bull Ground' which the Club soon set about enclosing, and for the first time admission could be charged, at 3d. (1p).

It wasn't until 1893 that the Club achieved Senior status, and still Amateur, they first entered the three major cup competitions (F.A., F.A. Amateur and Kent Senior), and also became founder-members of the Kent League (formerly the Kent Senior Cup) a year later. Around this time an impressive Grandstand was built, the basic structure of which remained until the ground was vacated in 1990. But it was not long before professionalism was adopted, in 1898.

Much of the Club's life has been spent in the Kent League, although they had a two season absence when they opted for the South-Eastern League in 1905, and a three year Southern League break from 1927. They resumed playing in the Kent League after the break caused by the Second World War, before returning to the Southern for the 1959/60 season, but once again this elevation was only for a few years.

With just three Kent League Championships to their credit, in 1903, 1958 and 1959, Sittingbourne were a fairly modest club with modest ambitions. During the rapid expansion of the Southern League, the Club rejoined in 1959, and for three seasons were reasonably successful, finishing 6th, 5th and 7th in the First (second tier) Division.

In the last two of those seasons, Sittingbourne made a serious challenge for promotion. During the 1961/62 season, their 2-0 set-back at Dartford in the last match of 1961 - their first defeat in 14 games - signalled the start of a slump. Two home defeats followed early in the New Year, but the exciting 5-3 Bull Ground victory over fellow Kent club Margate (watched by a way above average 2,100) gave reason for hope.

Indifferent form to the end of the season saw the team fade away, when more typical home attendances of 1,100 (for the 1-0 victory over Trowbridge) and 1,200 (a 3-2 defeat to Barry) were produced. A last few games surge was not enough to gain a coveted place, and the last match, a 2-0 victory over Hinckley, attracted only 900 fans to the match.

In 1962, the carrot of a definite election vacancy to the Football League (due to the mid-season resignation of Accrington Stanley) was dangled before the non-League world, and a mad rush to be the favoured club saw a near record 26 teams put their names forward. With Oxford United the clear favourite, virtually all the remainder had no hope whatsoever.

Sittingbourne were one of the 15 complete no-hopers who correspondingly received no votes. They, like Poole Town who also applied, were only an above average Southern League club from the First Division, whilst there were far worthier names such as those from the three cities of Chelmsford, Guildford and Bath, all three being prominent Premier Division clubs.

A dismal period in the league followed before the Club finally resigned and rejoined the Kent League in 1967, where they enjoyed reasonable success with two title wins, and several runners-up placings, to 1990. In February of that year the Club's life took a dramatic turn, following the selling of their Bull Ground, a prize building site, for £6½ million, and their move to the new Central Park ground that was being built on the outskirts of town.

Fairly rapidly Sittingbourne F.C. was transformed. An amazing all-seater 40,000 capacity dream Stadium began to unfold, a 23 acre venue that would host several other sports, not least Greyhound racing. A modest temporary seated Stand was first built whilst the first giant Stand was started behind it.

The Club swept all before them in the 1990/91 season and they were immediately re-admitted to the Southern League. Just two years later they walked away with the First Division title, and Gillingham F.C. suddenly had to treat the new boys on the block with a degree of trepidation. From attendances of just a few hundred a few years earlier, Sittingbourne suddenly had a team worth supporting - including several full time professionals - with nearly 6,000 present for the official opening of the Ground when Tottenham Hotspur appeared, and 3,074 for the local derby with Gravesend and Northfleet.

Then things suddenly started going wrong. Gross over-ambition led to gross overspending, and work on the Stadium was called to a halt. The temporary Stand seating 200 became the only seated Stand, and the planned 40,000 capacity dropped to a fifth of that number. For a while things were not too bad, with an initial 8th place in the Premier Division and crowds of up to 2,000, but the money situation soon caused the bubble to burst and hopes of a rapid rise to the Football League itself in a Stadium far surpassing many others in that competition, became no more than a dream as the nightmare continued.

Relegation, followed by promotion and demotion again in 1998, sees Sittingbourne once again as a modest club, presumably with modest ambitions.

SOUTH LIVERPOOL

(1914, 1921, 1937, 1938, 1939, 1947-51)

This is really a story of two clubs with the same name. The original South Liverpool was founded around the mid-1890's, and were initially named Africa Royal F.C. (a Shipping Company, and hence presumably a 'works' team at this time). A name change followed plus an entry to their first major league, The Combination, in 1898. Although their stay was brief, just one season (this competition was at the forefront of the non-League world with a total of eight of its members during its history who were to later join the Football League).

Two teams with the same name - but both with the same ending; rejection and oblivion.

Another short period was spent, this time in the Lancashire League, before several years out of Senior football. In 1911, the team came upon the scene again, entering the Lancashire Combination Division 2, yet amazingly a few months earlier they had been one of twenty clubs who had applied to join the proposed new Third Division. This proposal was turned down, and another ten years was to elapse before this addional division came to fruition.

Two successful seasons in the Combination led to promotion in 1913 to the First Division. Support for the team at this time was incredibly good, for an attendance of around 18,000 was attracted to the quaintly named Dingle Lane Ground in the affluent area of Toxteth, for the first home game, against neighbours Tranmere Rovers. Their first season in the First Division produced a final placing in the table of 6th, and with such excellent support it is little wonder that the Club felt worthy of election to the Football League. But taking into account they had virtually no track record, not surprisingly their effort produced no votes.

The team carried on playing during the First World War years and were quite successful, then in 1919 they were devastated to learn that their Dingle Ground had been sold to the Mersey Docks and Harbour Board, and in November that year they played their last match at this venue. Forced to ground-share with other clubs, their fortunes on the pitch deteriorated, yet they made another forlorn attempt for Football League status in 1921, and this time it was no surprise when they finished bottom of the voting table, despite the large influx of new clubs for the new Third Division North. Homeless, the Club folded during the Summer of 1921.

Despite the obvious football potential for a Senior club in the area, it was not until 1935 that the second South Liverpool was formed, following a meeting on the 15th February. The idea of a new club had been instigated by Arthur Joynson, who had been associated with the former outfit.

A suitable Ground was soon found, at Holly Farm, and with good financial support, the Club entered the Lancashire Combination for the 1935/36 season. Success was immediate, and after topping the 1937 final table, the Club applied for League status. Although reasonably well established they received only four votes of support, even though there were only three new applicants.

The following two years produced further applications, and on each occasion their votes only improved to five.

The Club must have understandably been greatly disappointed with these outcomes, for they had proved themselves worthy contenders having captured the Championship of the Combination twice again, to make it three in a row. Not only on the field were they successful, but the, now named, Holly Park Ground was gradually improved. Crowds at top games often topped 5,000, and good F.A.Cup runs had been enjoyed. Overall, the Club surely deserved a place with the elite, as much or more than any other.

War took its toll on the Club, as the earlier one had on the previous South Liverpool, and the team were never able to dominate as before. For a few years they played in the Cheshire League but without any outstanding success, and it was during this period that a run of five consecutive applications for Football League status were made. The first in 1947 was a wasted effort since all the re-election clubs were voted back in without a vote being taken. A year later, when the team finished in only a moderate ninth place in the final table, just one vote was gained. Even so, five clubs received none, including Workington who three years later, were voted in!

In 1949, when there were six applicants for the Northern section, the only two to receive any support were Shrewsbury and Scunthorpe, clubs that were also to make it a year later. Countrywide, football was enjoying a boom in support in post-War England, and although South Liverpool could attract two or three thousand to matches, these numbers were well down on their own halcyon days before the hostilities. Even so an all-time record attendance was attracted to Holly Park for the visit of the often quoted 'bare-footed' (none in fact were) Nigerian team in 1949, when 13,007 crammed into the Ground. However, by the early 1950's support for the team plummeted, and three figure attendances became the norm.

The 1949/50 season was a very disappointing one for the Club, for they finished in 18th place of 22, yet still persisted in making a Football League bid.

The resulting single vote was perhaps more than they deserved. Their final application was made the following year, despite performances on the field that were hardly an improvement, with a final finish one higher than a year earlier, at 17th. South Liverpool, along with Northwich Victoria were the only Northern clubs to receive no votes. Sensibly the Club decided that these efforts were futile, at least in their position at that time, and no more applications to join were made.

An even worse season followed in 1951/52, finishing second from bottom, and at that time the Club decided to return to the Lancashire Combination. The change of scenery brought little in the way of a change of luck, and only occasionally did the team rise above mid-table. The one bright spark was the Championship in 1966, but by now all hope of Football League status had been abandoned.

In 1968, the Club became founder-members of the Northern Premier League, *"I am confident that within 12 years South will be in the League and attracting 30,000 attendances without harming Liverpool or Everton,"* was the pipe dream stated by a Club Director at the time! The reality 12 years later was that South Liverpool finished 3rd from bottom of the Northern Premier League and attracted average attendances at Holly Park of around 200.

This once highly successful non-League club struggled on with success at a premium, and frequent vandalism at the Ground added to their woes. Despite two life-saving transformations by way of new blood, the Club finally had to leave Holly Park following further acts of vandalism and arson, and South Liverpool finally threw in the towel in 1991.

An enthusiastic band of supporters reformed South Liverpool, but currently playing in the Liverpool County Combination, it's a long, long way back to the top.

SOUTH SHORE

(1889)

It is questionable whether South Shore should be included here, for the Club amalgamated with Blackpool F.C. in 1899. However, since the two clubs lived very separate existences until that year this Club surely deserves its own independence! In fact South Shore's application to join the Football League pre-dates that of Blackpool by five years, and by applying in 1889, this makes the Club (jointly) the first ever to make an application and be refused; along with Sunderland Albion and Mitchell St. George's they are not only the first, but also the only ones never to have made it to the top.

One of three clubs to make the first ever Football League application, and who never made it to the top.

Football first came to this Seaside town in the late 1870's, and in 1879 (Blackpool) South Shore F.C. - as they were prefixed at the time - was founded, in those early days playing home matches off Lytham Road. At this time there was also a 'Blackpool F.C.' but the Football League club of that name was not founded until 1887 (a breakaway group from Blackpool St. Johns who formed their own club after the Chairman and Vicar of St. Johns refused to delete the suffix to their name). Therefore, South Shore was the Senior club in Blackpool around the late 1880's, and in fact as early as the 1882/83 season they first entered the F.A.Cup, although their initial match was lost 5-2 at Darwen Ramblers in the first round.

For their first ten years, South Shore had to depend on Friendly matches, local cup competitions, and most importantly F.A.Cup games. Their first victory in the latter competition came in the 1883/84 season when they beat Clitheroe at home 3-2, but then faced Blackburn Rovers in the 2nd round. There was a crowd of only 700 to see the homesters thrashed 7-0; but they had lost to the eventual winners.

The 1885/86 season was without doubt the Club's most successful in the Cup, for they fought through to the 6th round, the quarter-finals, when they entertained the London club - Swifts - and were narrowly defeated 2-1.

With the formation of the Football League in 1888, competitive football radically changed. South Shore were not invited or considered to be worthy of inclusion in the competition that first season, but they did join The Combination (despite their name not being put forward amongst the original 18 clubs), a league which attempted to run parallel with the Football League, but became far less disciplined with regard to the regular playing of fixtures. The Combination closed down on the 5th April 1889 with many games still outstanding. South Shore's record was reasonable having played 14 matches, of which five were won and two drawn.

On the 3rd May 1889, the first re-election meeting took place at the Douglas Hotel Manchester. The bottom four League clubs were required to stand for re-election, whilst there were applications from nine others to join. Seven of the applicants were represented at the meeting (Grimsby Town and Walsall Town Swifts applied in writing!), and South Shore were one of the hopefuls.

But there was no place for any of the newcomers, as all four clubs were comfortably re-elected. The only new clubs to receive any votes were the four teams that had been considered for the inaugural season of the Football League (headed by Mitchell St. George's from Birmingham with five votes) plus 'newcomers' Sunderland F.C.

This rejection must have been a disappointment for the South Shore club, and unlike most of the unsuccessful applicants who joined the new Football Alliance for the 1889/90 season, the Club opted to continue to play Friendly and cup matches. In the F.A.Cup that season they lost 4-2 at home to Aston Villa of the Football League in the 1st round.

Whilst South Shore may not be one of the most famous of clubs to grace the competition, they have gone down in history in respect of an additional rule that they instigated. Drawn to play Chatham in Kent in the 1st round during the 1888/89 season, South Shore were dismayed to find that the home club played on an open field where no gate money could be taken, and therefore they would not be recompensed in any way for their long journey (they also lost the game!). South Shore wrote to the Lancashire F.A. who in turn proposed the change that: *"A club not having an enclosed ground where 'gate' money may be taken should play on its opponents' ground."* This proposal was sent to and adopted by the Football Association.

In 1891 the Club joined the Lancashire League, by which time neighbours Blackpool F.C. - who were founder-members - were already a major force in the competition. With runners-up placings on four occasions and Champions once in the first six seasons, Blackpool by now had surged ahead to become the major football force in the town.

During this period the record of South Shore was far less impressive with final finishes of 8th, 10th and 8th again (of 12) in their first three seasons. But financially South Shore may well have been the better off, for attendances at their Cow Gap Lane were not unreasonable with 3,000 in attendance for the league visit of Bury, and a 2,305 crowd present in the F.A.Cup versus the same team.

Despite their election to the Football League in 1896, Blackpool F.C. found it hard going both on and off the field, and before their election, there had been an agreement on the 18th of April between the two local rivals to pool their resources and amalgamate. But South Shore later pulled out of the deal. That year Blackpool became a Limited Company but this did not halt their financial problems, caused principally by a big wage bill and gates that barely averaged 2,000.

By the late 1890's, South Shore were also suffering financially, and in the 1899/1900 season when they vacated their cramped Cow Gap Lane Ground which included just one covered seated Stand for around 300 and generally narrow flat standing areas elsewhere, it must have strained their resources. Their new Ground was unfinished when they moved in, with no roped enclosure or Grandstand, and was located in Bloomfield Road.

The first match there saw the 1st South Lancashire Regiment beaten 6-3 on the 21st October, and the formal opening of the enclosure brought Newton Heath (later Manchester United) as visitors in the 3rd qualifying round of the F.A.Cup, which was won 3-1. In the next round there was another big crowd present for the 1-1 draw with Southport Central, but in the replay South Shore lost 4-1, their last ever game in the competition.

Meanwhile Blackpool, rejected from the Football League in 1899, were desperate to find a new Ground as the development of their Raikes Hall Ground was imminent. They visited Bloomfield Road on the 9th of December, and that evening, after the Lancashire League match with South Shore, the two clubs decided at long last to amalgamate, and to use the Bloomfield Road Ground as 'home'.

STALYBRIDGE ROVERS

(1900, 1901)

At the end of the 1922/23 season, the local newspaper stated that: *"The town is not big enough to sustain a Third Division team."* This was in reference to the resignation of Stalybridge Celtic from the Third Division North after just two seasons as a middle of the table club in the Football League. These sentiments would no doubt have also applied around the turn of the century when the town's top team at that time - Stalybridge Rovers - made their two applications to join the League. With a population at this time of around 20,000 and situated on the Eastern periphery of Manchester it is difficult to see how a club in the town could attract sufficient support.

After two good seasons, the second attempt at election could well have been successful - but Bristol City upset the party!

Apart from the large numbers of Football League and Senior non-League teams in the big city itself, within easy travelling distances there are also the clubs in Oldham, Ashton-under-Lyne, Hyde and Mossley, and therefore there always has been competition for support from such catchment areas.

The Rovers were probably formed in the early 1890's, entering the Lancashire League in 1895 (after a season in The Combination), and within a few years they became a formidable force in the competition. The club had secured a very well appointed Ground just to the North-east of the town centre, off the currently named Waterfield Road, which included a large seated Stand (with standing room to the front). The Club won no honours the first season in the League, but finished in a satisfactory 6th position.

They made their first entry to the F.A.Cup a year earlier, where their progress was immediately halted by Wrexham who won 3-2 at Stalybridge. The 1896/97 season produce similar records in both league (one place higher) and the F.A.Cup, but the following campaign they did have limited success in the Cup, first beating Halliwell Rovers 2-1 at home in the first qualifying round, then Southport Central (3-1, also at home) before losing at Chorley.

After a slight dip in form a year later, when the team ended up just below half way, in 1899 their winning habit returned and they were back up to 5th, of 13 teams. The 1899/00 season produced a very satisfying Lancashire League campaign, for they finished as runners-up and also had what transpired to be their best run in the F.A.Cup. South Liverpool (1-0), Stockport County (Lancashire League Champions that season), and Port Vale were beaten in the early rounds, before the team met their match at Southern League Bristol City's St. John's Lane Ground, when they lost 2-1 before a 5,000 crowd.

After such an overall good campaign the Club decided to make their first election bid for a place in the Football League. But in what was only their second attempt, Stockport County scraped in with a narrow 'victory' over Doncaster Rovers after initial tied voting, and this left little for the other three bidders, Loughborough, Kettering, and lastly Stalybridge, who received the fewest number, with just one vote. A year later, with Stockport now out of the way (even so the County only just survived a re-election bid), the Rovers went one better.

For the Rovers became the Lancashire League Champions. It was, however, a close fought affair with only goal average separating them and Southport Central. The Rovers made another bid to join the League, and although they received seven votes (the same as rejected Walsall), it turned out to be an unfortunate year for their attempt. For Bristol City (with no past attempts) won by a mile, securing 23 votes, their popularity being probably encouraged by the Football League itself who welcomed an extension of the competition to two in the overall South, and the first in the South-west of the country.

Whether Rovers would have made it if it had not been for the 'intrusion' of Bristol City is open to conjecture. But in any event the Stalybridge club were destined never to apply again. In 1902, they dropped to fifth in the Lancashire League, and a year later - the last for this competition - they could only manage fourth place of 12.

In any event the Football League did not receive any more bids from the clubs of the ailing Lancashire League. In fact such was the lack of prestige of this league that Stalybridge Rovers and several other members were only invited to join the Lancashire Combination within the new Second Division! But Rovers proved themselves by finishing third and were promoted to the First Division for the 1904/05 season.

After several good, or at least reasonable, seasons, the Club suffered a slump, which was to become terminal.

They finished second from bottom in 1905 - but escaped relegation - and after an improvement to mid-table a year later, at the end of the 1906/07 season they finished bottom. It had been a dreadful season when only five games were won and four drawn of the 38, and 137 goals were conceded. In keeping with this form the Club's last F.A.Cup match ended as a 7-1 defeat at St.Helen's Recreation the next season.

At this juncture, Senior football in Stalybridge becomes somewhat difficult to identify in detail. Stalybridge Celtic were a completely separate club to the Rovers, and in fact were probably formed in 1906 (not 1909 as some records show), thereby overlapping Rovers' existence.

However at this time they were very minor and probably played only Friendly matches until 1909 (when they entered the Lancashire and Cheshire League). However, this big rise in status could be attributed to one man, Herbert Rhodes, who not only played in the Celtic's first match in 1906, but many years later personally ploughed many thousands of pounds into the club, which saw them eventually become a member of the Football League.

Celtic's elevation was relatively easy for they were elected into the new Third Division North in 1921, but who knows, if Bristol City hadn't been around at the right (or wrong) time, Stalybridge may at this time have already been represented by the Rovers!

STOCKTON

(1947)

Over the past century and more, there have been a number of Senior clubs carrying the name of 'Stockton' within their title. But the first on the scene was plain 'Stockton F.C.', who were founder-members of the Cleveland Association in 1882, and this original club was also the longest lived, surviving until 1975; their nickname 'The Ancients' was therefore particularly appropriate.

It was to be many years before the Club made their single application to join the Football League, and they spent the interim period principally as a prominent Amateur club.

A futile attempt (along with several others in the North-east) to be elected.... and it didn't even go to the vote!

After several seasons of Friendly and Cup fixtures, Stockton became founder-members of the second oldest League in the World (and still operating) - The Northern League - in 1889. Initially the competition was open to both professional and amateur clubs, but in 1906 it became purely amateur, by which time the Club had themselves adopted this status. The introduction of the F.A.Amateur Cup in 1893 found favour in the North-east of the country, and the early years of the competition saw several clubs from this area make their mark.

South Bank reached the semi-finals in the 1894/95 season - having beaten Stockton in the first round proper - and Middlesbrough (the current Football League club) actually won the competition. Two years later Stockton were Finalists themselves, losing out only after a replay to the renowned Old Carthusians team. The Club reached the Final again in 1899, and this time won it by beating Harwich and Parkeston 1-0 at Middlesbrough.

A member of the team was Chatt, a reinstated Amateur player, who had the unusual distinction of also earlier winning an F.A.Cup medal whilst playing (and scoring) for Aston Villa in 1895. In the years leading up to the First World War, The Ancients won the Amateur Cup on two more occasions, and vied with Bishop Auckland for the title as top Amateur club in the North-east.

The early days also saw a few successes in the Northern League, despite the competition during part of this period being dominated by the reserve teams of the local Football League clubs.

The inter-war years were the heyday for the Club, and support was at a high. Even during the depression years of the 1920's the team could attract crowds of 5,000 to their Victoria Ground, and in the early 1930's attendances of seven or eight thousand were common. After losing 4-1 to Kingstonian in the 1933 Amateur Cup Final, a match in which they were clear favourites, The Ancients suffered a dramatic loss of form, from which they never really recovered. The following season they lost in the Cup to 'unknown' locals Portrack Shamrock, and could only finish 5th in the Northern League.

On the 7th February 1939, the Club decided to turn professional, a perhaps surprising choice in view of their past dominance in the Amateur field, but presumably undertaken in an effort to rekindle their past glories. They applied to join the North-Eastern League for the 1939/40 season, but the War soon intervened and therefore they were unable to judge whether this change in status was beneficial.

A full programme recommenced as early as 1944 for the North-Eastern League, but once again the inclusion of several Football League clubs in the competition, as experienced earlier in the Northern League, limited the opportunities for honours for the majority non-League contingent.

The end of the War signalled a euphoric rise of interest in football throughout the country, and clubs everywhere - both professional and amateur - enjoyed vastly increased support at the turnstiles. Optimism tended to dictate sensible thinking at many clubs, all of whom considered they could do better at a higher level, and some considered themselves worthy of the Football League itself.

Stockton did not win any major honours during the 1946/47 season, and finished a moderate 7th in the league, although notably they did reach the 1st round proper of the F.A.Cup (for the fifth time from 1925), when they lost 4-2 to Lincoln City before an 8,058 attendance at the Victoria Ground. Yet this was the year they considered making a bid for Football League status.

The situation was bordering on farce for the 1947 re-election stakes, since an unprecedented 27 clubs made a bid. Worse still for Stockton was the fact that no less than four other clubs from the area were also attempting to join the League - Annfield Plain, Ashington, Consett, and North Shields.

None of these clubs would have stood a chance even in normal circumstances, and none of the remaining 22 teams who applied were sufficiently dominant in the non-League world. But the circumstances turned out to be abnormal, for it was decided that after the upheaval of the War, and the difficulty for many clubs in re-adjusting to peacetime conditions, the four re-election candidates that year would be reinstated without a vote being taken.

'Only' 18 clubs applied for election the following year, and from the North-east just one - North Shields - made the attempt. Stockton, obviously now with a better sense of reality, appreciated that another try would be futile, although ironically they did have further successes in the F.A.Cup that season. For only the second time (since 1925) the team reached the second round, and narrowly lost at this stage after an extra time replay, to Notts County. The first tie at the County Ground drew a crowd of 30,158, and such was the interest in the replay that it was staged at Ayresome Park Middlesbrough, where an incredible crowd of 34,261 was present.

The Ancients won the North-Eastern League title in 1951, but this was to be their last major success as the crowds disappeared, and financial problems arose. In 1958 they reverted to Amateur status, by the mid-1960's they had dropped in to the relatively humble Wearside League, and in 1973 plunged even lower to the Northern Alliance.

Two years later the Club folded, and their well developed Victoria Ground - which had been home since their formation - soon became a housing estate; but at least the former football club's exploits were remembered in the naming of the roads thereon - 'Wembley Court' and 'Wembley Way'.

Three 'other' Stocktons have since evolved; 'Stockton F.C.' who until 1999 played in the Northern League, 'Stockton Buffs' (later 'Town') who came and went in the 1980's, and 'Norton and Stockton Ancients', who are also members of the Northern League. It would be far to fanciful to consider that either of these two survivors could ever grace the Football League.

SUNDERLAND ALBION

(1889 - 1891)

Bristol, Liverpool and Sheffield each have two; London and Manchester have several; but in the football-mad North-east of the Country, Middlesbrough, Newcastle and Sunderland only have one each. Albeit Middlesbrough did have another Football League team - i.e. Ironopolis, for one season, but Middlesbrough F.C. only came upon this scene some years later. Newcastle had two aspirants - in East End and West End - before United were established, whilst on Wearside, both Sunderland F.C. and Sunderland Albion vied for the honour.

At one time it looked as if the Albion would become the top club in Sunderland.

In 1879, Sunderland F.C. was one of the first clubs to be formed in the area, founded by John Graystone and James Allan, two schoolteachers, they were initially known as 'Sunderland and District Teachers Association (Football Club)'. They joined the newly formed Northumberland and Durham F.A., and a year later their title was abbreviated to 'Sunderland Association F.C.', by which time they had established a home Ground at the Blue House Field, in the Hendon district.

After three short tenures elsewhere, the club finally settled in Newcastle Road, playing their first match at this venue in April 1886. Cup and Friendly matches were the only fare on offer, and during the 1887/88 season they were drawn against Middlesbrough in the F.A.Cup. Support for the team was good, and 8,000 were at Newcastle Road to see the 4-2 replay victory, but the match was declared void due to Sunderland playing three Scottish professional players who did not fulfil the necessary residential qualifications.

The repercussions that followed led to disquiet at the club, which lingered on until one of the founder-members of the club - James Allan - set up a meeting on 13th March 1888, when he, plus several members and most of the Scottish players, met in the Empress Hotel and formed a breakaway club, Sunderland Albion. For a home Ground they settled on the former home of Sunderland F.C., the Blue House Field, and within two months played their first match there, versus Shankhouse Black Watch.

For the 1888/89 season the Albion fielded four sides, and obviously became a threat to their older local rivals. There was great animosity between the two clubs, and Sunderland F.C., in an effort to maintain their lionshare of support in the town, built a clubhouse for the players and carried out improvements to the Ground to create the best enclosure in the North-east with a 15,000 capacity.

By coincidence the two clubs were drawn to play each other in successive weeks in the F.A. and Durham Cups. The prospect created much interest amongst the local football fans, then amazingly a week before the first game, Sunderland withdrew from both ties. Sunderland F.C. used the rather lame excuse that the club felt that Cup-ties had outlived their purpose of generating interest in the game and could now be abandoned. However, the general consensus was that the financial rewards that would come to the Albion by playing the two games would help to financially establish these rebels.

This unpopular decision by Sunderland F.C. led to pressures which eventually led to a Friendly between the two clubs - Albion refusing to donate their share of the gate to Charity as suggested - and a 10,000 crowd at Newcastle Road saw the newcomers lose 2-0.

A second meeting of the two clubs was played on the 12th January 1889, the older club refusing to play at Hendon, and this boiled up into violence when an Albion goal was disallowed. The visiting players left the field in protest, the Sunderland supporters retaliated by stoning the visiting officials as they left, and James Allan (in effect a founding member of both clubs) was hit in the eye and had to receive medical treatment.

Albion had a successful first (complete) season, winning the Durham Cup and reaching the first round of the F.A.Cup, and both clubs decided to apply for membership of the Football League in its first ever re-election meeting. There was no way in for any newcomers, but significantly the older established Sunderland team received two votes, whilst the newcomers, Albion, received none. For the following season, Sunderland Albion fielded their first team in the new Football Alliance (league), and another successful campaign followed with the Club finishing 3rd.

In March 1890, the Albion became the 'Sunderland Albion Football and Athletic Club Limited', with a share capital of £3,000, whilst the Blue House Ground now had *"the only cinder cycling track in Sunderland and grandstands well and substantially built."* Once again the two Sunderland clubs both made applications to join the Football League that year.

But to their dismay, Albion were rejected (no votes were recorded), and worse still, Sunderland F.C. were welcomed in at the expense of Stoke. This must have been a severe blow to the Albion, for their rivals already commanded greater support in the town, and now they would be playing at a higher level.

But the Club plugged on, and by the end of the 1890/91 season they again showed that they had a formidable team; they were runners-up (of 12) in the Football Alliance, and now also playing their first team in the Northern League, achieved a respectable 3rd place. That year the Club made their third, and as it transpired, final bid to join the Football League.

But once again they failed, and despite the increase in membership by two - Stoke regaining their place plus newcomers Darwen - Sunderland Albion were virtually shunned, receiving just one vote, with Newton Heath (later Manchester United) the only club to fare worse with none.

As Sunderland F.C. began soaring to the top, Albion were left in the cold, and support dwindled further, with a reported huge financial loss in 1891 of £748. They resigned from the Football Alliance (ironically if they had remained they may well have gained a coveted place in the Football League a year later when this competition was virtually voted en block to become the new Second Division), and concentrated on just the Northern League.

But things gradually got worse, and they finished 6th of 9 in the league, and on Sunderland F.C.'s eventual first (and last) visit to the Blue House Ground in April, the homesters were slaughtered 8-0 before a crowd of only 2,000.

On the 12th of May 1892, the Club's Directors and a large number of Shareholders met at the Empress Hotel to consider the financial position of the Club, and whether it could carry on. It was announced that a £500 guarantee was necessary from those present, and when this was not forthcoming, the Directors announced that they would see the season out, then wind-up the company. Sunderland Albion went into voluntary liquidation in August 1892.

WAKEFIELD CITY

(1921)

Another claimant for the 'Biggest City in England without a Football League team', and this could be extended to the 'Biggest without even a Senior non-League club'. Wakefield is, and always has been, virtually a football barren town, where Rugby League dominates, and in all likelihood will continue so. Or will it? The nearby successful village team of Emley are now playing in the City, and although unlikely to say the least, there is always the chance.......

It would be difficult to find a more Rugby orientated City and surrounds than that which exists in Wakefield, and consequently the oval ball form of football has completely dominated Winter sporting pursuits since the 1870's. Wakefield Trinity (Northern Union) rugby club was formed in 1873 as a section of the Holy Trinity Church Young Mens' Society, and they played their first games on Heath Common, not far distant from the Club's later Belle View Ground, where they finally settled.

The first serious effort to field a Senior football club in the town came with the formation of Wakefield City in 1906. The Club played their home matches on the old Elm Tree Street Ground, and started immediately as a professional club. Despite the status they chose, they played in the relatively minor, 17 strong former West Yorkshire League (the 'Leeds League' adopted this title in 1928). The Club entered the F.A.Cup in the 1907/08 season, and no club could surely have had a worse baptism.

Founded in 1920, applied in 1921, and encouraged by the League itself... yet the attempt was a dismal failure.

Drawn at home to Denaby United in the 1st qualifying round they were completely outplayed by the strong Midland League club, and lost 13-0! This club's bold attempt at establishing itself soon fizzled out, and the name was not heard of again until after the First World War.

Another (or possibly a reformation of the original) Wakefield City came upon the scene again in 1920, when 70 enthusiasts met on the 17th March at the George Hotel in Wakefield. The intention was to form a professional club again and hopefully enter the Midland League or failing that the Lancashire Combination, despite the town being located in Yorkshire!

Promises of help had come from Bradford (Park Avenue), Castleford Town and Yorkshire Amateurs clubs, and the new 'City' were encouraged when they received over 100 applications from players..

Wakefield City played their first match exactly one month later when a 'Mr. Mailey's XI' (the Secretary/Manager of Bradford P.A. who included several of his players in his team), won 4-1 before a crowd of 1,300. Further defeats to Leeds United and Huddersfield Town followed. Unlike their predecessors, home matches were played at the Coach Road Ground in Outwood, off the current main A61 road, about 3/4 mile to the North of the City. This was a well-banked Ground with a railed pitch perimeter fence and capable of holding 8 to 10,000.

Harry Tufnell (ex-Barnsley) was appointed the Manager, and season tickets were priced at 7/6d. (37p) for the coming season, their first complete one. The Club became founder-members of the Yorkshire League, but an unremarkable campaign saw them finish 6th of 13.

The Club was also professional from the start, but even with gates in the early days averaging a moderate 1,500 (although Yorkshire Amateurs attracted 3,000, and Acomb around 4,000), this was not sufficient to avoid financial losses - *"expensive hasbeens"*, as the players - several from Football League clubs - were referred to.

With the intention of applying to join the League, the Club were formed into a Limited Company on the 2nd February 1921, and there is little doubt that the Football League gave the Club every encouragement as they attempted to spread the influence of football into rugby dominated districts.

But Wakefield's application was wasted for they hardly had a good track record, although no doubt the possibility of election was considered reasonable due to the introduction of the Third Division North that year.

Amongst the attempts from Yorkshire clubs, Castleford Town received 18 votes, and Wakefield City managed four - another indication that as much as possible the League was encouraging the 'Rugby towns'; Wombwell, who it was said were attracting 7-10,000 crowds due to their inclusion of many ex-League players, had intended to apply, but then withdrew their application.

The Club's failure to secure a place with the elite could not have been very surprising, but to aid their future credibility they applied for, and were accepted into the Midland League.

Well out of their depth, the season was little short of disastrous for the team finished second from bottom, with just two points more than tail-enders Lincoln City Reserves. With nine victories and 24 defeats, from their 42 matches they conceded 103 goals - the worst defensive record in the league. By now the Club had taken out a lease on a Ground in Thornes Lane, to the South-east of the City centre. The new venue had two or three rows of terracing, but no Stand or seating, but the intention was to develop it to give a final capacity for 15 to 20,000.

For the 1922/23 season the club opted to play their first team in the Yorkshire League, for their Midland exploits had proved to be even more financially draining. But the ambition to join the Football League must have already been abandoned, for the rest of their years they did not even enter the F.A.Cup again.

A final move was made to Westgate Common, back in the Outwood area, but the Club was unable to win any honours, and during their remaining six seasons they could not even better their mid-table placing back in 1921. In fact their last two seasons were appalling for they won just a single Yorkshire League match in total, and that was away from home! Paid professional players had long since been abandoned, and now financially crippled after their second successive wooden spoon position they folded at the end of the 1927/28 season.

Football lives on in Wakefield - just. There is a 'Wakefield F.C.' playing in the moderate (modern) West Yorkshire League, and village side Emley, who have moved in to groundshare with Wakefield Trinity, are a fairly successful Northern Premier League club. It is rumoured that they will change their name to include 'Wakefield', in which case it is just possible that Football League matches could be played in the City one day.

WALLASEY UNITED

(1923)

Over the years there have been many clubs - of the 80 or so - that have attempted to join the Football League, who were complete no-hopers, and none more so than Wallasey United F.C.! Wallasey's story has to be traced back to New Brighton F.C. to whom they were inextricably linked. Since the formation of the Football League in 1888, there have been three clubs from the Wirral Peninsular (and it is highly unlikely that the future will produce anymore); Tranmere Rovers have held their place since 1921, New Brighton Tower had a brief existence in the League from 1898, and lastly the separate team of New Brighton had a long run which started in 1923.

New Brighton Tower was formed with the express purpose of providing a Winter attraction at this Seaside resort - which sadly has now lost its glamour as a holiday destination. The club was formed principally to make a profit, and when they were unable to gain promotion to the First Division, they resigned. Conversely, New Brighton F.C. was a club for the average local football fan.

The Tower club was formed in 1897, were elected to the Second Division one year later, and folded in 1901, and it was 20 years before a serious attempt was again made to field a Senior club in the town.

During the interim the only clubs of note in this area were New Brighton Tower Amateurs (who's only claim to fame was that they once reached the first round of the F.A.Amateur Cup), Harrowby - who were of little consequence - and Wallasey Borough, of similar stature, who became defunct around 1916.

A split in the club led to another being formed... and both applied to join the League in the same year. The result for United was inevitable.

The tip of the peninsular was deserving of higher quality football entertainment, and a unique opportunity suddenly presented itself. The former flourishing South Liverpool F.C. (just on the other side of the Mersey) were soon to lose their Dingle Park Ground, and in November 1919, the idea was mooted, but was never progressed, to transfer themselves to New Brighton.

With no ground by the Summer of 1921, all that was left of the club was a few assets, their name, their Lancashire Combination fixtures, and a large debt!

A packed public meeting in late June 1921 was held at the Egerton Street Schools, New Brighton, with Doctor Tom Martlew very much to the fore, when it was decided that a New Brighton Football Club would be formed, that would - with the approval of the South Liverpool Directors - take over their liabilities and Lancashire Combination fixtures, and hence create an instant Senior club. Unlike the former Tower club, it was agreed that this new organisation would be created by, and for, football.

Ironically, the name agreed was to be 'Wallasey United F.C.' (that has great significance later), but the original proposers to form a club, carried away in their enthusiasm, had already registered the name of 'New Brighton F.C.', and this it had to stay. South Liverpool's debts were paid, shares were issued, a Ground was secured (which became Sandhey Park), and the new Club were ready to embark on their Lancashire Combination fixtures.

Ironically another new club sprung up in the area at the same time, Wallasey County, who were formed in July 1921, but the plans of this ambitious Liverpool County League team soon floundered. Meanwhile, The Rakers as they became known due to the Ground's proximity to Rake's Lane, got off to a flying start, securing the double over Rochdale reserves, and crowds of around 5,000 were often attracted to Sandhey's Park. By the season's end they had finished third from top in the Combination, and somewhat prematurely applied for Football League, when although turned down, they received encouragingly seven votes.

The next season was as successful, for although the team slipped to fourth in the Combination, an excellent F.A.Cup run was only terminated at Second Division Sheffield Wednesday, after victories had included the 3-0 beating of Coventry City from the same Division.

But by early March, the Club was beginning to have doubts about making another application to join the League, for many Third Division clubs were reporting severe financial hardships. However, when Player/Manager Bob Alty acrimoniously resigned after a disagreement with the Directors, his subsequent actions may well have only spurred the Rakers to change their thoughts, for on the 26th March a definite decision was made to apply. Meanwhile, another football situation was developing nearby!

On the departure of Bob Alty, there was a minor split within the Club, and he plus some of his 'supporters' decided to form another club. In what appears to be a show of pique, these rivals, with obvious bad financial judgement, also decided to apply for Football League recognition for their newly created team - Wallasey United.

Whether this was an attempt to split the voting, or a serious attempt at election is not known, but this was clearly no more than a bunch of fans plus an established Manager, with no team, no Ground and hence no football credentials.

At the League meeting New Brighton, along with Durham City received the maximum votes and duly took the two additional places available; Wallasey United received none.

Wallasey gained a place in the Cheshire League, and as a home Ground conveniently were able to take over the Tower Ground, that Harrowby F.C. vacated when they folded that Summer. A reasonable team was assembled, and a creditable draw was gained in their first league match, but the next - on a Monday afternoon - they lost 3-2 at home to Port Vale Reserves, *"before a small crowd."* Somebody must have heard of the Club, for Mold United invited the team to come and open their new Ground!

After drawing 1-1 at Llandudno in the F.A.Cup, the replay was won before a very reasonable 2,000 crowd, but they lost in the next round at home to Winsford. Then things went bad for they had dropped to bottom in the table by mid-October, and just to add to their woes the home game on the 3rd of November attracted a crowd of less than 100, when another defeat ensued at the hands of Congleton.

The Club did pick up towards the end of the season and managed to finish 15th of 22, but financially they were drained. Along the road at Sandheys Park, The Rakers although only managing 18th (of 22) were well supported, averaging 6,425 in their home matches.

Clearly the area could only support one Professional team, and Wallasey's illusions of coming out top dogs failed miserably. They folded during the Summer of that year, and remain one of the strangest - and least heard of - clubs that have ever attempted to enter the Football League.

WELLINGTON TOWN/TELFORD UNITED

(1962, 1963, 1965 - 68 / 1970 - 76, 1982)

A rare club that had a complete name change, reflecting the change in status of the locality in 1969, yet they remained the same club. Wellington, in Shropshire, was nothing more than a small town on the road between Wolverhampton and Shrewsbury with a pre-War population of around 10,000, yet with the post-War 'New Town' creation of Telford, this number was rapidly multiplied by more than tenfold. There-fore on catchment area alone Telford United could well boast a Football League club, yet their many attempts in the past have always been woefully poor.

A name change and many election attempts, now leave the Club having to rely on automatic promotion... and it could just happen one day.

Wellington Town was formed as early as 1876, and adopted this name three years later. Appropriately the Club became founder-members of the Shropshire League in 1890, becoming Champions in 1897 and 1898. They then moved on to the Birmingham League, where they remained for most of the next 40 years, during which time various honours came their way, including the League title in 1921, 1935 and 1936. Somewhat unsuited geographically for an upward move to one of the leading non-League competitions, they opted for the Cheshire League in 1938 where they remained for 20 years.

The reformation of this league following the War saw Wellington Town become immediate Champions in 1946, and also the following year. They continued as a leading club in this competition, repeating their table top success in 1952, yet ironically their worst season was also their last in the Cheshire League, when they finished 12th of 22.

The attendances at home matches, in common with most clubs, gradually slumped as the 1960's approached, despite the rapidly increasing population in the area, and from the 4,000 or so in the 1940's, barely four figures were being achieved by 1960. Wellington became one of the many new clubs to join the Southern League in 1958, and joining the Premier Div-ision a year later they held this status (one of only three clubs) until 1979, when they became founder-members of the Alliance Premier League. Yet the Championship of both the Southern and Alliance Leagues has always eluded them, despite several notable runs and victories in various cup competitions.

Wellington's first stab at the Football league was made in 1962, the year when everybody wanted to take the place of Accrington Stanley! A below mid-table finish in the Southern League did not help their case, and consequently they received no votes.

A better season followed, but their application only received one vote, and in 1964 they, along with several other Southern Leaguers were barred from applying due to the signing of Football League players controversy; in any event a poor campaign had left the Club in the lower reaches of the final table. The team gradually came back to the fore in the Southern League, but although this period did not produce any outstanding clubs, there were none-the-less far worthier clubs who deserved Football League recognition than Wellington.

This was reflected in the voting figures at the re-election meetings when they maintained a constant vote of one each year.

The year of the name change - 1969 - did not produce an application, but the 'new' Telford United wasted no time in taking up where Wellington had left off, although the League clubs were not impressed, and the Club's application received no votes in 1970. Strangely, Telford's bid in 1971 actually received two supporting votes, despite a disappointing season that saw the team finish well down in the bottom half of the table, although a run through to the second round of the F.A.Cup may have helped their case. Continuous applications to join the Football League were made until 1976, but regular mid-table finishing positions were hardly inspiring, and correspondingly two votes on one occasion was the best the Club could achieve.

In 1977, the Football League took the sensible step of only allowing two non-League clubs to apply for election, and this effectively barred Telford United from further attempts for several years. The 1978/79 season was to prove to be one of the best for the Club, although they never really seriously challenged for the Championship, with Worcester City the runaway leaders.

However, they managed third place, but were denied a stab at the Football League by second place Kettering Town who finished as runners-up. Fortunately the team could not have chosen a better year for good performances, for their high ranking in the Southern League allowed them entry to the newly formed Alliance League, which years later was to become the unofficial 'Fourth Division' (fifth level) of the Football League.

Although never having taken the title, the early years of the Alliance were generally good ones for Telford. In three successive years the Club had excellent runs in the F.A.Cup, reaching the second round in 1983, having beaten Wigan Athletic and held Tranmere Rovers to a draw, and the fourth round the following season.

On this latter occasion, no fewer than three Football League teams were dispatched (Stockport County, Northampton Town and Rochdale - by 4-1 at Spotland). But the 1984/85 season produced one of the best set of F.A.Cup results ever achieved by a non-League team. Four League scalps were taken; Lincoln City (after a 1-1 draw), Preston North End (an excellent 4-1 victory at Deepdale), Bradford City, and Darlington by 3-0 following another 1-1 drawn match.

United met their match in the 5th round when they went down 3-0 at Everton. If only their Alliance Premier League performances could have matched their F.A.Cup exploits, then 'promotion' to the Football League may well have followed.

Earlier, in 1982, the Club made its last election attempt. Runcorn surprisingly were the Alliance Champions, winning the title by a clear seven points, but neither they or runners-up Enfield wished to apply for election, therefore this honour was reserved for third placed Telford United who trailed Runcorn by 16 points. Their case for 'promotion' was clearly not strong enough (if only their Cup runs had preceded this season!), and they received only 13 votes, the lowest ever in the 'only one club application' period.

Telford United could reasonably be described as a 'sleeping giant'. After Ground improvements they will have a Football League rated stadium, have run a fully professional squad, and with a sizeable catchment area, on paper they must be considered one of the few clubs with a genuine strong case.

But should Football League status become a reality in the future, this is a promotion that is unlikely to be welcomed by neighbours Shrewsbury Town!

WEST HARTLEPOOL

(1903)

It is little wonder that the current Hartlepool United of the Football League have consistently struggled, for there are few, if any, provincial towns where the population is divided in its support for the two leading Winter sports - Football and Rugby (Union). In success terms, Rugby leads, in support numbers Hartlepool United probably fare reasonably well, but outside of the 'big three' in the North-east, this situation will always prove a struggle. Formed as relatively late as 1908, Hartlepool United were preceded by an earlier, completely unrelated, Senior club, West Hartlepool F.C.

Finishing bottom of your league is hardly good credentials for making a bid to join the League - but West did, and failed dismally.

The Amateur club, West Hartlepool, was formed in 1881, despite a previous attempt two years earlier, the year when in fact the famous Hartlepool Rovers first saw the light of day; from the earliest times, there was obviously serious competition for support between the two sports! Initially the Club became members of the Northumberland and Durham Football Assoc-iation, before becoming founder-members of the Durham F.A. in 1883.

But Rugby had immediately taken a dominant hold on the population, and the fairly short history of West Hartlepool was to become blighted with difficulties. This was reflected in the many years when the Club struggled, with frequent changes of ground, and at times when their very existence was threatened.

Even in football terms the Club was not without its local challengers, for there were others of a reasonably high status, two of whom were entrants to the F.A.Cup; the railway team of West Hartlepool NER (from 1894 to 97), and sur-prisingly Hartlepool Rovers (a football section of the Rugby Club?), who played three matches between 1891 and 1893. Eventually, towards the end of the 19th century, with the influx of new players and officials - notably J.P.Hender-son of Sunderland F.C. who became the President for a while - West Hart-lepool became a reasonably viable club.

In 1898 they became members of the Northern League Second Division, but started their campaign in a disastrous fashion, losing 9-0 to other newcomers Stockton St.John's at their Trafalgar Street Ground in Thornaby. Fortunately the Club improved sufficiently to finish seventh of ten teams. The next season, in an eight team division, they improved to fifth place, one above Scarborough F.C. who were beaten 5-0 in Hartlepool, and they won their first major honour, the Durham Amateur Cup.

For the 1900/01 season the Club was 'promoted' (the Second Division closed down), and finished second from bottom in the 11 strong Northern League. Amongst their many defeats was a 7-0 thrashing, on their own Park Road Ground, by Bishop Auckland. Conversely Scarborough were beaten with the same scoreline.

Notable other teams in the league that season were Darlington, Crook Town and Stockton.

The Club continued to struggle, finishing bottom of the table in 1903, the year when they chose - ludicrously it would seem - to apply for election to the Football League! However, there is no doubt that West Hartlepool were chosen by the Football League for one of their attempts at 'colonizing' a Rugby stronghold town (although probably uniquely a Union base rather than Rugby League). The clubs were unimpressed, and the seven votes were in reality far in excess of the number the Club deserved; finishing bottom of a league, but which admitedly included the reserve teams of the 'big three' from the North-east, who appropriately shared the top three positions.

No further attempts were made to join the League, and with another wooden-spoon position a year later, they no doubt would have received no support from the clubs. After these unimpressive seasons, there was no reason to suspect that the 1904/05 season was to be anything different. In respect of the Northern League, it wasn't, for West Hartlepool finished mid-table, albeit a big improvement from a year earlier.

But the Club shot to fame with their performances in the F.A.Amateur Cup. Along the way the team beat Grangetown Athletic, Notts Jardines, Darlington St.Augustines, and Bishop Auckland in the Semi-Final played at Stockton. Having reached the Final, the club had to make the long journey to London to meet Clapton at Shepherds Bush, which was played before a crowd of 4,000. The team held a comfortable 2-0 half-time lead, and increased this to three, before a dramatic recovery by Clapton in the last 15 minutes produced a final score of 3-2.

The latter half of that season saw better results and crowd figures, 3,000 turning up at Park Road for the visit of Bishop Auckland in late February.

But this Cup success did nothing to lift the team, and a year later they were back in familiar territory, finishing third from bottom. But a good result could virtually be guaranteed against the hapless Scarborough, who were beaten 13-0 at Park Road! West Hartlepool continued their career in the Northern League until 1910, never having reached the heights in the meantime, when they finally gave up. With poor support and financial problems they decided to throw in the towel, and their assets and liabilities were taken up by Hartlepools United.

Hartlepools United was formed as a professional club in the Summer of 1908, and were registered as a Limited company in June that year. Although West Hartlepool, an Amateur club throughout their existence, had hardly flourished, their 1905 Amateur Cup success probably awakened the district into the realisation that there was a place for a top level football team.

Although a completely new club, the pair ran in tandem for two years, and during this period shared the Victoria Ground, the former home of West Hartlepool R.F.C. After the demise of West Hartlepool F.C., several of their players joined the professional club, including T. and R. Hegarty, the full-backs in the F.A.Amateur Cup Final side.

United gained instant entry to the Professional North-Eastern League in 1908, and immediately became a success, so much so that two failed attempts were made to join the Football League before the onslaught of the First World War; they finally made the grade in 1921.

WEST STANLEY

(1921)

Probably an unfamiliar name to many non-League enthusiasts, West Stanley (who effectively folded in 1959), came moderately close to gaining admission to the League in their one attempt. Although they failed, unlike many, they did have a reasonable case for inclusion.

First find 'West Stanley'! The name of 'Stanley' as a place name is quite common in the North-east of the Country, but it is the town of Stanley (between Consett and Chester-le-Street), in County Durham, where this Club lived. As early as the late 1880's there were several clubs based in the town, but the intriguingly named 'Oakey's Lily-whites' became the most prominent, and after one season in the North-West Durham Alliance League, they moved up to the Northern Alliance in 1896, at which time they were renamed 'Stanley F.C.' Until 1906, when a further name change to 'West Stanley' was adopted, they played at Oakey's Oval, which could boast a Grandstand, before moving on to Murray Park in the High Street. West Stanley F.C. was located adjacent to the East Stanley Cemetery, but the apparent misnomer in their title related to the former nearby farmhouse of this name, and also the 'West Stanley Colliery' which opened in 1833.

Although they failed with their one attempt, they - unlike many - had a reasonable case for inclusion.

The first match at Murray Park was a Durham County Cup encounter versus (confusingly) Stanley United (from near Crook), on the 27th September 1906, which was won 2-1, having moved up another rung on the non-League ladder, to the highest in the area, when they became founder-members of the professional North-Eastern League.

This league catered for the 'A' teams (reserves at that time) of the local Football League clubs, and other founder-members included Carlisle United and Workington. This was a big step-up for West Stanley, and with £10 per week budgeted for players' wages, there was at this time talk of forming the Club into a Limited Company. £130 was spent on fencing the ground, however the funds did not stretch to providing much in the way of facilities for the players: *"It is not necessary to have baths. If players have a good place to wash in, then that will be sufficient"*, it was announced!

Although the team started badly in the league, they gradually improved, as did their home attendances which rose from around 3,000 to 6,000 by March 1907. A very satisfactory season saw the team finish third in the North-Eastern League, and their ambitions were voiced when the local newspaper reported that: *"They (West Stanley) are anxious to provide their patrons with the very best class of football that it is possible to secure. There is talk in Stanley of a League Division Two team there, and I should say that the club is drawing better gates than many of the present Division Two teams...... they have such a large and loyal following."*

This enthusiasm spread to undertaking improvements at Murray Park, with a pitch enlargement, an extension of the Grandstand, large changing rooms (presumably with Baths!), and banking behind both goals with terracing elsewhere; in the Summer of 1907, the Club became a Limited Company.

Although attendances for the 1907/08 season were somewhat disappointing after those of the previous year, a big match could always entice the locals, and for an Exhibition match between Sunderland and Newcastle United (who disappointingly sent mostly reserve players), a new record crowd of around 10,000 was set. No honours were won that season (although the team did reach the Final of the Durham Senior Cup), nor were they in the years leading up to the First World War, but the team could usually be seen placed in the top half of the table.

After the hostilities, the North-Eastern League recommenced for the 1919/20 season, a poor one for West Stanley who could only finish in the lower half of the table, but the main interest lay in their F.A.Cup run. After overcoming matches in the preliminary rounds, the Club entertained Second Division Rotherham County in the final qualifying tie, West Stanley's biggest ever match.

Over 8,000 roared the locals on to a 1-0 victory, and the first round brought Gillingham of the Southern League to Murray Park. The attendance was, at 10,000, *"the biggest crowd that ever watched a football match in North-west Durham",* and the team surprised even their own fans with an emphatic 3-1 win. In the second round (the last 32), the team travelled to London to take on Tottenham Hotspur, but before a 35,000 crowd, there was no fairytale ending, for the Wests were beaten 4-0.

The 1920/21 season got off to a flying start, and Murray Park attendances were at a high, with crowds of up to 6,000 flocking there, but these early hopes were dashed, and the team finished well, at a reasonable 7th in the table. Of all the seasons, this was the one when the Club wished to do well, for the opportunity presented itself to join the Football League.

Six of the available places had been taken by the en-bloc inclusion of Central League teams, and with four from the North-east, plus several other unvoted inclusions, there were just four vacancies left for the fourteen hopefuls. With already a strong representation from their part of the Country, West Stanley were never in with a real chance, despite a worthy Ground and good home crowds, and they received only six votes. Yet newcomers Ashington and Durham City (who both finished below the club - together with Hartlepools - in the North-Eastern League that season) were to flounder a few years later, and it can only be hypothesized on the outcome should West Stanley have been amongst the chosen few in 1921!

Despite this setback the Club maintained their popularity, and the following season an all-time record attendance of 12,585 packed Murray Park for the second replay of the relatively minor North-West Durham Charity Cup Final versus Leadgate Park, which had been held over from the previous season (a 1-0 defeat).

The team carried on in the North-Eastern League until 1958, by which time they were in desperate financial straits, and they opted for the local Northern Alliance. But after the season's end, they gave up the struggle, which was not helped by an undersized pitch (due to the introduction of Greyhound Racing) which prevented the staging of F.A.Cup matches.

The Club was held in limbo for three years, confident of finding another suitable Ground and resuming their playing career at a higher level once again, but this never came to pass. West Stanley F.C. finally died a peaceful and unheralded death at an indeterminate date early in the 1960's.

WEYMOUTH

(1963, 1964, 1975)

"Shows potential, but an under-achiever; should do better" could well be the end of term report for Weymouth F.C.! Not unlike Chelmsford City, the Club is based in a good sized town, with a population of over 50,000, and has a reasonable catchment area. Yet, like their Essex counterparts, they had/have a good Ground (a fairly new one in the case of the Dorset team), and although considered to be one of the top non-League clubs up to the recent past, their playing career in the late 1990's left much to be desired.

A potentially big non-League club that have never quite realised their expectations - will they make it eventually?

Weymouth F.C. was founded in 1890, the 1893/94 season becoming their first as a Senior club, which produced their first entry to the F.A.Cup. They then made steady progress via the Dorset League followed by the Western League (from 1907 to 1949 - except for two post-First World War years in the Dorset League, plus their absence in 1946/47). Frequent honours in the Western led to admission to the Southern League from 1923 for five years, and a return in 1949 which lasted until 1979.

For much of their existence the Club played at the Recreation Ground, in the centre of town, which almost inevitably became a more commercialised venue, when it was developed as a Supermarket, in 1987. The Club moved into a brand new Stadium, which lay virtually on the site of the Speedway Stadium, and was built to Alliance Premier League standards.

The venue has a 6,600 (800 seated) capacity, which could fairly easily be expanded if required, and there would be no difficulty in attaining Football League status in this direction.

The team had made steady progress in the pre-First World War Western League, and after four seasons in the early 1920's they were Champions and runners-up once each. Weymouth were admitted to the Southern League (Western Section), when they became a Limited Company and turned professional.

But those years in the Southern League were not very fruitful, and after finishing 13th of 16 in 1928, and then struggling both on and off the pitch, they took over their Reserves' team place in the Western League Division 2 (the first team had also played in the First Division during their Southern League days). After several poor seasons, the team finally fought their way back to the top in 1934, but continued in the Second Division (in a strangely sectionalised league which had only a few teams in the first division - mostly reserve XI's - but normally 18 in the second), until 1948. After just one season in the First Division they moved up to the Southern League.

The Club soon established themselves, and for many years always finished in the top half of the table, although the Championship eluded them until 1965.

Meanwhile two attempts were made to join the Football League. In 1963, there were 12 non-League clubs competing, but with the four re-election candidates securing the lionshare of the votes, there were few left for the rest. In a year when there were no outstanding candidates, Weymouth received just one vote.

That season, the Dorset team had finished in third place, but could not consolidate and slipped to seventh a year later. Therefore, in 1964 when there was a similar number of hopefuls, with again no outstanding candidate, Weymouth again received just a single vote.

In 1965, the Club at last were Champions of the Southern League, which they achieved with the aid of a number of former Football League players. This factor may have deterred them from applying for election in view of the situation a year earlier when a number of clubs were barred from making such an attempt due to the signing of Football League players on free transfers.

However, it is a mystery why the Club did not try again in 1966, for they claimed the Championship again, and now, after several years of proving themselves, this would surely have been the best time. The Uniteds' of Cambridge and Hereford, from the South, applied that year but they were well down the pecking order in the Southern League, indeed the Bulls had only just been promoted to the Premier Division.

For the next dozen years or so, the Club lost its way to a certain degree, and although never in danger of relegation, they were unable to recapture the title. Weymouth's sixth place in the Southern in 1979, having retained an unbroken membership of the Premier Division since its inception in 1959, was sufficient for them to gain admittance to the new Alliance Premier League.

Yet in 1975, the Club again appeared to act irrationally, for they made their third and final application to join the Football League, at the end of one of their worst seasons which saw them finish well down in the bottom half of the table! Perhaps the Club were previously acting cautiously and only decided to apply when they felt they were in a good financial position, but a poor league position inevitably produced reduced gates, and hence an unlikely time of great prosperity.

The team made a good start in the new Alliance, claiming the runners-up spot the first year, and winning the League Cup two years later, yet with now just a single club, from the Alliance, allowed to apply for a place in the Football League, Weymouth's name was not put forward. Despite the big advantage of their brand new Stadium, the Club's fortunes soon began to dip, and in 1989 after a dreadful season, and average home attendances failed to reach four figures, they found themselves relegated back to the Southern League.

Continued financial problems led to a further demotion in 1991, the Club's Centenary year. The next decade was a far from happy one as the Club spent most of the period in the lower, Southern division, at one time appearing to be on the way back, but then rapidly suffering relegation again. Weymouth were promoted to the Premier Division in 1998, and after a few years of consolidation, at last they appear to have stabilised.

Although the first big hurdle has yet to be realised, promotion back to the Conference, and then an even bigger final step-up, it is not beyond the realms of possibility that one day, in the not to distant future, the Club will receive an endorsement to their the report; *"late developer, but made it in the end....well done"*!

WIGAN COUNTY/ WIGAN TOWN

(1899 and 1906, 1907)

How strange that one of the strongest of Rugby League strongholds can also boast of being the provincial town that has had the most number of clubs applying for election to the Football League! Not only that, but the town has had a long succession of various Senior Wigan Football Clubs, the majority of whom have played on the same Ground. Although completely separate clubs, it is appropriate that the pair that made unsuccessful bids to join the Football League have been grouped together here.

Football (soccer) was first seriously started in the town with plain 'Wigan F.C.', who were formed from the local Cricket Club in 1872, and played their first match at Warrington on the 18th January 1873. In October 1876, Wigan F.C. combined with Upholland F.C. and became 'Wigan & District', playing their home matches at the Cricket Ground off Frog Lane, but they never recovered from debts incurred and disbanded in February 1878.

Another serious attempt was made to form a town Senior club with the formation of 'Wigan A.F.C.' in 1883. For a time interest in football increased, and after the visit of Blackburn Rovers in September 1884, such was the popularity that for a time the rival 'Wigan F.C.' (Rugby) to ensure continued support had to admit spectators free of charge to their matches! But this football prosperity was fairly brief, and Wigan A.F.C. folded around 1897.

Borough, Athletic, Town and County have all made bids for election to the Football League ....two made and two didn't.

Wigan County became the fourth major club in the town. Founded in 1897, they were the first to enter a seasonal competition, the Lancashire League. This club was formed by the Wigan Trotting and Athletic Club who had built and owned the Springfield Park Ground.

County were therefore the first of several clubs that used this venue as their home, and they assembled a strong squad, composed mainly of former Everton and Preston North End players. The team established themselves reasonably well, finishing the season in 8th place of 14, in competition with the likes of Stockport County, Rochdale, South Shore and Stalybridge Rovers. In addition they were the first team from the town to enter the F.A.Cup and fought through to the 1st round proper (the last 32), when they only narrowly lost, 1-0, to Manchester City.

The 1898/99 season was similar to the first for the team finished 7th in the Lancashire League, which now contained 13 clubs. For a brief period the association game appeared to be making a serious challenge to rugby in the town, and, perhaps carried away with over ambition, the Club decided to apply for election to the Football League at the end of the season. Surprisingly, County received seven votes of support, the same as Lancashire League Champions Chorley, but far too few to challenge the support given to the re-election candidates; Coventry City who were later to grace the League received no votes.

This rebuke seemed to have disheartened the Club and the 1899/1900 season was poor, with the team ending up fourth from bottom in the Lancashire League. In the F.A.Cup they lost 3-1 at Crewe Alexandra in the third qualifying round, having beaten Swinton Town 8-0 in an earlier tie. But the Club quickly came to the realisation that they couldn't carry on and folded during the Summer of 1900.

Coinciding with the demise of County, 'Wigan United' were formed (and indeed may well have arisen out of the ashes of the former club), and like their predecessors arranged to play home matches, also in the Lancashire League, at Springfield Park. Their three seasons were something of a roller coaster ride - finishing second from bottom in 1901, third the following year, and finally bottom in 1903.

The last season was a complete disaster for the team won just one match, with 5 points total from 22 games. The Club's demise during the Summer of 1903 coincided with the earlier expiry of their Springfield Park lease in January that year, and no attempt at renewal led to the team playing their remaining home matches on their opponents grounds.

'Wigan Town' became the next Senior club in the town, having been formed in December 1905. On the resignation of Middlewich Athletic from The Combination in January 1906, the new Wigan club were allowed to take over their fixtures. They had a severe handicap, starting at the bottom of the table, and were unable to improve on this position by the season's end. Even so they immediately made their first application to join the Football League, an attempt that was no doubt encouraged by the Football League who at this time were anxious to establish their clubs in Rugby 'fortresses'.

Wigan Town obtained a surprising number of five votes, but even so this number was far too few.

The team continued in The Combination, alongside the likes of Chester and Tranmere Rovers, plus the reserve elevens of Wrexham and Crewe Alexandra, and in this, their first complete season, they finished third in the final table, albeit trailing by many points the two teams above them Whitchurch - Champions - and Chester).

In view of the result of their League application a year earlier, their second attempt, in 1907, may well have been more successful. But on this occasion, albeit with more competition - five other clubs - they disappointingly received no support. They entered the F.A.Cup for the first and only time the following season, and this was as short a record possible for they lost 4-1 at Macclesfield Town in the preliminary round.

The Club resigned from The Combination, and spent the 1907/08 season in the Lancashire Combination Second Division. But it was a miserable campaign, as the team finished second from bottom, and at this time appeared to have disappeared from the football scene. The Club may have carried on at a lesser level, but in any event they had folded by the First World War, and so came to an end the career of the 6th Wigan.

There was then a quick succession of further 'Wigans'; in the immediate pre-war period, Wigan Amateurs, for one season, in 1919, and another 'United' (who played in the West Lancashire League), before being elected to the Lancashire Combination in 1920. Irregular payments to amateur players led Wigan United (the second) to reconstitute itself mid-season, and they became 'Wigan Association' in November 1920, but only for a month, before the title of Wigan Borough was finally adopted.

Borough soon gained election to the Football League, but embroiled in a financial crisis they resigned mid-season, on 26th October 1931. It was many years before Wigan Athletic (founded 1932) gained election to the Football League (in 1978) after a record number of 25 applications, and between times there was yet another Wigan - Rovers - who were around between 1959 and 1983.

WILLINGTON ATHLETIC

(1903)

Football clubs from the North-east applying for election to the League have tended to appear within three distinct periods. In the early days and into the early 20th century there were several, including the successes of Sunderland, Newcastle and Middlesbrough; the creation of the Third Division North in 1921 brought in Darlington, Hartlepools and the short careers of Ashington and Durham, whilst soon after the Second World War there was a host of unsuccessful attempts by clubs. Willington Athletic F.C. slot into the first period.

Willington Athletic are something of an enigma, for despite their solitary attempt, in 1903, there is no particularly valid reason, other than unrealistic enthusiasm and ambition, why they tried even then, although two league championships soon after may well have been marginally more productive! Easily confused with 'Willington F.C.', founded in 1911, from County Durham (near Spennymoor), Willington Athletic came from the small town of Willington Quay, North of the Tyne, and just to the East of Newcastle.

This unheralded application from the Willington Quay club received just one vote - probably coming from neighbours Middlesbrough.

The Club was founded around 1890, and gained entry to the Northern Alliance a year after its formation. Now regarded as only a moderate Senior competition, in the early days it had a far greater standing, and although no immediate honours were won, the Club did capture the Northumberland Challenge Bowl (a success repeated the next year), and the Senior Cup twice before the turn of the century.

One of the earliest of leagues, the Northern League - the oldest after the Football League itself - was formed in 1889, and therefore with two such competitions in such close proximity, this illustrates the serious manner in which football was considered during the late 19th century. In 1891, the Sunderland 'A' (reserve) team were Northern Alliance members (soon to be followed by Newcastle United 'A' and Ashington), plus the likes of Gateshead North Eastern Railways, and Birtley.

With only nine teams in the league during the 1891/92 season many Friendly matches were played to supplement the fixture list, and of course the F.A.Cup. Willington entered the Cup at the second round qualifying stage, but their run was shortlived, for after drawing 2-2 at home to fellow newcomers to the Alliance, Shankhouse, they lost the replay 4-1.

The Club received no honours that season, but with a continuous membership of the Northern Alliance, until 1915, they occasionally hit the headlines. One major success, the Northern Alliance Championship in 1905 (and twice more repeated), came two years after their one shot at the Football League. They also achieved little of merit in the F.A.Cup, the first run of any note being the 1893/94 season, when the end came at the final qualifying stage with a 4-1 home defeat to Middlesbrough (also their conquerors the following season).

In the 1902/03 season, when they applied for League membership, the team lost 3-0 at home to Sunderland Royal Rovers in the first qualifying round, therefore this was hardly an encouraging endorsement to add to their credentials.

That campaign came to an end following a 2-2 draw at home - the sloping Howdon Station Ground - with Wallsend Park Villa. This improved the Athletic's final league placing to a modest sixth, having won 10 matches and lost 11 of the 26; but with only 25 points they trailed the runaway Champions Morpeth Harriers by 24, and even their last opponents who finished runners-up were 16 points ahead. But despite such a modest campaign, by an equally modest club, Willington naively set out their stall that they hoped would lead to membership of the Football League.

On the 27th April 1903, there was a meeting of Club officials and supporters at the Ship Hotel, Willington Quay, who met to discuss, *"the scheme for the formation of a Second League (Second Division) club"*. Before a good attendance, the Athletic Chairman stated that: *"The general opinion is that the Northern Alliance card was almost played out..... to keep interest they must provide a better class of football"*. He reasoned that if the Club could gain election, then they could hold onto their better players instead of seeing them move on to League clubs; they had plenty of talent within the Club. There was no reason why they could not: *"provide one of the finest League teams in existence."*(!)

Middlesbrough F.C. had promised to be very supportive of their bid (probably the direction from which their one solitary vote was later to come), and with a catchment of around 45,000, there should be no reason why they could not achieve break-even gates of 3,000, which would realise around £100 per match. The main disadvantage was they were off the main route, which would add to their travelling expenditure.

The proposal at the meeting was to make an application at the 1903 Football League re-election meeting, when they could set out their case.

The Club had already the offer of two 'fields' (grounds), their current one, and another at the top of Church Bank in nearby Wallsend (currently the main A193 road), but after further discussion they decided to stay with their Howdon Station enclosure. The Club already had promises to take up 300 shares, and Arthur Thompson of the Willington Cycling Club promised the support of his members, providing they were allowed to use the ground during the Summer months. Finally, Mr.J.J. Pearce moved that the scheme should be adopted, and this was carried unanimously. It was also agreed that forms would be printed and circulated, stating the Club's ambitions, and appeals for further support. On the 5th May, *"Another Step Forward"*, was reported. It was confirmed that the proposed five shilling (25p) shares would not be issued until the Club was in the League, and realistically they realised they may not be accepted (!), but confirmed that if unsuccessful another attempt would be made in 1904.

On the 25th May at the Tavistock Hotel in Covent Garden, London, there was a full attendance of representatives from clubs of both divisions, to listen to the cases for the three clubs that were seeking re-election, and those of the five new applicants, of which Willington Athletic was one. Quite clearly the Club did not stand a chance, considering the proximity of the 'big three' that were already members and the far more realistic bid that came that year from West Hartlepool. Willington did receive one vote - West Hartlepool also failed, with seven - that solitary vote probably coming from Middlesbrough F.C.

Willington Athletic never made another attempt, and after continuing to play in the Northern Alliance until the First World War, their name never reappeared on any major fixture lists after the cessation of hostilities.

WORCESTER CITY

(1947 - 1957, 1959, 1960, 1962, 1968, 1969)

Worcester City F.C., founded in 1902, were late developers when it came to seeking election to the League. Yet once they started they made many determined bids, sixteen in total.

The Club, created from the amalgamation of Worcester Rovers and Berwick Rangers (not the one on the Scottish borders!), first played at the latter's ground in Severn Terrace, and were immediately accepted into the most suitable Senior competition, the Birmingham & District League.

One year on they moved to the Rovers' old ground at Thorneloe, and their wandering continued in 1904 when the Royal Grammar School's grounds at Flagge Meadow (still a sports field) was utilized. Maintaining their 'one year-a-ground' policy they made the final move to St. George's Lane (close to Flagge Meadow), after appeals for donations to develop the Ground were successfully answered.

The Birmingham & District League after the turn of the century was totally dominated by the reserves of Aston Villa for well over a decade, but Worcester City made a notable breakthrough when they captured the title in 1914 (Stoke, a non-League team in 1911, were also Champions, and played their first team in both the Birmingham and Southern Leagues). They remained in this company until 1938, during which time they repeated their top of the table achievement on three occasions, plus a trio of runners-up finishes in the early 1930's.

Another club with so much potential...yet their many attempts were all failures - will the future be any more rewarding?

During their career in this Midland competition the Club enjoyed their best victory (18-1 over Bilston in 1931), and eleven years earlier suffered their worst defeat, of 10-0 to Wellington Town (later Telford United).

Although the team could only manage a moderate 7th place of 14 in the Birmingham & District League, in 1938, they applied, and were accepted into the Southern League for the final full pre-War season. The Club remained in the Southern until the formation of the Alliance Premier League in 1979, a period which encompassed all their many bids to join the Football League.

An attempt was made in 1947, the abortive year when all hopefuls were excluded without a vote, the first of eleven successive tries. They were one of only three clubs to receive any votes (one in their case) in 1948, following a good Southern League campaign in which they had finished in third place, and the following year tied with Gillingham in the southern section election, by receiving five votes, woefully short, but the best of the non-Leaguers. In the league their performances declined somewhat for a few years, which culminated in their worst season to that date, when they ended up fourth from bottom in 1956.

Yet during this period they continued to make their annual pilgrimage to the re-election meetings, gaining the best chance in 1950 - when the Football League was extended by two clubs in each Third Division.

City gained 11 votes, second only to the two successful favourites, Colchester United and Gillingham. Despite their indifferent performances on the pitch, the Club normally received at least one vote each year, a period when they were particularly difficult to come by, and even topped the 'chart' on occasions, albeit with way below the number of votes necessary for election.

The early to mid-1960's were not very fruitful for Worcester City, and finally, in 1967, they were relegated to the First Division after finishing third from bottom in the Premier section. But during the 1958/59 season they achieved one success that eclipsed all others. Never a particularly good F.A.Cup club (prior to 1958 they only reached the first round on four occasions), they surprised the football world when they beat Fourth Division Millwall in the second round, 5-2, and positively stunned it with their victory over one of the leading Second Division sides, Liverpool, in the third. In the next round the team went out to Sheffield United at St. George's Lane, by now one of the biggest of non-League grounds, before an all-time record crowd of 17,042.

After two years when no votes were obtained, a year was missed before the 1959 F.A.Cup successes rekindled the flame, and the League clubs were obviously impressed for the Club received seven votes, although far fewer than the emerging non-League 'giants' Peterborough United. The two attempts made in 1960, and two years later, received little support, and the next bid was not made until 1968.

In their first major success for nearly forty years, the team took the Southern League First Division title.

But having only been playing in the competition's 'second level', the voters were unimpressed, and just one vote came Worcester's way. Even a year later, the Club's last attempt, they only managed a single vote, despite a good season that saw them finish fifth from top in the Premier Division.

Worcester City could only manage to maintain a place in the Premier Division until 1974, although they were back again three years later, but by now all hopes of election to the Football League had disappeared. With founder-membership of the Alliance Premier League, following their first and only Southern League Championship, this presented the far better chance of a move up, since applications were then restricted to just one club. But without ever achieving a high enough position for such a move (they declined to apply in 1979), the team was relegated in 1985 and have since struggled to recover the necessary status.

If potential, locality, and ground capacity were the only requirements, then Worcester City would probably have been members of the Football League by now. The Club is still regarded by many as one of the major forces in non-League football, despite many seasons away from the top, and with a population of well over 75,000 there is a suitable catchment for good support; ironically their two nearest major non-League neighbours, Cheltenham (to the South) and Kidderminster (to the North) have both attained League status by promotion.

After its glowing past history, St.George's Lane is likely to prove the main stumbling block to progress, for with no parking, hemmed in within residential areas, and dilapidation that is rife, a move to a new venue is almost certainly a pre-requisite for promotion even to the Conference.

YEOVIL & PETTERS UTD./ YEOVIL TOWN

(1927/ 1947 - 1960, 1962 - 1964, 1966 - 1968, 1970 - 1976)

How fitting that alphabetically the last of this long list of non-League clubs should be Yeovil. The many superlatives that can be used are all fully deserved. The most famous non-League F.A.Cup side of all time, with numerous appearances in the later rounds, and numerous Football League 'scalps'; a near continuous record at or near the top; support normally far in excess of their contemporaries; an excellent new Ground which is far better than many others even in the lower levels of the Football League - with a capacity for 8,761 including seating for 5,253 - even the former and famous Huish Ground (despite its notorious slope) was one of the best outside the League; relatively isolated football-wise, with the nearest Football League club - Exeter City - 46 miles distant; a good sized town with a population of over 30,000 and a wide catchment net; and so the list goes on.

They may be last alphabetically, but for determined efforts - which arguably deserved to have produced the desired result - Town are first!

The Club has not only made the record number of Football League applications - 28 - but also made the record number of consecutive attempts of 14. There is only one real mystery regarding the Club, and that is, how on earth have they not made it already!

Yet, despite all these glowing references, as is usually the case, the Club were formed as just another minor outfit - in 1890. Created as a mixed Rugby and Football club (they played the different 'codes' on alternate weeks), the team, as 'Yeovil Casuals' was soon entered into the Somerset Senior League.

The team won the title on four occasions up until the outbreak of the First World War. In 1908, the 'Casuals' in their title became 'Town', and six years later the Club combined with the works' team 'Petters United', to become a formidable local organisation, now known as 'Yeovil & Petters United'.

In 1919, United joined the Western League, and a year later moved from their Pen Mill Athletic Ground ('Town's' former home venue), to Huish. After the Western League Championship in 1922, the Club became members of the Southern League, one of the earliest new entrants after the mass movement of member clubs to the new Third Division in 1920. Going from strength to strength, the team won the Western Section in 1924, but the high travel costs for the Club resulted in a financial crisis which was only alleviated by the intervention of local businesses.

On the field the Club maintained a good record, and in 1926 a set of electric lights were erected at Huish for training purposes; floodlights were a taboo subject with the football authorities. As well as two runners-up finishes in the Southern League during the early 1930's, Yeovil also established a good F.A.Cup record, reaching at least the first round on most occasions from 1932, and appearing in the third three times. But prior to these successes, Yeovil & Petters United made their first bid for election to the Football League as early as 1927.

Torquay United were the clear favourites amongst the four southern section contenders, and they made it in preference to re-election candidates Aberdare Athletic, but only after a second vote count. Discarding Ebbw Vale, just two votes had been left for Yeovil and Kettering, and they had one each. Whilst this was no surprise, perhaps more surprising was the fact that the Club made no further attempts in the pre-War period. With their F.A.Cup runs and good performances in the Southern League, one could have expected an effort. Or was it the 'Petters' in their title, a works connection, which may well have displeased the football authorities!

When football returned to normality for the 1946/47 season, Yeovil had dropped the 'Petters United' and added 'Town', which presumably gave them more 'respectability'. The Club's post-War record as a giant amongst giantkillers commenced in the 1948/49 season when - after first beating Second Division Bury - mighty Sunderland of the First Division were overcome, before an all-time record all ticket 16,318 crowd; in the fourth round the team lost 8-0 at Manchester United. The two notable victories were to kick-start an incredible run of Football League scalps which has continued unabated.

But the Cup exploits have tended to hide the fact that in their league battles the Club have a largely unremarkable record. It will come as a surprise to many that the Southern League was won on only three occasions in a post-War period of over 30 years. Therefore in this light, despite their many attempts, the fact that so few votes have been obtained is, perhaps, not so surprising; between 1947 and 1960, two votes in 1949 and 1953, plus one in 1950 were the grand total!

Strangely after their record run of 14 seasons, no bid was made in 1961, despite the team finishing third in the league. But they were back in the fray a year later, although no votes were gained.

As the F.A. victories piled up, at last the Club became a more familiar name, and in 1964, coupled with a Championship success, they received their best support to that time - all of three votes!

The rest of the 1960's proved little better towards reaching their target - The Football League - and into the early '70's this indifference continued. But a runners-up place in 1973 was definitely noticed for with no obvious contender, the Town came from nowhere to gain 14 votes, the best of the non-League contingent. 1976 nearly became their greatest triumph, for although their F.A.Cup exploits were moderate by their standards - taking Millwall to three matches before they were defeated - they were Southern League runners-up to the up and coming Wimbledon. When it came to the Election meeting, Yeovil just failed to gain recognition, claiming 18 votes to Workington's 21. The role was reversed a year later when Wimbledon stepped up in place of the Cumbrian team.

1976 was to be Yeovil's last attempt, for with initially only two (and later one) clubs allowed to try their luck from 1977, the Club were never in a position to be nominated. The team experienced an unheard of major slump in the mid-1980's which saw them relegated to the Isthmian League, but soon bounced back, and since 1988, except for one short 'hiccup', have remained at the peak of the non-League pyramid.

The 2000/01 season saw a mighty battle with Rushden and Diamonds for the Conference Championship, but they eventually narrowly lost out on automatic promotion.

Surely there can be little doubt that in the case of Yeovil Town it is not a case of 'if', but 'when' they became members of the Football League. With everything geared up for this elevation, it surely cannot be long coming.

****

Convincing Arguments

When the idea of the Football League was originally conceived, in some quarters there was little more than a lukewarm reception of the idea. Indeed when plans were made to extend the League to two divisions, in 1892, an advertisement was placed in the *Athletic News,* inviting applications from interested clubs! Even a year later, Accrington - after losing their play-off matches - opted for the Lancashire League rather than play in the Second Division. But this attitude changed, and over the ensuing years, non-League clubs clamoured to join the elite, while the incumbents who had to seek re-election appreciated their privileged position and did all they could to convince the other clubs that their place should remain intact.

THE FOOTBALL LEAGUE.

The FOOTBALL LEAGUE, having decided to establish a First and Second Division of Clubs in their Competition, invite application for admission.

There will be six vacancies for the First Division and twelve for the Second Division.

Forms of application, stating the conditions in detail, can be had from the Secretary, Mr. H. LOCKETT, 8, Parker-terrace, Stoke-on-Trent.

In those early years, those seeking re-election and those attempting to join would often only apply in writing, and at best their representatives would attend the election meeting and put forward their case, being allowed just five minutes to convince those present. But by the dawn of the 20th century, a more professional approach by those election-seeking clubs began to evolve. In 1907, Oldham Athletic were possibly the first to produce a written plea, by way of a brochure, which extolled their claim; turned down the year before, they at first narrowly missed out in 1907, but did gain entry at a late date by way of Burslem Port Vale, who resigned. In 1919, South Shields' manager, Jack Tinn, visited every League club canvassing support, and the club also issued a prospectus. This showed that the club was well supported, their Horsley Hill Ground had benefitted from £2,000 spent on it, and the club had enjoyed pre-War success in both their league and F.A.Cup matches; their efforts bore fruit, for the club was duly elected.

Eventually re-election or being elected for the first time became a serious undertaking, and not only brochures stating the newcomers claims became the norm, but so did publicity, usually by way of canvassing Football League members, particularly from those attempting to retain their status.

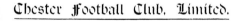

Chester Football Club, Limited.

Telephone :

706 CHESTER.

Registered Office :

SEALAND ROAD,

CHESTER.

GENTLEMEN,

The Chester Football Club Limited desire to make application for admission to the Football League, Division III (North), and have authorised their Directors to submit for your consideration the following facts in support thereof. The application is based upon a genuine desire of the members of the Club, and of all football enthusiasts within the City of Chester and districts, who have no hesitation in stating that if this application be favourably considered, the Club will be able to discharge its obligations in its new sphere, and would prove an asset to the present distinguished Associate Members of the Football League. Your support is confidently solicited to enable the Club to attain its desire, and we have pleasure in appending the following particulars for your consideration and support.

The City of Chester.

The ground is situate in the confines of the City of Chester, which City is known throughout Great Britain for its historical associations. It has a population with its suburbs of more than 60,000 people; in addition, Chester is the Capital of the County.

ALDERSHOT FOOTBALL CLUB, LTD.

Colours :
BLUE AND RED, WHITE KNICKERS
Ground :
RECREATION GROUND, HIGH STREET

Winners :
SOUTHERN LEAGUE CHAMPIONSHIP, 1929-30
LONDON COMBINATION, Division II, 1930-31
HANTS COMBINATION CUP, 1929-30 & 1930-31
HANTS SENIOR CUP 1927-28

Winners :
ALDERSHOT CHARITY CUP, 1927
RUSSELL COTES CUP, 1928-29
ALDERSHOT CHARITY CUP 1929

TELEPHONE :
9 a.m. till 5 p.m. ALDERSHOT 11

Hon. Secretary :
W. DAWS

Manager :
W. McCRACKEN

OFFICE

RECREATION GROUND,
ALDERSHOT

17th June, 1937.

Dear Sir,

At the Annual Meeting of the Football League our representative, on behalf of this Club, tendered to those responsible for our re-election to Associate Membership our cordial thanks.

Our indebtedness, however, is so fully appreciated by us that we desire to proffer this further expression of gratefulness to all who so kindly voted in support of our re-election.

I am, yours faithfully,

For and on behalf of,

ALDERSHOT FOOTBALL CLUB, LTD.,

In 1931, Chester just scraped in, at their third attempt. Six years later, after the Shots successful re-election, they took the trouble to write and thank the clubs.

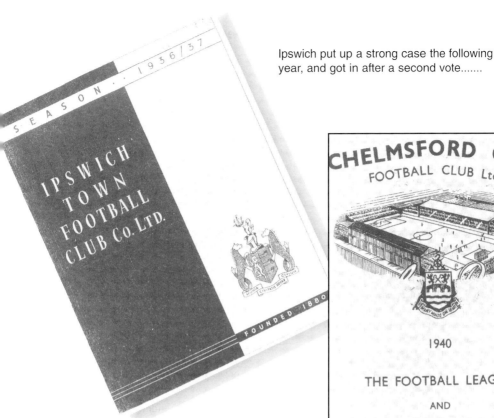

Ipswich put up a strong case the following year, and got in after a second vote......

.......but despite so many attempts, their fellow East Anglians never made it

CHELMSFORD CITY
FOOTBALL CLUB Ltd.

1940

THE FOOTBALL LEAGUE

AND

CUP COMPETITIONS

May we come in ?

Football League Division III. (Northern Section).

Hon. Secretary:
HARRY MANSLEY.

Phone: Residence 2600.
Business 2141.

11, SELKIRK ROAD,

CURZON PARK,

CHESTER.

To The Secretaries of all 1st & 2nd Division Clubs of the Football League.

May 1948.

Dear Sir,

At the Annual General Meeting of our Section held in Leeds on 11th May, it was resolved that every endeavour should be made to defeat the proposal to be put forward by The Football League Management Committee at the Meeting to be held in London on Tuesday, June 8th. Re alteration of Rule 80, viz. "That the four bottom Clubs, two in the Northern Section and two in the Southern Section should automatically retire and not be eligible for re-election." This very drastic proposal is of such grave importance that it cannot only concern Third

NATIONAL ASSOCIATION OF NON LEAGUE
FOOTBALL CLUBS

37, Riverbank Road,

LIVERPOOL, 19.

Dear Sirs,

This appeal is in the nature of an S.O.S. from junior Clubs anxious to improve their status.

The Football League Annual General Meeting is to be held on May 30th and we have to admit failure insofar that we have been unable to find any League Club to sponsor our cause.

Although any reference to an extension of the League does not appear on the Agenda of the League A.G.M., we have it on the highest authority that the subject could be

1948: Panic in the Third Divisions! The suggestion had been voiced that the two bottom clubs in each section would be automatically relegated, and replaced with new clubs.

Conversely, a year later, the non-Leaguers were doing everything to try and make their lot better, and encourage the inclusion of their members.

The net result was that the clubs for re-election invariably retained that status, and the non-Leaguers had to endure many more years of a near 'closed shop' within the Football League.

173

Club Colours :
BLUE & WHITE SHIRTS
WHITE KNICKERS

HALIFAX TOWN

Members of
FOOTBALL LEAGUE Div. III
YORKSHIRE LEAGUE

ASSOCIATION FOOTBALL CLUB, LIMITED,

TELEPHONE
3 4 2 3

Shay Grounds,
Halifax,

SECRETARY-MANAGER
J. H. THOMSON

19th June.   194 7

The Chairman and Directors,
Dear Sirs,

As Chairman of Halifax Town I shall be greatly obliged
if you will read the following and give our club your support.

No doubt you are aware we are in the unfortunate
position of finding it necessary to apply for reinstatement in
Division Three, Northern Section, in which we have finished
badly this season.

We were established thirty years ago and have had many
difficulties to overcome, but we have managed successfully
until now.

We are as well placed financially as most clubs in the

MANSFIELD TOWN
FOOTBALL CLUB
LIMITED

Chairman: W. M. HORNBY.
Hon. Sec.: H. N. MEE.
Sec.-Manager: F. R. GOODALL.

REGISTERED OFFICE:
FIELD MILL GROUND
MANSFIELD
PHONE 567

OUR REF: YOUR REF: DATE

June, 1947.

For the consideration of the Board of Directors:-
Dear Sir,

Having unfortunately finished the 1946-47 Season
at the bottom of Division 3 Southern Section, we now find it
necessary to make application for re-election as Associate Members
of the Football League.

The Club has been in membership since 1931 having had
spells in both the Northern & Southern Sections, so for the first time
in 16 years we find ourselves in this unenviable position.

Mansfield Town, in the Third Division South,
found themselves in the same position as
Halifax Town !

In 1947 Halifax Town got the jitters when
they finished bottom of the Third North, and
sent out a plea to First and Second Division
clubs for support.......

SHREWSBURY TOWN FOOTBALL CLUB LTD.

President :   MAJOR R. E. RHODES

Chairman:
Mr. B. D. J. HAYES

Secretary-Manager:
A. LESLIE KNIGHTON

Registered Office:
GAY MEADOW
SHREWSBURY
Telephone 5027

26th May, 1948

Gentlemen,

We have made an application to the Football League for admission to the Third Division
Northern Section, this being for the Seventh successive time, and the increased encouragement given
us each year at the Annual Meeting of the Football League clubs leads us to hope that we might be
successful on this occasion.

Last year a proposition was accepted that the Clubs seeking re-election should be given one
more chance as some of their difficulties might reasonably have been caused through the war and to
some extent no fault of their own. We appreciated and agreed with the proposition. This practice
of course should not for the sake of the game develop and make the League a closed shop.

As a reminder, the following was the result when voting last took place :—

Hartlepools United	...	...	...	38 votes
Accrington Stanley	...	...	...	29 ,,
Shrewsbury Town	...	...	...	22 ,,
South Liverpool	...	...	...	5 ,,
Scunthorpe	...	...	...	4 ,,
Burton Town	...	...	...	0 ,,
Wigan Athletic	...	...	...	0 ,,

In submitting our claim for election we feel that we have

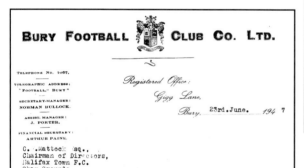

BURY FOOTBALL ⬥ CLUB CO. LTD.

TELEPHONE No. 1067.

TELEGRAPHIC ADDRESS:
"FOOTBALL," BURY

SECRETARY-MANAGER:
NORMAN BULLOCK.

ASSIST. MANAGER:
J. PORTER.

FINANCIAL SECRETARY:
ARTHUR PAINE.

Registered Office:
Gigg Lane,
Bury, 23rd. June.   194 7

C. Mattock Esq.,
Chairman of Directors,
Halifax Town F.C.
Shay Grounds,
Halifax.

Dear Mr. Mattock,
I am in receipt of your letter of the 19th.inst.
with reference to your application for re-election to the Third
Division North.

You may rest assured that you will have the support
of the Bury Club at the forthcoming League meeting. I fully realise
that your Club has had to face up to the difficulties occasioned
by the War and hope that,like all other our friends in football,
Season 1947-48 will be the beginning of a new era for your Club.
Kind regards and all best wishes.

..... to which Second Division Bury promised
their support; a struggling team in their
division, they no doubt realised that they
could well find themselves in a similar
position in the future!

Whilst these two clubs were desperate to retain
their status, the Shropshire club (above) were still
struggling to gain recognition, along with............

...... (bottom right) The Iron, who produced an impressive brochure for their 1948 attempt.

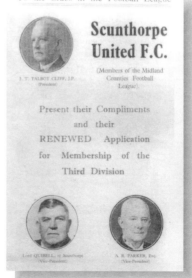

To the Clubs in the Football League

Scunthorpe United F.C.

(Members of the Midland
Counties Football
League).

J. T. TALBOT-CLIFF, J.P.
President

Present their Compliments

and their

RENEWED Application

for Membership of the

Third Division

Lord QUIBELL, of Scunthorpe
(Vice-President)

A. R. PARKER, Esq.
(Vice-President)

174

Gillingham Football Club Co., Ltd.

FOUNDED 1893

Members of the Football Association, Southern Football League and Kent Senior League.   Affiliated K.C.F.A.

SECRETARY—E.W.FLETCHER,
96, THIRD AVENUE,
GILLINGHAM, KENT.
Phone 5559

MANAGER—ARCHIE CLARK
Phone 5854
TREASURER—S. H. MARTIN

DIRECTORS :—
Chairman—W. S. C. COX.
Vice-Chairman—J. W. LEECH
T. W. BOWMAN, J.P.
S. H. MARTIN
H WOOD
A. E. WELLER

COLOURS :
Blue Shirts with White Collars
and Cuffs.

GROUND :
PRIESTFIELD STADIUM,
GILLINGHAM, KENT.
Phone 5854

The Secretary,

20th May, 1949.

3rd Division Football League (Southern Section)—Season 1949/50

Dear Sir,

On behalf of my Board of Directors I have much pleasure in stating that we have again made another application for membership to the 3rd Division Football League (Southern Section) for Season 1949/50, therefore it would be appreciated if you will kindly place this letter before your Board at the next Meeting.

To support our application for election to the Football League, it should be noted that despite the unanimous vote of all the Southern Section Clubs for re-election to the League at the end of Season 1937/38, Gillingham F.C. lost their place at the Annual League Meeting by a close majority in favour of Ipswich Town.

Both Shrewsbury and Scunthorpe finally made it in 1950, when both Third Divisions were extended by two clubs each......

.....Colchester United and Gillingham, became the new additions to the Southern section.

Colchester United Football Club Limited

LAYER ROAD GROUND
COLCHESTER

Workington (below) made it a year later, in 1951......

......But no such luck for South Liverpool (bottom right), who that year made their 10th and final attempt before giving up

DEAR SIR,

I have pleasure in enclosing herewith various Press cuttings with reference to our claim for recognition and admittance to the Football League.

The whole of the great British sporting public would acclaim the decision of the League clubs in the event of Colchester United being admitted to the Football League, and you yourself could be instrumental in satisfying the people's wishes. I therefore consider the present moment to be most opportune to bring before you certain facts and figures.

The playing achievements of the Club during the last season, and in particular our successful F. A. Cup run, speak for themselves, including as they did victories over such redoubtable League Clubs as Huddersfield, Bradford, and Wrexham.

HAVE WE CONVINCED

You

THAT WE ARE ENTITLED TO

League Status?

IF SO, WE RESPECTFULLY APPEAL FOR YOUR

SUPPORT. WE WILL NOT FAIL YOUR

CONFIDENCE IN US.

Vote for Workington

AND HELP LEAGUE FOOTBALL IN THE

RAPIDLY GROWING DISTRICT OF

WEST CUMBERLAND.

SOUTH LIVERPOOL

ATHLETIC AND ASSOCIATION FOOTBALL CLUB CO. LTD.

(INCORPORATED UNDER COMPANY'S ACT, 1929)

CHESHIRE COUNTY LEAGUE .·. LIVERPOOL COUNTY COMBINATION

President : Mr. W. COOK.   Vice-President : Mr. GEORGE HOSKER.
DIRECTORS :—H. D. ARROWSMITH, Chairman.   W. G. WILLIAMSON, Vice-Chairman.
G. H. DUCKETT, C.C. A. E. GILLMORE, S. V. JACKSON, E. J. JOHNSON, R. NASH, C.C. F. O'FARRELL, G H. SIMCOCK.
J. TOPPING, W. WHITE.

TREASURER :
J. A. DUNCAN, A.C.R.A.
71, NORTH BARCOMBE ROAD,
LIVERPOOL, 16,
Phone : CHIldwall 4088.

RESERVE TEAM SECRETARY :
A. DERBYSHIRE,
38, CANTERBURY STREET,
LIVERPOOL, 19.
Phone : GARston 4888.

SECRETARY/MANAGER :
R. A. JOYNSON.
37, RIVERBANK ROAD,
GRASSENDALE,
LIVERPOOL, 19.
Phone : GARston 1387.

REGISTERED OFFICE AND GROUND :
HOLLY PARK, WOOLTON ROAD,
GARSTON, LIVERPOOL, 19.
Phone : GARston 1818.

..............18th May,.........194 9.

To THE BOARD OF DIRECTORS:-

F.C.

Dear Sirs,

We beg to advise you that we have applied for admission to the Third Division (Northern Section) of the Football League.

It is our sincere belief that we have a strong case for election and if you will bear with us for a few moments, we would like to indicate one or two of the main arguments in our favour.

By the 1950's, with the post-war football boom increasing attendances at all levels, many non-League clubs were making applications, and it was to be many years before such numbers were rationalised. However, back in the pre-War days, the number of clubs applying was more rational, as in 1932, when the Third Division South section (right) received applications direct, and then sought the opinions of its members, before recommendations were made at the Election meeting.

Telephone : LIBERTY 3078.

Football League.
Southern Section—Third Division.

Secretary :
W. J. DARBYSHIRE.

34, Cromwell Road,
Wimbledon, S.W.19.

Dear Sir,

Herewith I have pleasure in sending you Forms of Questionnaire and Analysis Sheets for four Clubs who are seeking admission to the League.

I shall be glad if you will place these before your Board as speedily as possible.

1960, and at last Peterborough United deservedly made it to the new (since 1958) Fourth Division. They had impressive credentials, not only on the playing front, but with their large and well appointed Ground that featured in their election brochure that year.

North Shields (below) also had an excellent Ground, but their eighth, and last, attempt in 1962 failed to impress......

......Similarly that year, Guildford (right) from the South were unable to gain 'promotion'.

A PPLEBY PARK can accommodate 15,000 spectators. There is covered accommodation for 3,500 and seating for 1,000. The playing pitch is a good one and changing rooms are up to the highest standard of a modern, forward-looking club.

The actual changing rooms are modern having been built within the last five years. They are centrally-heated and immediately adjoining them is a plunge bath, foot baths and showers.

Part of the same building is a spacious social club with a liquor licence. This is used for the entertainment of visiting clubs playing at Appleby Park.

In immediate proximity is the directors' boardroom, tea pavilion and small private stand.

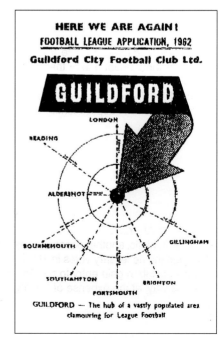

HERE WE ARE AGAIN!
FOOTBALL LEAGUE APPLICATION, 1962
Guildford City Football Club Ltd.

GUILDFORD

LONDON

READING

ALDERSHOT

BOURNEMOUTH

GILLINGHAM

SOUTHAMPTON

BRIGHTON

PORTSMOUTH

GUILDFORD — The hub of a vastly populated area clamouring for League Football

In 1961, Cambridge City (at that time the more senior of the two University town clubs), really thought the time would soon come for their election. They reinforced this view with an advert. in the 'Soccer Star'.

FINANCIAL STABILITY

The directors of Yeovil Town realise that the success of any club must be based on financial stability. With this uppermost in our minds, we have pursued a policy over many years which places the club in an extremely healthy monetary position.

The club which is situated in the centre of the town, is valued at over £400,000 together with six freehold houses, present value in excess of £70,000. The club is more than confident that the extra expenses involved in being a league club will cause no real problems, thanks to the financial base already established and the revenue obtained from the gates, and the 3 auxiliary bodies controlled by the club - namely the weekly lottery, social club and supporters club.

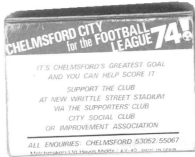

As a change from brochures, Chelmsford City produced souvenir boxes of matches for their bid in 1974.

Of all the clubs denied a place in the League, Yeovil are without doubt one of the most deserving of cases. The above is taken from a brochure in the late 1960's, when they were in the middle of their marathon run of applications.

AND FINALLY......
Wigan Athletic, another deserving case, managed to gain the necessary votes in 1978, and became the last club to gain entry to the Football League in this way, at the expense of Southport.

WIGAN ATHLETIC
ASSOCIATION FOOTBALL CLUB LTD.

APPLICANTS

for

ASSOCIATE MEMBERSHIP

of the

FOOTBALL LEAGUE

1978

Souvenir Edition

UPS AND DOWNS - AN OVERVIEW
The current League Clubs that have had to seek re-election:

Aston Villa (1890, 1891)

Barnsley (1900, 1911)

Birmingham (1910)

Blackpool (1899, 1909, 1913, 1983)

Bolton (1890)

Bournemouth (1924, 1934)

Bradford City (1949, 1963, 1966)

Brentford (1921, 1925)

Brighton & H.A. (1948)

Bristol Rovers (1939)

Burnley (1889, 1890, 1903)

Cambridge United (1986)

Carlisle United   (1935)

Cardiff City (1934)

Charlton Athletic (1926)

Chesterfield (1902, 1906, 1907, 1908, 1909)

Colchester United (1954, 1955, 1973)

Crewe Alexandra (1893, 1895, 1896, 1956, 1957, 1958, 1972, 1973, 1974, 1979, 1980, 1982, 1983)

Crystal Palace (1949, 1951, 1956)

Darlington (1933, 1937, 1952, 1970, 1973, 1975, 1979 1980)

Derby County (1889, 1891)

Exeter City (1922, 1929, 1936, 1937, 1952, 1958, 1961, 1986)

Gillingham (1921, 1929, 1930, 1932, 1938)

Grimsby Town (1908, 1910, 1920, 1955, 1969)

Halifax Town (1922, 1930, 1947, 1948, 1950, 1954, 1965, 1977, 1979, 1981, 1984, 1985)

Hartlepool United (1924, 1929, 1939, 1960, 1961, 1962, 1963, 1964, 1970, 1971, 1977, 1978, 1983, 1984)

Leicester City (1904, 1915)

Leyton Orient (1906)

Lincoln City (1893, 1895, 1897, 1898, 1907, 1908, 1911, 1914, 1920, 1963, 1965, 1966, 1967, 1971)

Manchester City (Ardwick) (1894)

Mansfield Town (1947)

Millwall (1950, 1958)

Northampton Town (1972, 1973, 1982, 1985)

Norwich City (1931, 1947, 1948, 1957)

Nottingham Forest (1914)

Notts County (1889, 1890)

Oldham Athletic (1959, 1960)

Port Vale (1893, 1895, 1896, 1905)

Preston North End (1986)

Queens Park Rangers (1924, 1926)

Rochdale (1922, 1931, 1932, 1934, 1966, 1967, 1978, 1980, 1982, 1984)

Rotherham United (1934)

Scunthorpe United (1975, 1982)

Shrewsbury Town (1953)

Southend United (1922, 1935)

Stockport County (1901, 1902, 1903, 1904, 1913, 1965, 1972, 1974, 1976, 1985)

Stoke (City) (1889, 1890, 1892)

Swansea City (1975)

Swindon Town (1933, 1956, 1957)

Torquay United (1928, 1985, 1986)

Tranmere Rovers (1925, 1957, 1981)

Walsall (1893, 1895, 1901, 1926, 1938, 1939, 1952, 1953, 1954, 1955)

Watford (1927, 1951)

West Bromwich Albion (1891) *

Wrexham (1966)

York City (1950, 1964, 1967, 1968, 1969, 1978, 1981)

* West Brom. Finished third from bottom in 1892, but by winning the F.A.Cup they were not required to seek re-election.

Current/recent League Clubs that have never had to seek re-election (With year of entry shown):

Arsenal	(1893)	Manchester United	(1892)
Barnet *	(1991)	Middlesbrough	(1899)
Blackburn Rovers	(1888)	Newcastle United	(1893)
Bristol City	(1901)	Oxford United	(1962)
Bury	(1894)	Peterborough Ut .	(1960)
Chelsea	(1905)	Plymouth Argyle	(1920)
Cheltenham Town **	(1999)	Portsmouth	(1920)
Coventry City	(1919)	Reading	(1920)
Everton	(1888)	Rushden & Diamonds **	(2001)
Fulham	(1907)	Scarborough *	(1987)
Huddersfield Town	(1910)	Sheffield United	(1892)
Hull City	(1905)	Sheffield Wedneday	(1892)
Ipswich Town	(1938)	Southampton	(1920)
Kidderminster Harriers **	(2000)	Sunderland	(1890)
Leeds United	(1920)	Tottenham Hotspur	(1908)
Liverpool	(1893)	West Ham United	(1919)
Luton Town †	(1897)	Wigan Athletic	(1978)
Macclesfield Town **	(1997)	Wimbledon	(1977)
Maidstone United *	(1989)	Wolverhampton W.	(1888)
Manchester City (Ardwick)	(1892)	Wycombe Wanderers **	(1993)

*   Only entered League after period when re-elections were necessary, but later relegated/folded.

**   Only entered League after period when re-elections were necessary.

†   Finished second bottom in 1900, resigned before re-election vote.

The Clubs voted out of the League:

Stoke (1890) *	Glossop (1915)
Walsall (Town Swifts) (1895) (1901)*	Aberdare Athletic (1927)
(Burslem) Port Vale (1896) *	Durham City (1928)
Crewe Alexandra (1896) *	Ashington (1929)
Burton Wanderers (1897)	Merthyr Town (1930)
Blackpool (1899) *	Newport County (1931)
Loughborough (1900)	Nelson (1931)
Doncaster Rovers (1903) (1905) **	Gillingham (1938) *
Stockport County (1904) *	New Brighton (1951)
Burton United (1907)	Gateshead (1960)
Lincoln City (1908) (1911) (1920)*	Bradford P.A. (1970)
Chesterfield (Town) (1909) *	Barrow (1972)
Grimsby Town (1910) *	Workington (1977)
Gainsborough Trinity (1912)	Southport (1978)

*   Club re-elected at a later date (current members)

**   Club re-elected, twice, but subsequently relegated.

Clubs resigned, retired or forcibly removed
(month shown only if during the season):

Accrington	(After losing 1893 1st Division play-off, declined to join new 2nd Division)
Middlesbrough Ironopolis	(Resigned 1894)
Northwich Victoria	(Resigned 1894)
Rotherham Town	(Resigned 1896)
Darwen	(Resigned 1899)
Luton Town	(Resigned 1900)
New Brighton Tower	(Resigned September 1901)
Burslem Port Vale	(Resigned 1907)
Stoke	(Resigned 1908)
Leeds City	(Expelled, October 1919)
Stalybridge Celtic	(Resigned 1923)
Wigan Borough	(Resigned October 1931)
Thames Association	(Resigned 1932)
Accrington Stanley	(Resigned March 1962)
Port Vale	(Expelled 1968, but immediately voted back in)
Aldershot	(Resigned March 1992)
Maidstone United	(Resigned August 1992)
Also:	
Peterborough United	(Demoted 3rd to 4th Division, 1968)
Swindon Town	(Won 1st Div. play-off but demoted to 2nd, due to financial irregularities, 1990)

Clubs relegated and promoted (since 1987)

1987:	Lincoln City	(replaced with Scarborough)
1988:	Newport County	(replaced with Lincoln City)
1989:	Darlington	(replaced with Maidstone United)
1990:	Colchester United	(replaced with Darlington)
1991:	No team relegated	(replaced with Barnet - Aldershot resigned during season)
1992:	No team relegated	(Colchester United promoted) (Maidstone U. resigned pre-season)
1993:	Halifax Town	(replaced with Wycombe Wanderers)
1994:	No team relegated or promoted	
1995:	No team relagated or promoted	
1996:	No team relegated or promoted	
1997:	Hereford United	(replaced with Macclesfield Town)
1998:	Doncaster Rovers	(replaced with Halifax Town)
1999:	Scarborough	(replaced with Cheltenham Town)
2000:	Chester City	(replaced with Kidderminster Harriers)
2001:	Barnet	(replaced with Rushden and Diamonds)

Clubs who have applied for the League but never elected
(See individual clubs' sections for years, etc.):

Some clubs from the same town have been 'paired up', or not included (a forerunner was a League member) even if not strictly the same club, whilst others who are distinctly different, have been included here separately.

Abertillery Town
Altrincham
Annfield Plain
Argonauts
Ashton North End
Ashton United
Bangor City
Barry/Barry Town
Bath City
Bedford Town
Bexleyheath & Welling
Bexley United
Blyth Spartans
Boston United
Bridgend Town
Burton Town
Burton Albion
Cambridge City
Castleford Town
Chelmsford City
Chorley
Consett
Corby Town
Cradley Heath
Dartford
Dudley Town

Ebbw Vale
Ellesmere Port Town
Enfield
Fairfield Athletic
Folkestone
Gloucester City
Goole Town
Gravesend & Northfleet
Guildford City
Hastings United
Hillingdon Borough
Kettering (Town)
Kings Lynn
Lancaster Town
Liverpool Caledonians
Llanelly
Lovells Athletic
Manchester Central
Mid-Rhondda
(Mitchell) St.George's
Morecambe
Newcastle City
Newcastle East End *
North Shields
Nuneaton Town/Borough
Pontypridd

Poole Town
Prescot Cables
Rhyl
Romford
Rossendale
Runcorn
Salford United
Sittingbourne
South Liverpool
South Shore
Stalybridge Rovers
Stockton
Sunderland Albion
Wakefield City
Wallasey
Wellington T./Telford Utd.
West Hartlepool
West Stanley
Weymouth
Wigan County
Wigan Town
Willington Athletic
Worcester City
Yeovil & Petters United/Town

* Club declined offer to join new Second Division in 1892.

Current members of League who were not elected (i.e. promoted), and never applied for election:

Wycombe Wanderers
Macclesfield Town (Forerunner 'Macclesfield' applied for election in 1896)
Cheltenham Town.
Kidderminster Harriers
Rushden & Diamonds

Club making the most applications, before being elected:
25 - Wigan Athletic

Most Re-election Applications:

14   Hartlepool United, Lincoln City (not re-elected three times, plus once relegated)
13   Crewe Alexandra (not re-elected once)
12   Halifax Town (plus once relegated)
11   Barrow (not re-elected once)
10   Newport County (not re-elected once, plus once relegated), Rochdale, Southport (not re-elected once), Stockport County, Walsall (not re-elected twice)
8   Darlington (plus once relegated) Exeter City (also finished bottom in 1995)
7   Workington (within period 1951 to 1977), York City

Clubs making most applications, but were never elected:

28   Yeovil & Petters United/Town
18   Bedford Town, Chelmsford City and Kettering Town/Kettering

Club with the most consecutive number of applications
14   Yeovil Town (1947 to 1960 inclusive).

Unluckiest club to not be re-elected:

Although open to debate, Gateshead's exclusion ranks high. Gateshead evolved from South Shields (entered League in 1919), and sought re-election on just two occasions, finishing second from bottom of the Third Division North in 1937, and third from bottom in 1960, when they were voted out!

Town from which applications have been made from the most clubs:

4 Wigan:	Wigan County -	1899.
	Wigan Town -	1906, 1907.
	Wigan Borough -	1921, successful, 1931 - folded mid-season.
	Wigan Athletic -	1932, 36, 37, 38, 39, 47 -51 incl., 62, 64-76 incl., 78- successful
4 Burton Upon Trent	Burton Swifts -	1892, successful.
	Burton Wanderers -	1894, successful.
	Burton Town -	1939.
	Burton Albion -	1955, 1956, 1957, 1958.

(N.B. Burton Wanderers and Burton Swifts combined as Burton United, in 1901)

Towns with most clubs (3), that have become Football League members:

Burton-on-Trent: Burton Swifts, Burton Wanderers, Burton United (Swifts and Wanderers amalgamated)
Rotherham: Rotherham Town, Rotherham County, Rotherham United (Town and County amalgamated)

Clubs that have had to seek re-election, and subsequently reached the First Division/Premier League:

Swansea City	(6 years later reached top division;	highest placing 6th)
Brentford	(10 years later, reached top division;	highest placing 5th)
Charlton Athletic	(10 years later reached top division;	highest placing 2nd)
Crystal Palace	(13 years later reached top division;	highest placing 3rd)
Cardiff City	(* 17 years later reached top division;	highest placing 10th)
Norwich City	(15 years later reached top division;	highest placing 3rd)
Brighton & H. Alb.	(31 years later reached top division;	highest placing 13th)
Watford	(31 years later reached top division;	highest placing 2nd)
Barnsley	(* 78 years later reached top division;	highest placing 19th)

* including War years.

First/Premier Div. clubs that have subsequently had to seek re-election:

(In multiple re-election bids, shortest period shown)

	Cardiff City	(5 years later sought re-election) †
	Northampton Town	(6 years later sought re-election)
	Grimsby Town	(7 years later sought re-election)
	Blackpool	(12 years later sought re-election) †
	Preston North End	(25 years later sought re-election) † ‡
	Bradford City	(27 years later sought re-election) * †
	Bradford Park Avenue	(35 years later sought re-election)
Also:	Burnley	(1987: 3rd bottom, 26 years later) ‡
	Carlisle United	(1988: 2nd bottom, 13 years later)
	Brighton & H. A.	(1997: 2nd bottom, 14 years later)

* Including War years.   † Also F.A.Cup winners.   ‡ Former League Champions.

Founder-members that have had to seek re-election:

Preston North End, Aston Villa, Bolton Wanderers, West Bromwich Albion, Accrington, Burnley, Derby County, Notts County, Stoke. (The only founder-members not to have sought re-election being: Wolverhampton Wanderers, Blackburn Rovers and Everton)

Since 1920: Re-election necessary at end of first season in Football League:

- 1920/21: Brentford and Gillingham
- 1921/22: Halifax Town and Rochdale
- 1923/24: Bournemouth (& Boscombe Ath.)
- 1927/28: Torquay United
- 1932/33: Newport County (second period in League)
- 1951/52: Workington

Re-election necessary at end of first season in Fourth Division:

- 1958/59: Oldham Ath., Aldershot, Barrow and Southport (first season of Fourth Division)
- 1962/63: Lincoln City.
- 1968/69: Grimsby Town.

Club elected to Fourth Division and required to seek re-election:

Hereford United (1972/1980 - relegated 1996/97)

Clubs promoted (not elected) to League and subsequently relegated:

- 1992   Maidstone United (folded - August)
- 1999   Scarborough.
- 2001   Barnet.

Current League member: Most unsuccessful re-election bids:

- 3   Lincoln City (1908, 1911 and 1920) (Also relegated 1987).

Re-election application only avoided on goal average:

- 1921/22: Tranmere Rovers and Newport County.
- 1922/23: Barrow.
- 1923/24: Watford.
- 1929/30: Bristol Rovers.
- 1930/31: Hartlepools United.
- 1932/33: Clapton (Leyton) Orient and York City
- 1936/37: Crewe Alexandra and Torquay United.
- 1937/38: Hartlepools United and Darlington.
- 1947/48: Bristol Rovers.
- 1948/49: Northampton Town.
- 1949/50: Walsall, Aldershot, Bradford City and Wrexham.
- 1951/52: Gillingham.
- 1954/55: Crewe Alexandra.
- 1955/56: Barrow.
- 1960/61: Exeter City
- 1962/63: Newport County.
- 1963/64: Rochdale.
- 1966/67: Notts County.
- 1975/76: Scunthorpe United. and Darlington.
- 1979/80: Port Vale.
- 1982/83: Rochdale.
- 1983/84: Wrexham.
- 1984/85: Halifax Town.
- 1985/86: Halifax Town and Tranmere Rovers.

Miscellany:

1962, (the year that Accrington Stanley resigned during the season) saw the most number of applications for election - 26 (plus three clubs standing for re-election) - see separate feature.

****

1931, Merthyr Town became the only club to apply, for both sections of the Third Division, in the same year.

****

1923, two clubs from - virtually - the same town applied for membership: New Brighton, who were successful, and Wallasey United who were not. Between 1959 and 1974, Cambridge City made thirteen unsuccessful applications, and between 1965 and 1970 Cambridge United made six applications before being elected. Between 1965 and 1967 incl. both City and United made applications.

****

1896, Macclesfield applied for membership of the League, but no other attempts were made from the town for 101 years before Macclesfield Town were automatically promoted in 1997. The original Macclesfield were founded in 1874, moved to the Moss Rose Ground in 1891, and folded in 1897. Hallfield F.C. moved into the Ground and changed their name to Macclesfield in 1904, later adding the 'Town' suffix.

****

Two different clubs from Ashton-Under-Lyme (Lancashire) have unsuccessfully applied for election: Ashton North End (1899) and Ashton United (1947).

****

In 1899, four clubs from the same League (which embraced only 13 teams), The Lancashire, applied for election: Chorley (1st), Ashton North End (3rd), Wigan County (4th) and Stockport County (5th) - all were unsuccessful, as were Blackpool (not re-elected) and Darwen (retired); all six clubs are/were located in Lancashire.

****

1899 Ashton North End made an unsuccessful bid for election, and then folded within weeks, hence never playing another match.

****

From 1928 to 1930, Argonauts made three unsuccessful bids, yet had not signed on players and hence never played a match.

****

Liverpool Caledonians applied for election in 1892, having never played a competitive league match. On being turned down by the League they played in the Lancashire League (1892/93 season), but completed only seven such matches before folding.

****

When Leeds City applied, and were accepted into the Football League in 1905, their playing record consisted of one season in the West Yorkshire League in which they had finished 11th of 14, the lowest level of league from which a club has ever been elected (due to the Football League's obsession with 'colonising' Rugby League strongholds). Chelsea were elected to the League on the 29th May 1905, just two months after the Club's formation, therefore they had no playing record whatsoever! Bradford City and Hull City were also elected soon after the formation of each club.

****

Clubs that may have sought election - but didn't !

This feature should be viewed as a very subjective list, in view of the many clubs that did seek election, who, in view of their status or past record, really had no right to do so! However, there have been others, that if they attempted, may have stood a chance.... or would they?

◆ ◆ ◆ ◆ ◆ ◆ ◆ ◆ ◆ ◆ ◆ ◆ ◆ ◆ ◆

Old Carthusians and **Halliwell** were both amongst the first eight clubs suggested by Mr. Bentley to be considered to form the Football League in 1888, but didn't make the final list, and never subsequently applied. Old Carthusians were a surprise suggestion since they were the only Southern based club and were strictly Amateur. A prominent team in the 1890's with two F.A.Amateur Cup Final victories plus the F.A.Cup (in 1881), they would probably have performed well. However in the rapidly diverging line (in that period) between Amateur and Professional clubs, their presence would probably have caused problems. Halliwell joined the Lancashire Combination for the (first) 1891/92 season, but did not complete their fixtures, and therefore would presumably have been totally unsuitable for the Football League. Halliwell Rovers were members of the Lancashire League for several seasons at the end of the 19th century.

For The Combination, which supposedly was to run in tandem with the Football League (but finished the 1888/89 season with many fixtures unplayed), twelve clubs were originally suggested, amongst them, Halliwell (again!), **Blackburn Olympic, Derby Junction, Derby Midland**, **Notts. Rangers**, **Witton** and **Long Eaton Rangers** none of whom ever applied for election to the Football League. Although Blackburn Olympic were F.A.Cup winners in 1883, they were soon overshadowed by their neighbours - Rovers - and no doubt would have had difficulties in competing with them. They never had the chance to compete in any league , for they folded soon after the first thoughts regarding the creation of The Combination. Witton (not the Witton Albion in Cheshire) were also based in the Blackburn area, and soon faded off the football map. They did not complete their 1890/91 fixtures in the The Combination, and would no doubt not have survived in the Football League.

Similarly Derby Junction and Derby Midland would have had problems with 'County'. Midland was an already well established club, made up of mostly railway workers, but ran into problems when the Company refused to continue to support a professional team and folded (or were taken over by Derby County) in 1891. Although, nearby, and much smaller, Burton-upon-Trent did manage to support two League clubs for several years but it is somewhat inconceivable to think of a maximum of five Football League clubs concentrated in two towns less than twenty miles apart! Notts Rangers would also have been a poor relation to County and a few years later Forest, and they didn't feature very prominently on the pre-League fixture lists of the two eventual Football League clubs. The club did become founder-members of the Midland League in 1889, but did not complete all their fixtures, were expelled from the competition at the end of the season, and presumably then folded. Long Eaton Rangers (near Nottingham), are the one club, in this sextet, that have continued to exist in some form, although the current team in the town was only founded in the 1950's. Perhaps they might have survived in the League, but located midway between Derby and Nottingham they would have had difficulty in competing for support. They joined the Midland League, but resigned after the 1898/99 season.

The Combination eventually embraced twenty teams, including the six above, others that either became Football League members (or applied for same), plus **Leek Town**. Rather like Long Eaton Rangers, there is currently a team of the same name, and playing in the Northern Premier League. But they too were founded in the early post-War years (originally as Abbey Green Rovers), their first predecessors having been founded in 1876. This earliest Leek Town did appear in the later Combination for a few unremarkable years, but then faded away, and therefore could not have been considered as serious contenders for a place in the Football League.

Berwick Rangers: The 'old chestnut' question - *"Which English club plays in the Scottish League?"* Berwick-upon-Tweed is located in England, just South of the Scottish border (although their former Ground was in fact situated in Scotland), and therefore the answer to the question is rightly - Berwick Rangers. Formed in 1881, for most of their existence, until 1905, they did indeed play in English Football, but that year joined the East of Scotland League, and in 1951 were elected to the Scottish League. In view of their status in 1905 (and before), an application to join the English Football League at either time would have inevitably failed, in the latter case when there were many more worthier clubs (in English Leagues) seeking election.

Bishop Auckland: Theoretically, being part of the 'Pyramid', the Bishops could become members of the League by promotions upwards from their current league, The Northern Premier. From the late 1800's until the mid-1950's, they were winners of the F.A.Amateur Cup on ten occasions, and even more frequent Champions of the Northern League, the competition in which they have spent most of their life. Their heyday was the early 1950's, and coupled with the boom in football around this time, if an attempt had been made this would have been the time. During this period the team was well supported, but being strictly Amateur, this factor would no doubt have gone against them.

Corinthians: A club that reflected everything that was honest in the game, it is even said that if awarded a penalty it would deliberately be missed, and a booking would have resulted in that player being asked to leave the club! But apart from this different world - in the pre-Second World War days - when cheating throughout football was not the problem it is in the modern game - the Corinthians (who later combined with the Casuals) were a very formidable club. Originally their rules forbade them from entering any competitive football, but eventually they succumbed and played in the F.A.Cup, from 1923, and almost continuously until 1939. So respected was the club that until 1933 they received a bye until the 3rd round (or its equivalent), and were a match for any club, especially from the Third Division (in 1929, Norwich City were beaten 5-0 on their own ground). If their rules had allowed it, a bid in 1932 could well have been successful (Thames Association resigned that year), especially considering the near success of the - proposed - Argonauts club in 1928.

Darwen: Brief members of the Football League in the early days, they resigned in 1899, and then reapplied two years later. If one, or more, applications had been made around 1930, then they may well have been more successful, having been Lancashire Combination Champions twice in succession and Combination Cup winners on two occasions around the same time. Indeed, it is possible that if a bid had been made in 1931, Darwen may have been preferred to Chester, who were voted in on a second vote, and displaced Nelson.

London Caledonians: Referring to the pre-First World War period, the Callies (ostensibly a club for exiled Scots, who in their early days were actually members of the Scottish F.A.), were one of the leading clubs in the top Amateur League, the Isthmian. But in this period it is even more unlikely that there would have been consideration to vote in an Amateur club. In addition, with no ground of their own, this factor would also have weighed against them. During the inter-War years, there were a number of other consistent leading clubs in the Isthmian League; notably **Dulwich Hamlet** thrice Champions and with undoubtedly one of the best non-League grounds, **Nunhead** (who folded in the 1940's), **Wimbledon** (who of course went professional and eventually made it), **St. Albans City, Ilford** (who much later disappeared under the Leytonstone/ Walthamstow Avenue/ etc. banner), and **Kingstonian** (who were, around the millennium, in with a chance of automatic promotion whilst in the Conference). Comparisons with their professional counterparts are difficult to make, but they may have fared well, although if at all successful they probably would have been forced to turn professional.

Pegasus: A combined Oxford and Cambridge University Amateur team composed of undergraduates. They were highly successful in the early 1950's, and well supported at their normal home ground in Iffley Road, Oxford. But they could never have entered a league of any kind, since the availability of players depended on the University term times. Their success was shortlived, for the early post-War period provided an influx of mature players (denied their further education due to the War), but as time was to tell, the experience gradually diminished. As a team, for a few years, they no doubt could have competed with lower division clubs.

Rushden and Diamonds: The most recent member of the Football League, who due very much to the immense wealth of their owner, managed promotion in 2001 via the Conference. Having only been in existence, in their present format, for a decade or so the question is somewhat irrelevant. The club was created from Rushden Town (Southern League), and Irthlingborough Diamonds (United Counties League), neither of whom would have had the finance, ground, or ability to compete at the higher level.

Wealdstone: For some years they have had to groundshare, most recently with Edgware Town, at an interesting but totally inadequate venue for Football League usage. In 1985 they achieved a unique double, the Championship of the Gola League (Conference), by four points, plus the winning of the F.A.Trophy, and therefore, certainly at that time, they had the playing ability for better things. This was two years before the introduction of automatic promotion to the League, but the inadequacy of their Lower Mead Ground would have prevented acceptance, the factor which no doubt prevented an application in 1985. On the sale of the Ground, the Club moved in with Watford F.C. for a while, whose Ground would have of course been perfectly acceptable, but with crowds even in the Championship season averaging of than 1,000, it would have been an inevitable financial disaster.

Since automatic (sometimes!) promotion was introduced in 1987, for three successive years, from 1994, Kidderminster Harriers, Macclesfield Town and Stevenage Town were denied promotion due to their Grounds not being up to the required standard. Whilst the former two have since been promoted to the Football League, **Stevenage Town** must be considered one of the unluckiest of clubs to be denied a place amongst the elite.

Finally....   In the Tilbury versus Erith and Belvedere programme dated 24th December 1966 (perhaps the writer had been having too much early Christmas cheer!), the following was included: *"We are now in a position to take stock of the various possibilities open to us as a very ambitious football club. The decisions that are taken now because of several reasons which cannot as yet be divulged, will be binding upon us for evermore. We must make this club the focal point of football for everyone in a radius of 20 miles at least."*

"We have the potential to do wonderful things to make Tilbury greater than even your wildest dreams. To illustrate this I will state emphatically that within the next 20 years this club should be in a position to grace the soccer fields of EUROPE. Where others fail we shall succeed. Twenty years is a long time but I hope that most of you will be supporting us as strongly in 1986 as you are now. Save this programme and see if our lads hopes are realised."

The Club in 1966 were playing in the (Amateur) Athenian League Division One (second tier) and finished the season in 11th place of 16. The programme **was** saved, and at the end of the 1986/87 season the club finished 19th of 22 in the Isthmian League Division One (second tier)!

Nearly Tried!

There are several known clubs, and probably there are others, who came close to making applications, but then withdrew before the election meeting. In 1921, at the time of the formation of the Third Division North, the well supported **Wath** (near Rotherham) and **Wombwell Town** both seriously considered making a bid to join the League, but did not get as far as the meeting. Both were elected to the Midland League the following season. **Wycombe Wanderers** also made a tongue in cheek application in 1981. Peeved that only an Alliance Premier League team could be considered, a ruling made previously but never agreed by the Isthmian League, the Club went through the formal procedure of applying. A Football League delegation subsequently inspected the Loakes Park Ground and, subject to a few minor details, confirmed that it was acceptable. Wanderers, having the satisfaction of knowing they had a suitable Ground, and having made their point, then withdrew their application before the meeting!

In 1921 South Wales clubs **Aberaman**, a small town near Aberdare plus **Bridgend** decided to have a go. The applicants were considered at the relevant meeting, but the clubs either withdrew before the voting or their names were formally removed. A few years after Aberdare Athletic's successful bid, they were voted out, and then in 1928, reapplied as the joint club '**Aberaman and Aberdare**', but withdrew their bid before the meeting.

The next year, 1929, **Mansfield Town** made an unsuccessful bid to join the Third Division North, and also applied for the South section, but withdrew their latter bid before the meeting convened. **Merthyr Town** are the only club to have applied for election in the same year to both sections (1931)! The same year **Connah's Quay and Shotton** made a bid. The team had earlier played in the Cheshire County League, then came a spell in the Welsh League (North), and they were Champions that year. But they, like others, withdrew their application before the meeting.

Bangor City, not for the first time, applied for the North section in 1950, but then felt better of it before the meeting. Much earlier**, Nelson** applied, then withdrew (in 1913) and two years later **Coventry City** did likewise, but of course, both were later destined to become members.

In 1911, for the third time, a serious suggestion was made with regard to the formation of a Third Division (ten years ahead of the actual event). Together with the names of many past and present members of the League, two others put their names forward, for the first and only time. **St. Helens Town**, who had, then, recently been relegated to the Second Division of the Lancashire Combination (and finished fourth that season) - hardly the right credentials - plus **Croydon Common** (earlier a report that the Club was to amalgamate with Crystal Palace was denied), of the Southern League Division Two, who had just completed a reasonably successful season. The Third Division proposal at this time was voted out at the League meeting.

In 1925, Manchester League **Manchester North End** first considered applying to join the League, and on the 4th February 1928, the Club Chairman announced that this move was seriously being considered, but it was never made. The Club folded in 1939.

The Southern League - The Alternative Football League:

Until 1893, the Football League was composed entirely of Northern and Midland clubs, and even then only Arsenal were added to the list. Luton Town (1897-1900), Bristol City (1901), Clapton (later Leyton) Orient and Chelsea in 1905 - the latter failing to gain election to the Southern League - were the only additions during this period. Admittedly the South had generally remained substantially Amateur during the early seasons of the Football League, but by 1892, there was moves afoot to get in on the action. A meeting was held in February 1892, which had been instigated by the Royal Arsenal club, regarding the formation of the Southern League. 12 clubs were elected, and 11 were unsuccessful, with the voting as follows:

Successful:		Unsuccessful:	
Chatham	29 *	Chesham	*10
Luton Town	29 *	Wolverton	9
Millwall Athletic	25 *	City Ramblers	8
Marlow	24	Woodville	8
Swindon Town	24 *	Uxbridge	*7
Reading	22 *	St.Albans	6
West Herts	21	Erith	3
Royal Arsenal	19	Westminster Criterion	2
Ilford	19 *	Old St.Stevens	2
Chiswick Park	18	Upton Park	2
Old St.Marks	15	Tottenham Hotspur	0
Crouch End	12		

For the record, the final composition of the Southern League (which after a few years was competing on a near equal footing with the Football League) for the 1894/95 season consisted of the following 16 clubs:
(1st Division) Millwall Athletic, Luton Town, Southampton St.Mary's, Ilford, Reading Chatham, Royal Ordnance Factories, Clapton, Swindon Town.
(2nd Division) New Brompton, Sheppey United, Old St.Steven's, Uxbridge, Bromley, Chesham, Maidenhead.

* Became founder-members in 1894.

Some clubs exist to this day, others had faded before the Southern League even started two years later; note a certain club from North London who was bottom of the voting!

Accrington Stanley - Who wants to take their place?

Accrington Stanley caused something of a sensation in 1962 when they resigned from the Fourth Division before completing their fixtures for the season; they tried to rescind their resignation letter but this was refused. For the first time in many years there was a guaranteed place available for one lucky non-League hopeful, instead of the almost impossible dream of being accepted in place of a non re-elected club (there had been only two such occurrences in the post-War seasons to that date). Coupled with the ludicrous number of clubs that by this time were applying for Football League status, the prize being offered in 1962 brought a veritable frenzy of clubs, all clamouring to be the chosen one. A record number of 26 clubs applied (plus the three re-election candidates), and there could well have been more. An article in the 1962/63 F.A.Year Book, conjectured on who might be worthy of applying. It is interesting to compare the fortunes of these clubs now, in the 21st century - 40 years later - and also to note those teams ground capacities (at that time) and their average attendances:

Club	League	Capacity.	Ave.Att.	Notes:
Ashington	Northern Counties	10,000	3,000	Former member
Bath City	Southern	21,000	5,000	#
Bedford Town	Southern	17,000	3,500	#
Bilston	Birmingham & Dist.	11,500	1,000	
Boston United	Central Alliance	10,000	1,800	
Bromsgrove Rovers	Birmingham & Dist.	8,000	1,400	
Burscough	Lancs. Combination	11,500	1,000	
Cambridge City	Southern	14,000	4,700	#
Cambridge United	Southern	6,500	2,800	*
Chelmsford City	Southern	18,000	4,750	#
Cheltenham Town	Southern	9,000	2,150	*
Chorley	Lancs. Combination	13,500	1,500	
Dorchester Town	Western	4,000	850	
Fleetwood	Lancs. Combination	4,000	500	
Gateshead	Northern Counties	20,000	4,000	Former member #
Guildford City	Southern	12,000	3,000	#
Hastings United	Southern	14,500	2,000	
Hereford United	Southern	12,000	3,250	#
Kettering Town	Southern	11,000	2,750	#
Kings Lynn	Southern	17,000	2,750	#
Lancaster City	Lancs. Combination	10,000	1,000	
Macclesfield Town	Cheshire	14,000	1,500	*
Morecambe	Lancs. Combination	10,000	2,000	#
Nelson	Lancs. Combination	19,000	3,500	Former member
New Brighton	Lancs. Combination	16,000	1,250	Former member #
North Shields	Northern Counties	11,000	2,000	#
Northwich Victoria	Cheshire	17,000	1,000	Former member
Oxford United	Southern	15,700	4,000	Elected that year
Rossendale United	Lancs. Combination	2,900	600	
Salisbury	Western	10,000	1,700	
South Shields	Northern Counties	24,000	3,000	#
Weymouth	Southern	12,000	2,750	
Wigan Athletic	Lancs. Combination	27,000	3,500	* #
Yeovil Town	Southern	15,000	3,980	#

Those clubs noted # (plus Oxford United) did in fact apply that year (plus many others that were not included in the list), and those marked * later became members of the Football League. Other clubs mentioned - in view of their ground capacities were: Ebbw Vale (23,000), Llanelly (22,000), Poole Town (20,000) and Merthyr Tydfil (19,000), plus Amateurs, Dulwich Hamlet, with an enormous ground capacity for 35,000. Significantly the article pointed out that none of those teams had the outstanding qualifications of Peterborough United (elected two years earlier), and in the majority of cases these potential hopefuls had lower average crowds than the hapless Accrington Stanley!

The Numbers Game

The re-election procedures were closely allied to the voting powers of the Management Committee, which was composed of members from the clubs themselves, and remained (presumably) substantially the same through the years, but with the lesser 'Associate' (i.e. Third and Fourth Divisions) members having far less of a say; although for at least one period, the hopefuls made their pleas to the Associate Members, who in turn made their recommendations to the voters at the election meetings. It is known that in the 1920's, the Associate Members *"had extra voting power"*, in 1974 they also *"gained representation on the Management Committee"*, and in 1981, their *"collective vote was increased "* (Ref: 'League Football' by Simon Inglis). Varying number of clubs and/or votes per club therefore definitely changed over the years, and even allowing for absentees and possible abstentions, the number of votes cast varied, sometimes substantially. One intriguing point is the figures in 1986 - the first, and last year, when half votes come into the equation (The First Division clubs had 1.5 votes each, the Second, one vote, and the Third Division believed to be a collective 12). 256 total votes were cast, but, 4 (number of votes-for-election clubs) x 67 votes = 268!

Notes: Below are the total number of votes cast per year (the next column shows the number of clubs required to stand for re-election). 'X' indicates no vote taken (or an unknown number), and where second votes were required these have been ignored. 1919 - 2 votes taken (1st and 2nd Div.). 1921 - (New) 3rd Div.North votes. * 1922-58 - 3rd South and 3rd North figures (2 clubs from each) ** 4 clubs from Fourth Division.

A study of the detailed seasonal voting figures, explains some of the widely differing vote numbers.

Year	Votes	Clubs		Year	Votes			Year	Votes	
1889	48	4		1921	270	4*		1957	98/97	
1890	X			1922	90/90			1958	89/107	
1891	48			1923	135/180			1959	192	4**
1892	50			1924	X			1960	192	
1893	X			1925	88/92			1961	196	
1894	112			1926	X/90			1962	192	
1895	80			1927	88/88			1963	192	
1896	84			1928	90/90			1964	196	
1897	87	3		1929	90/90			1965	196	
1898	87			1930	90/90			1966	188	
1899	102			1931	98/98			1967	194	
1900	92			1932	147/49			1968	193	
1901	97			1933	98/98			1969	182	
1902	93			1934	96/X			1970	193	
1903	102			1935	93/98			1971	196	
1904	102			1936	99/98			1972	196	
1905	112			1937	98/98			1973	196	
1906	114			1938	98/98			1974	192	
1907	114			1939	98/97			1975	196	
1908	108							1976	192	
1909	78	2		1940-1946 (WW2)				1977	184	
1910	86							1978	196	
1911	78			1947	X			1979	203	
1912	78			1948	98/96			1980	196	
1913	78			1949	96/96			1981	196	
1914	78			1950	98/118 98			1982	212	
1915	78			1951	98/98			1983	212	
				1952	98/98			1984	208	
1916-1918 (WW1)				1953	98/98			1985	X	
				1954	98/98			1986	256	
1919	41/164			1955	98/98			Promotion and relegation		
1920	84			1956	96/96			introduced in 1987		

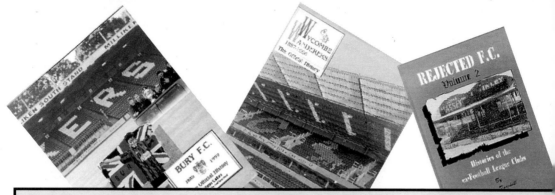

~ Yore Publications ~

Established in 1991 by Dave Twydell, Yore publications have become the leading publishers of Football League club histories. Nearly thirty have been produced, and although many are now out of print, some clubs for which copies are still available include - Scarborough, Wycombe Wanderers, Lincoln City, Notts County, Rochdale, Barnsley, Bury and Scunthorpe United. Each history is a large page quality hardback with dustjacket and contains a well illustrated written history, full statistics and line-ups for at least all Football League seasons are included, with many named team groups.

A number of Football League Who's Who books (biography and statistics of every League player) have also been produced, including Chesterfield, Reading, Portsmouth, and Hull City .

Non-League football is another feature of our publications, especially the 'Gone But Not Forgotten' series (published twice yearly), each of which contains around six (written and illustrated) abbreviated histories of defunct clubs and/or former grounds (also Videos available).

The Rejected F.C. series consist of the compilation histories of former Football League and Scottish League clubs (several clubs per book), plus a much acclaimed 90 minute video. Other nusual titles (e.g. 'The Little Red Book of Chinese Football') are also included in our current stocks.

We only publish football book - normally of an historic nature, for which two or three free
Newsletters are posted each year. For your first copy, please send a S.A.E. to:
Yore Publications (Ref R/W),
12 The Furrows, Harefield, Middx. UB9 6AT.
Or visit our web sites:
www.yorepublications.sageweb.co.uk... or .....www.yore.demon.co.uk/index.html